SELF-ACTUALIZATION FOR NURSES

Issues, Trends, and Strategies
for Job Enrichment

Contributors

Mark Abrahamson
I. Robert Andrews
Kishan Shyamlal Bagadia
M.M. Bakr
Cedil H. Bell, Jr.
Janet K. Bishop
Mary Blount
J.E. Bragg
Suzanne Burge
V.R. Buzzotta
Bishop Clarkson Memorial Hospital
Lee Crigler
Diane Ramy Faulconer
Betty A. Finkelmeier
Eliot Freidson
Barbara Fuszard
Jacob W. Getzels
Frank Goble
Alvin Gouldner
Ernest Greenwood
Egon G. Guba
P.R. Harris

Frederick Herzberg
Dorothy Jongeward
Dolores Kaulbach
R.E. Lefton
Douglas McGregor
Walter R. Mahler
Donald L. Mills
Terence R. Mitchell
James A. Moses, Jr.
Elayne Lowe O'Loughlin
Thomas H. Patten, Jr.
Diane M. Reeves
Margaret Riley
Cindi Sanborn
Mannie Sherberg
Douglas S. Sherwin
Mark Silber
Marie Tobin
Denis D. Umstot
Howard M. Vollmer
Roy W. Walters and Associates
Lyle York

SELF-ACTUALIZATION FOR NURSES

Issues, Trends, and Strategies for Job Enrichment

Edited by

Barbara Fuszard, Ph.D., R.N.
Professor, Nursing Administration
School of Nursing
Medical College of Georgia
Augusta, Georgia

AN ASPEN PUBLICATION®
Aspen Systems Corporation
Rockville, Maryland
Royal Tunbridge Wells
1984

Library of Congress Cataloging in Publication Data
Main entry under title:

Self-actualization for nurses.

"An Aspen publication."
Edited versions of articles which have been previously published in various sources.
Includes bibliographies and index.
1. Nursing—Social aspects—Addresses, essays, lectures. 2. Self-actualization (Psychology)—Addresses, essays, lectures. 3. Job enrichment—Addresses, essays, lectures. I. Fuszard, Barbara. [DNLM: 1. Job Satisfaction—collected works. 2. Nursing—collected works. 3. Personnel Management—collected works. WY 16 S465]
RT86.5.S45   1984   610.73   84-16874
ISBN: 0-89443-871-9

Publisher: John R. Marozsan
Associate Publisher: Jack W. Knowles, Jr.
Editorial Director: N. Darlene Como
Executive Managing Editor: Margot G. Raphael
Managing Editor: M. Eileen Higgins
Editorial Services: Martha Sasser
Printing and Manufacturing: Debbie Collins

Copyright © November 1984 by Aspen Systems Corporation
All rights reserved.
Aspen Systems Corporation grants permission for photocopying for personal or internal use, or for the personal or internal use of specific clients registered with the Copyright Clearance Center (CCC). The consent is given on the condition that the copier pay a $1.00 fee plus $.12 per page for each photocopy through the CCC for photocopying beyond that permitted by the U.S. Copyright Law. The fee should be paid directly to the CCC, 21 Congress St., Salem, Massachusetts 01970.
0-89443-871-9/84 $1.00 + .12.

This consent does not extend to other kinds of copying, such as copying for general distribution, for advertising or promotional purposes, for creating new collective works, or for resale. For information, address Aspen Systems Corporation,
1600 Research Boulevard, Rockville, Maryland 20850.

Library of Congress Catalog Card Number: 84-16874
ISBN: 0-89443-871-9

Printed in the United States of America

1   2   3   4   5

For my dear parents,

Margaret and Harold Fuszard,

with love

Table of Contents

Preface xi

Introduction xiii

PART I. THE PROFESSIONAL AND THE INSTITUTION: GOAL CONFLICT 1

Section 1. Social Behavior and the Administrative Process 3
Jacob W. Getzels and Egon G. Guba

Section 2. The Concept of Professionalization 11
Howard M. Vollmer and Donald L. Mills

Section 3. Attributes of a Profession 13
Ernest Greenwood

Section 4. Professions and Professionalism 27
Eliot Freidson

Section 5. Role Specialization in a Formal Organization 28
Mark Abrahamson

PART II. MOTIVATION OF THE PROFESSIONAL 33

Section 6. The Esteem Needs 35
Frank Goble

Section 7. The Self-Actualization Needs 37
Frank Goble

Section 8. Theory X and Theory Y 39
Douglas McGregor

Section 9. The Problem of "Close Supervision" 42
Alvin Gouldner

Section 10. The Hazards of Close Supervision 44
Roy W. Walters and Associates

Section 11. The Screening Functions of Rules 45
Alvin Gouldner

Section 12. Job Rotation, Job Purfication, and Job Enlargement 47
Barbara Fuszard

PART III. JOB ENRICHMENT DEFINED 51

Section 13. One More Time: How Do You Motivate Employees?
(Part I) 53
Frederick Herzberg

Section 14. The Human Need for Work 59
Frederick Herzberg

Section 15. One More Time: How Do You Motivate Employees?
(Part II) 63
Frederick Herzberg

Section 16. An Update on Job Enrichment 75
Kishan Shyamlal Bagadia and M.M. Bakr

Section 17. Team Production (Semi-Autonomous Work Groups) 81
Lyle York

Section 18. Theory Z 83
Barbara Fuszard

PART IV. RESTRUCTURING WORK FOR JOB ENRICHMENT ... 87

Section 19. "Adhocracy" in Health Care Institutions? 90
Barbara Fuszard and Janet K. Bishop

Section 20. Participative Management 100
Frederick Herzberg

Section 21. Participative Decision Making: An Experimental Study in a Hospital 102
J.E. Bragg and I. Robert Andrews

Section 22. Primary Nursing's Effect on Professional Development 111
Marie Tobin

Section 23. Extending the Influence of the Clinical Nurse Specialist 113
Mary Blount, Suzanne Burge, Lee Crigler, Betty A. Finkelmeier, and Cindi Sanborn

Section 24. Clinical Ladders and Specialty Teams 116
Diane Ramy Faulconer and Diane M. Reeves

Section 25. Professional Synergy 120
P.R. Harris

Section 26. Coordinated Care: Making It a Reality 129
Margaret Riley and James A. Moses, Jr.

PART V. A PERFECT TOOL OF JOB ENRICHMENT: EVALUATION ... 137

Section 27. An Uneasy Look at Performance Appraisal 139
Douglas McGregor

Section 28. Job Evaluation and Job Enrichment: A Collision Course? 147
Thomas H. Patten, Jr.

Section 29. Goal Setting and Job Enrichment: An Integrated Approach
to Job Design 153
*Denis D. Umstot, Terence R. Mitchell, and
Cecil H. Bell, Jr.*

Section 30. The Evaluation Process 167
Bishop Clarkson Memorial Hospital

Section 31. Peer Review: A Perspective for Performance Appraisal 180
Elayne Lowe O'Loughlin and Dolores Kaulbach

PART VI. THE MANAGER AS CLIMATE SETTER FOR JOB ENRICHMENT 193

Section 32. Strategy for Winning Employee Commitment 194
Douglas S. Sherwin

Section 33. Is There Love in Your Leading? 203
Mark Silber

Section 34. Management Concepts That Work: Sponsorship 209
Barbara Fuszard

Section 35. The Effect of Management Style on Job Enrichment 212
Dorothy Jongeward

Section 36. Coaching and Counseling 222
V.R. Buzzotta, R.E. Lefton, and Mannie Sherberg

Section 37. The Pygmalion Effect 235
Walter R. Mahler

Index **239**

Preface

The future of professional nursing is the concern of many in the health care field. Health care administrators, including nursing administrators, see their institutions increasing in size and complexity. They feel responsible not only for the efficiency (to the board) and effectiveness (to the patients) of these institutions, but also for the satisfaction and growth of the employees. The key employee of the health care agency is the professional nurse.

The health care administrator sees the available number of competent, dedicated professional nurses dwindling at a time when, because of expansion and diversification, health care agencies need more and more professional nurses. New delivery systems compete for professional registered nurses. Furthermore, there are increased demands for higher salaries as the role of the professional nurse becomes more demanding and complex, the initial education required more time-consuming and expensive, and continuing education more essential for currency. The profession of nursing is moving ever closer to the traditional "professions" on the professionalization continuum, and nurses are expecting the recognition and rewards concomitant with that status. To these pressures is added the "ogre" of collective bargaining with the nurses who have been hired. Both recruitment and maintenance of nursing staff require cost commitments that institutions are finding difficult to meet.

Individual professional nurses, too, are concerned about the future of professional nursing. First of all, newly emerging types of health care providers have nibbled at what had traditionally been the professional nurse's role. Nurses sometimes appear to be left with the distasteful paperwork that services other departments. Countless articles in the literature attest to the job dissatisfaction that nurses are experiencing with their roles in health care institutions.

Second, professional registered nurses are striving for the right to perform, to be respected, and to grow as true professionals. The professional nursing association has been working to help nursing meet the criteria for a profession identified so many years ago by Abraham Flexner. Educational programs for nursing are growing closer to those of the "traditional professions" in time and personal commitment. Nurses have long embraced a code of ethics and are accepting personal responsibility for constant updating of their knowledge and skills. They are accepting more responsibility for their independent functioning and are increasingly aware of their independent moral and legal responsibilities in this functioning. Yet they see evidence every day that society does not yet accord nursing professional status.

Finally, nurses have seen the discrepancy between their rewards for professional, autonomous, responsible functioning and the rewards that other professionals receive. History shows that salaries of nurses have always been low, that part of their remuneration was expected to be their personal satisfaction in service to their fellow man. While the salaries of others, such as clerks, laborers, and the new health technicians, have spiraled, nursing salary increases have often been less than cost of living increases. Is it any wonder that nurses look to collective bargaining for what they feel it did for other workers?

Thus, the problem of the future of the professional nurse is multifaceted. Health care administrators seek a solution to the shortage of competent professional nurses in their institutions that is cost effective and can be reached without the hassle of collective bargaining. Individual professional nurses seek job satisfaction, growth in status as a true health care professional, and a salary commensurate with that status. The thesis of this book is that the needs of the health care system and the individual professional nurse can be met simultaneously within the concept of job enrichment.

Barbara Fuszard, Ph.D., R.N.

Note: The editor, Barbara Fuszard, has inserted comments within the text of many of the articles included here. These editorial comments have been set in italics to set them apart from the original article.

Introduction

Can the existing image and reality of professional nursing in an institutional setting be changed before we lose all professional nurses from our health care institutions? Yes. The nursing administrator, who is both nurse and manager, can influence the role of nurses through job enrichment.

The concept of job enrichment is not new. Herzberg, who coined the term, has been developing and writing about his concept since the 1950s, but we in nursing have been slower than other groups to realize its potential. Herzberg sought to identify what motivates employees. Five factors stood out as strong determiners of job satisfaction among the workers in his studies:

1. achievement
2. recognition
3. the work itself
4. responsibility
5. advancement

The last three were found to be the most important for lasting change of attitudes.[1] In 1977, Godfrey polled 17,000 nurses to determine what they found most satisfying about their jobs. They listed the four greatest satisfiers as helping people, worthwhile work, intellectual challenge, and interesting work,[2] items comparable to those found by Herzberg in his earlier, more extensive studies.

In reviewing these findings, it appears that management personnel fulfill their obligations to their employees only partially by meeting their needs for security, safety, and social contacts. Herzberg related the motivators of workers to the opportunities required on the job if employees are to experience continual satisfaction in performing it:

Motivator	Growth Principle
Achievement and recognition for achievement	Opportunity to increase knowledge
Responsibility	Opportunity to increase understanding
Possibility of growth	Opportunity for creativity
Advancement	Opportunity to experience ambiguity in decision making
Interest	Opportunity to individuate and seek real growth[3]

Herzberg also explained how the job can help employees reach new levels of psychological growth:

> First, the job must allow for some achievement opportunities, and these achievements must result in the employee's knowing more about his occupation or job than he did previously. The recognition for achievement is the reinforcement that is necessary at the early stages of all learning. Eventually, it is hoped, the employee will develop his own generator and will thus rely less on outside recognition of his growth and more on his own evaluation.
>
> Second, increased responsibility suggests a more complex task. Increasing the complexity of the job can provide the opportunity for understanding the relationships among the various components of the assignment and thereby provide for the next level of psychological growth.
>
> Third, the task must contain an open end in its description, to allow for possible growth. If the job allows for possible growth, it may then provide the opportunity for the employee to be creative and satisfy the third level of psychological growth.
>
> Fourth, advancement in the formal sense, or even without change in rank, requires in either case that a higher order of task be presented to the employee. This higher-order task gives the opportunity to be successful in ambiguity and thus leads to a still higher level of psychological growth.
>
> Finally, if the employee finds that the actual task he has to do is of direct interest to him, then his job can provide a sense of personal worth and individuality. Furthermore, if the job has intrinsic attractive powers, the employee is less likely to be concerned with other people's hygiene and less tempted to seek substitute growth from his own hygiene needs. In this latter instance, he is enabled to experience the highest level of psychological growth—self-actualization.[4]

The use of the terms *motivators, satisfaction,* and *needs* is founded in Maslow's theory that a person's basic needs are motivators.[5] Both Maslow and Herzberg felt that people are satisfied ("happy") when their needs are met. They, however, disagreed on what these needs are.

The Getzels-Guba model offers a framework for the discussion of job enrichment and its application to the problems facing the health care administrator and the individual nurse.[6] This model interrelates the achievement of the goals of the institution, which are the concern of the nursing administrator, with the goals of the individuals who work in the institution. The goals of the institution are met only through the actions of individuals, however. It is the aim of management to direct the actions of the individuals in the organization so that the goals of the organization will be met. At the same time, which sometimes leads to conflict, individuals are seeking to meet their own needs and achieve their own goals.

Herzberg identified the actions of management that help individuals meet their personal goals. Since registered nurses are reaching toward professionalism, they feel a need to be permitted to function, to be recognized, and to be rewarded as professionals. Therefore, the discussion of the Getzels-Guba model in this book is followed by a review of professionalization and the problem of a professional in an organization.

A brief review of motivation leads to a discussion of the role of leadership and the precursor to job enrichment, job enlargement. Job enrichment then rises as a strange child of the motivation theories, taking the genes of these theories and rearranging them to elicit new views of motivation. The concept of job enrichment assumes form when concrete examples are offered to the nursing administrator. A smorgasbord of structural changes, such as decentralization, specialization, and the establishment of lateral positions, are available to the top-level manager. Attitudinal changes involve opportunities for professional control by individual nurses, new types of evaluation, and new ways of looking at the nursing administrator's responsibility for counseling and disciplining. Many of the suggestions in this text involve tapping the creativity of nurses, their drive for growth, and their acceptance of further responsibility.

Any text is limited by its front and back covers. This text will expose nursing administrators and students of nursing administration to the concept of job enrichment and will stimulate their own creativity by offering examples of job enrichment that have already proved successful. Other ideas drawn from management literature will be applied to institutional nursing. This book will then be completed by the ingenuity of the individual readers who take the appropriate, applicable suggestions of this book and institute them in their own setting.

NOTES

1. Frederick Herzberg, *Work and the Nature of Man* (New York: New American Library, 1966), p. 92.
2. Marjorie A. Godfrey, "Job Satisfaction—or Should That Be *Dis*satisfaction? How Nurses Feel About Nursing: I," *Nursing 78* (April 1978): 92.

3. Herzberg, *Work and the Nature of Man*, p. 196.
4. Herzberg, *Work and the Nature of Man*, pp. 196–197.
5. Maslow, *Motivation and Personality*, 2d ed. (New York: Harper & Row, 1970).
6. Getzels, Lipham, and Campbell, *Educational Administration as a Social Process: Theory, Research, Practice* (New York: Harper & Row, 1968), p. 80.

Part I
The Professional and the Institution: Goal Conflict

Registered nurses (RNs) traditionally seek employment at institutions such as hospitals to fulfill their personal and professional goals. Yet these health care institutions were established to meet, not the needs of RNs, but the health needs of society.

The model presented in "The Getzels-Guba Model" offers a framework that can be used not only to study the dilemma of employees in an institution whose goals differ from the goals of the institution, but also to examine various ways to resolve this conflict. This classic model includes an individual's unique goals and activities (which they call "idiographic"), the organization's goals and activity requirements (which they call "nomothetic"), and ways in which the interrelation of the two can be used to study administration as a social process. Getzels and Guba define administration as a process dealing with social behavior in a hierarchical institution. Therefore, it is the responsibility of an administrator, such as the nursing administrator, to orchestrate the two dimensions of the Getzels-Guba model so that both the needs of the nurse and the role expectations of the institution are met. The nursing administrator is in a strategic linking position between personnel needs and institutional needs. In order to function adequately in this position, the administrator needs to understand both the personnel (in this case the registered professional nurse) and the institution.

The case for the RN is presented by Vollmer and Mills in "The Concept of Professionalization." The administrator must remember, first, that the nurse is a product of the times. Herzberg reported that persons in all types of occupations, from common labor to the professions, derive satisfaction from the work itself.[1] Examining the values of persons who entered the workforce in the 1940s, 1950s, 1960s, and 1970s, he found that the common value among these workers was a *desire to serve*:

A sound labor philosophy for the eighties must rest on the basic need of human beings to be needed. People want to be responsible and efficient when they can perceive that their work serves a meaningful purpose.[2]

This orientation to service dovetails perfectly with the need of today's nurses to achieve professional status. Vollmer and Mills see professionalization as a process, a continuum.

Nursing's position on this continuum can be compared to those of other occupations by utilizing criteria for a profession identified by Flexner in the early 1900s,[3] as explained by Greenwood in "Attributes of a Profession." Greenwood's explanation is congruent with later concepts of professionalism, such as professionalism as autonomy[4,5] and as decision making.[6]

In "Professions and Professionalism," however, Freidson throws a pall over the hopes of those who would raise nursing to a profession within the existing social system of health care. Freidson, a medical sociologist, says that the relationship between nursing and medicine must change before nursing can become a profession—that meeting all the Flexner criteria, such as organization and code of ethics, are valueless trappings.

Abrahamson, in "Role Specialization in a Formal Organization," examines the institution in which the professional works, describing the ponderous bureaucracy first identified by Weber.[7] Many of the characteristics of a pure bureaucracy apply to health care institutions, especially large hospitals. Compounding the bureaucratic, hierarchical structure of health care institutions are the two lines of authority that impinge on the nurse—the hospital's authority and the physician's authority. Abrahamson also identifies the role of the professional in the organization.

NOTES

1. Frederick Herzberg, "Herzberg on Motivation for the '80s: Piecing Together Generations of Values," *Industry Week*, 1 October 1979, 63.

2. Ibid., p. 63.

3. Abraham Flexner, "Is Social Work a Profession?" *Proceedings of the National Conference of Charities and Corrections*. (Chicago: 1915), pp. 576–590.

4. Eliot Freidson, ed., *Profession of Medicine* (New York: Dodd, Mead, 1970).

5. Eliot Freidson, *Professional Dominance: The Social Structure of Medical Care* (New York: Atherton Press, 1970).

6. Allen B. Rosenstein, *A Study of a Profession and Professional Education* (Los Angeles: Department of Engineering, University of California at Los Angeles, 1968).

7. Max Weber, *The Theory of Social and Economic Organization* (translated by A.M. Henderson and T. Parsons; Glencoe, Illinois: Free Press, 1947).

1.
Social Behavior and the Administrative Process

Jacob W. Getzels and Egon G. Guba

The process of administration deals essentially with the conduct of social behavior in a hierarchical setting.[1] Structurally, we may conceive of administration as a series of superordinate-subordinate relationships within a social system. Functionally, this hierarchy of relationships is the locus for allocating and integrating roles, personnel, and facilities to achieve the goals of the system.

We conceive of the social system as involving two major classes of phenomena, which are at once conceptually independent and phenomenally interactive. There are, first, the *institutions* with certain *roles* and *expectations* that will fulfill the goals of the system. Second, inhabiting the system there are the *individuals* with certain *personalities* and *need-dispositions*, whose interactions comprise what we generally call "social behavior." Social behavior may be apprehended as a function of the following major elements: institution, role, and expectation, which together constitute the *nomothetic*, or normative, dimension of activity in a social system; and individual, personality, and need-disposition, which together constitute the *idiographic*, or personal, dimension of activity in a social system.

To understand the nature of the observed behavior and to be able to predict and control it, we must understand the nature and relationships of those elements. The term "institution" has received a variety of definitions, but for our purposes it is sufficient to point out that all social systems have certain imperative functions that come in time to be carried out in certain routinized patterns. These functions—governing, educating, policing, for example—may be said to have become "institutionalized," and the agencies established to carry out these institutionalized functions for the social system as a whole may be termed "institutions." These institutions have certain noteworthy characteristics.

Reprinted and modified with permission from Jacob W. Getzels and Egon G. Guba, "Social Behavior and the Administrative Process," *School Review*, 65 (Winter, 1957), 424–433.

a) Institutions are *purposive*. They are established to carry out certain ends, and these ends serve as the criteria against which institutional practices are ultimately evaluated.
b) Institutions are *peopled*. If institutions are to carry out their prescribed goals, human agents are required. It should be noted, however, that here we are concerned with people, not in the personalistic sense, but in the actuarial sense. To avoid the possibility of confusion, we may adopt the term "actor" instead of "person" for this level of analysis.
c) Institutions are *structural*. To carry out a specific purpose requires an organization, and organization implies component parts and some rules about how these parts should be interrelated. If the goals and purposes of the institution are known, the tasks to achieve the goals may be specified, and these may be organized into *roles*. Each role is assigned certain responsibilities and concomitant resources, including authority and facilities for implementing the given tasks. A significant feature of such a blueprint or "table of organization" of roles is that it is most frequently set up *before* the selection of any real incumbents for the roles; it is set up in terms of *actors*, in the sense previously defined. And if we may anticipate ourselves a little here, the real person may or may not exactly fit the given roles. As we shall see, this question of fitness poses, in many ways, one of the critical dilemmas of administration.
d) Institutions are *normative*. The fact that tasks for achieving the institutional goals are organized into roles implies that the roles serve as "norms" for the behavior of the role incumbents or actors. The role expectations are obligatory upon the actor if he is to retain his legitimate place in the institution.
e) Institutions are *sanction-bearing*. The existence of norms is of no consequence unless there is adherence to them. Accordingly institutions must have at their disposal appropriate positive and negative sanctions for ensuring compliance with the norms, at least within broad limits.

The most important subunit of the institution is the role. Roles are the structural elements defining the behavior of the role incumbents or actors. The following generalizations may be made about the nature of roles.

a) Roles represent *positions, offices,* or *statuses within the institution.* The role itself may be described, in the words of Linton, as the "dynamic aspect"[2] of such positions, offices, or statuses.
b) Roles are defined in terms of *role expectations*. A role has certain normative rights and duties, which may be termed "role expectations." When the role incumbent puts these rights and duties into effect, he is said to be performing his role. The expectations define for the actor, whoever he may be, what he

should do under various circumstances as long as he is the incumbent of the particular role.
c) Roles are *institutional givens*. Since the role expectations may be formulated without reference to the particular individuals who will serve as the role incumbents, it is clear that the prescriptions do not depend on individual perception or even on typical behavior. Although the expectations may be misperceived or even serve as points of departure for the actual role incumbents, their crucial significance as blueprints for what *should* be done is not thereby nullified.
d) The behaviors associated with a role may be thought of as lying along a *continuum from "required" to "prohibited."* Certain expectations are held to be crucial to the role, and the appropriate behaviors are absolutely required of the incumbent. Other behaviors are absolutely forbidden. Between these extremes lie certain other behaviors, some of which would be recommended and others perhaps mildly disapproved, but all of which would be considered permissible, at least in the ordinary case. It is this flexible feature of roles that makes it possible for role incumbents with different personalities to fulfill the same role and give it the stamp of their individual styles of behavior.
e) Roles are *complementary*. Roles are interdependent in that each role derives its meaning from other related roles in the institution. In a sense, a role is not only a prescription for the role incumbent but also for incumbents of other roles within the organization, so that in a hierarchical setting the expectations for one role may, to some extent, form the sanctions for a second interlocking role. For example, the role of sergeant and the role of private in the army cannot really be defined or implemented except in relation to each other. This quality of complementariness fuses two or more roles into a coherent, interactive unit and makes it possible for us to conceive of an institution as having a characteristic structure.

So far in our analysis it has been sufficient to conceive of the role incumbents as only "actors," devoid of personal or other individualizing characteristics, as if all incumbents of the same role were exactly alike and implemented the given role in exactly the same way. But roles are filled by real, flesh-and-blood persons, and no two persons are exactly alike. An individual stamps the particular role he fills with the unique style of his own characteristic pattern of expressive behavior. Even in the case of the relatively inflexible roles of sergeant and of private, no two individual sergeants or privates fulfill the roles in exactly the same way. To understand the observed behavior of a specific sergeant and a specific private, it is not enough to know only the nature of the roles and of the expectations (although their behavior cannot be understood apart from these), but we must know the nature of the individuals inhabiting the roles and reacting to the expectations as well. That is, in addition to the nomothetic, or normative, aspects, we must also consider the idiographic, or individualizing, aspects of social behavior. Now, just as we were able to analyze the institutional dimension into the component elements of role and expectation, so we may analyze the individual dimension into the component elements of personality and need-disposition.

The term "personality," like that of "institution," has been given a variety of meanings. For our purposes, "personality" may be defined as the dynamic organization within the individual of those need-dispositions that govern his unique reactions to the environment. The central analytic elements of personality are the need-dispositions, which we may well define, with Parsons and Shils, as individual "tendencies to orient and act with respect to objects in certain manners and to expect certain consequences from these actions."[3] Or, as the same authors go on to say: "The conjoined word 'need-disposition' itself has a double connotation; on the one hand, it refers to a tendency to accomplish some end state; on the other, it refers to a disposition to do something with an object designed to accomplish the end state."[4]

Returning to the example of the sergeant and the private, we may now make an essential distinction between the behavior of two individuals with a need-disposition for "submission" in the roles of sergeant and private and the behavior of two individuals with a need-disposition for "ascendance" in the same roles. In short, to understand the behavior of specific role incumbents in an institution, we must know both the role expectations and the need-dispositions. Indeed, needs and expectations may both be thought of as *motives* for behavior, the one deriving from personal propensities, the other from institutional requirements. What we call social behavior may be conceived as ultimately deriving from the interaction between the two sets of motives.

The general model we have been describing may be represented pictorially as indicated in Figure 1–1. The nomothetic axis is shown at the top of the diagram and consists of institution, role, and role expectations, each term being the analytic unit for the term next preceding it. Thus the social system is defined by its institutions; each institution, by its constituent roles; each role, by the expectations attaching to it. Similarly, the idiographic axis, shown at the lower portion of the diagram, consists of individual, personality, and need-dispositions, each term again serving as the analytic unit for the term next preceding it. A given act is conceived as deriving simultaneously from both the nomothetic and the idiographic dimensions. That is to say, social behavior results as the individual attempts to cope with an environment composed of patterns of expectations for his behavior in ways consistent with his own independent pattern of needs. Thus we may write the general equation: $B = f(R \times P)$, where B is observed behavior, R is a given institutional role defined by the expectations attaching to it, and P is the personality of the particular role incumbent defined by the incumbent's need-dispositions.

Figure 1-1 General Model Showing the Nomothetic and the Idiographic Dimensions of Social Behavior

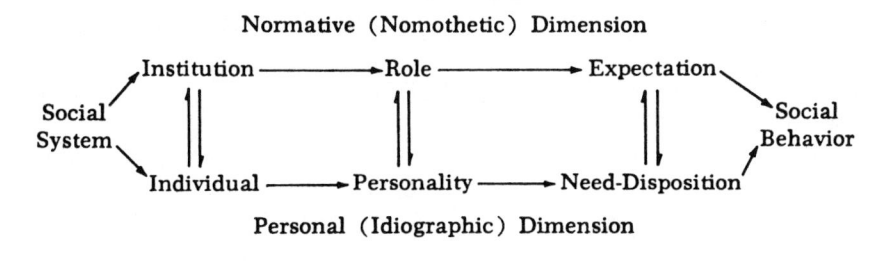

```
                Normative (Nomothetic) Dimension
           ╱Institution ─────────▶ Role ──────────▶ Expectation╲
    Social╱       ⇅                  ⇅                  ⇅        ╲Social
   System╲                                                        ╱Behavior
          ╲Individual ─────────▶ Personality ──────▶ Need-Disposition╱
                    Personal (Idiographic) Dimension
```

The portions of role and personality factors determining behavior vary with the specific act, the specific role, and the specific personality involved. The nature of the interaction can be understood from another graphic representation shown as Figure 1-2. The factors entering into a given behavioral act may be conceived as occurring at a line cutting through the role and personality possibilities represented by the rectangle. At the left, the proportion of the act dictated by considerations of role expectations is relatively large, while the proportion of the act dictated by considerations of personality is relatively small. At the right, these proportions are reversed, and considerations of personality become greater than considerations of role expectations. In these terms, for example, the behavior of our army private may be said to conform almost entirely to role demands (Line A), while the behavior of a free-lance artist derives almost entirely from personality dispositions (Line B). In either case, behavior, insofar as it is "social," remains a function of both role and personality although in different degrees. When role is maximized, behavior still retains some personal aspects because no role is ever so closely defined as to eliminate all individual latitude. When personality is maximized,

---

Figure 1-2 The Interaction of Role and Personality in a Behavioral Act ($B = f[R \times P]$)

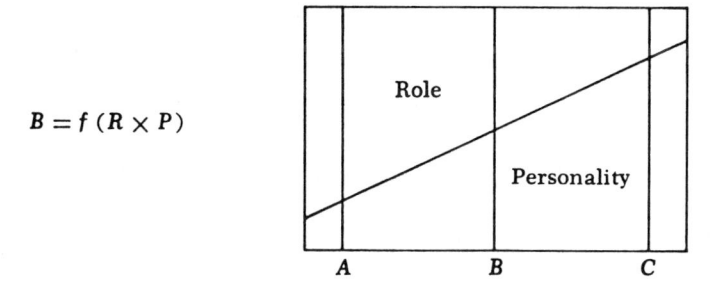

$$B = f(R \times P)$$

```
    ┌─────────┬─────────┬─────────┐
    │  Role   │         │        ╱│
    │         │        ╱│       ╱ │
    │         │      ╱  │     ╱   │
    │         │    ╱    │   ╱     │
    │         │  ╱      │ ╱       │
    │        ╱│         │ Personality│
    │      ╱  │         │         │
    │    ╱    │         │         │
    └─────────┴─────────┴─────────┘
         A         B         C
```

social behavior still cannot be free from some role prescription. The individual who divorces himself entirely from such prescription ceases to communicate with his fellows and is said to be autistic.

The relevance of this general model for administrative theory and practice becomes apparent when it is seen that the administrative process inevitably deals with the fulfillment of both nomothetic role expectations and idiographic need-dispositions while the goals of a particular social system are being achieved. The unique task of administration, at least with respect to staff relations, is just this: to integrate the demands of the institution and the demands of the staff members in a way that is at once organizationally productive and individually fulfilling.

In the framework outlined here, we may proceed to a reformulation of certain recurring administrative problems and to a clarification of the issues involved.

INDIVIDUAL AND INSTITUTIONAL CONFLICT

When an individual performs up to role expectations, we may say that he is *adjusted* to the role. Conversely, when an individual fulfills all his needs, we may speak of him as *integrated*. Ideally, the individual should be both adjusted and integrated, so that he may by one act fulfill both the nomothetic, or institutional, requirements and the idiographic, or personal, requirements. This would obviously be the case if institutional expectations and personal needs were absolutely congruent, for the individual would always will what was mandatory, and both his adjustment and his integration would be maximized. But absolute congruence of expectations and needs is seldom, if ever, found in practice, and as a consequence there is inevitably a greater or lesser amount of strain or conflict for the individual and the institution. In the present context this strain or conflict may be defined simply as the "mutual interference of adjustive and integrative reactions." The model points to three primary sources of conflict in the administrative setting.[5]

  a) *Role-personality conflicts* occur as a function of discrepancies between the pattern of expectations attaching to a given role and the pattern of need-dispositions characteristic of the incumbent of the role. Recall again our example of the individual with high need-dispositions for "ascendance" who is placed in the role of private. There is mutual interference between nomothetic expectations and idiographic dispositions, and the individual must choose whether he will fulfill individual needs or institutional requirements. If he chooses the latter, he is liable to unsatisfactory personal integration. If he chooses the former, he is liable to unsatisfactory role adjustment. In practice there is usually compromise, but, in any event, the nature of the forthcoming behavior is quite different when the expectations and the dispositions are discrepant than when they are congruent.

b) *Role conflicts* occur whenever a role incumbent is required to conform simultaneously to a number of expectations which are mutually exclusive, contradictory, or inconsistent, so that adjustment to one set of requirements makes adjustment to the other impossible or at least difficult. Role conflicts in this sense are situational givens and are independent of the personality of the role incumbent. They are evidence of disorganization in the nomothetic dimension and may arise in several ways:

   (1) Disagreement within the referent group defining the role. *For example, some head nurses may expect the nursing supervisor to give them specific direction, whereas other head nurses may expect the nursing supervisor to let them use their own professional judgment to solve unit problems.*

   (2) Disagreement among several referent groups, each having a right to define expectations for the same role. *For example, the hospital administrator may expect the nursing administrator to standardize supplies throughout the hospital in order to contain costs, whereas an individual physician may expect the nursing administrator to obtain special supplies for specific patients.*

   (3) Contradiction in the expectations of two or more roles which an individual is occupying at the same time. *For example, the nursing administrator is often torn between the roles of manager and nurse, since time constraints can make it impossible to practice both.*

c) *Personality conflicts* occur as a function of opposing needs and dispositions within the personality of the role incumbent. The effect of such personal disequilibrium is to keep the individual at odds with the institution either because he cannot maintain a stable relation with a given role or because, in terms of his autistic reactions, he habitually misperceives the expectations placed upon him. In any case, just as role conflict is a situational given, personality conflict is an individual given and is independent of any particular institutional setting. No matter what the situation, the role is, in a sense, detached by the individual from its institutional context and function and is used by him to work out personal and private needs and dispositions, however inappropriate these may be to the goals of the social system as a whole.

In the terms of our model, these three types of conflict represent incongruence in the nomothetic and the idiographic dimensions, or the interaction between the two dimensions of the social system under study. Such incongruence is symptomatic of administrative failure and leads to loss in individual and institutional productivity.[6]

NOTES

1. Our indebtedness to the work of Talcott Parsons will be self-evident throughout this and subsequent sections of the paper. See also J.W. Getzels, "A Psycho-sociological Framework for the Study of Educational Administration," *Harvard Educational Review*, XXII (Fall, 1952), 235–46.
2. Ralph Linton, *The Study of Man*. New York: D. Appleton-Century Co., 1936.
3. Talcott Parsons and Edward A. Shils, *Toward a General Theory of Action*. Cambridge, Massachusetts: Harvard University Press, 1951.
4. For some attempts at research in this area, see (*a*) Samuel A. Stouffer and Jackson Toby, "Role Conflict and Personality," *American Journal of Sociology*, LVI (March, 1951), 395–406; (*b*) J.W. Getzels and E.G. Guba, "Role, Role Conflict, and Effectiveness: An Empirical Study," *American Sociological Review*, XIX (April, 1954), 164–75; (*c*) J.W. Getzels and E.G. Guba, "The Structure of Roles and Role Conflict in the Teaching Situation," *Journal of Educational Sociology*, XXIX (September, 1955), 30–40.
5. The term "satisfaction," as it is used here, is more or less synonymous with "contentment" and should not be taken to include such additional concepts as fundamental agreement with institutional objectives or the feeling that the institutional environment lives up to the incumbent's standards of technical or professional adequacy. These concepts involve certain additional factors, as, for example, the level of aspiration of the incumbent, which are too complex to be handled here.
6. The relation of theory, research, and practice in administration generally has been discussed by J.D. Thompson, "On Building an Administrative Science," *Administrative Science Quarterly*, I (June, 1956), 102–11; and in educational administration specifically by A.P. Coladarci and J.W. Getzels, *The Use of Theory in Educational Administration*, Monograph No. 5. Stanford, California: School of Education, Stanford University, 1956.

* * * *

Orchestrating the two dimensions of the Getzels-Guba model is a challenge for the nursing administrator, who not only must ensure that institutional goals are met, but also must offer RNs the opportunity to meet their own needs. One need of RNs is becoming ever more dominant—the need for professional recognition. What is the interface between professionalism and job satisfaction? What does a professional seek from work? In discussing their view of professionalization—a process in which an occupation becomes a profession—Vollmer and Mills introduce the concept of professionalism, a further complication of the diadic Getzels-Guba model.

2.
The Concept of Professionalization

Howard M. Vollmer and Donald L. Mills

The constituent elements of social life are neither "black" nor "white." Human behavior, however we want to describe it, exhibits varying shades of "gray." Max Weber, the eminent German social scientist, recognized this when he wrote about "ideal types" in the last decade of the nineteenth century and the first decade of the twentieth. He described changes in political organization as movements from "traditional" to "rational-bureaucratic" forms of administration. These he called "ideal types," or what we today might term "models," of administrative behavior. Needless to say, no individual organization is completely bureaucratic or completely traditional in its structure and behavior. The chief use of ideal types or models, then, is to describe and understand administrative behavior; they permit us to locate particular administrative patterns along a *continuum* ranging from traditional forms at one end to rational-bureaucratic patterns at the other. Insofar as the elements in the continuum are unidimensional, we can describe organization X as being more or less bureaucratic in comparison with organization Y. Having made this description, we have then established the basis for making certain predictions about the behavior of these organizational entities and about the individuals within them. Adequate description along meaningful base dimensions is the first task in the social as in the natural sciences.

Those who have studied occupational institutions in recent years have begun to establish the basis for what promises to be a useful classification scheme similar in method to Weber's use of ideal types to describe administrative organization. It focuses in large part upon the way human beings tend to organize their work activities along a career perspective, rather than the way they administer, coordinate, and control collective efforts in a particular organizational context. Individual patterns of work transcend administrative boundaries. In modern industrial

---

Modified with permission from Howard M. Vollmer and Donald L. Mills, eds., *Professionalization* (Englewood Cliffs, N.J.: Prentice-Hall, 1966), pp. 1–2.

society, at least, people tend to move from one job position to another, and from one employer to another. Yet there is often some continuity between one job and the next; people are not randomly assigned from job to job. Whatever skills or knowledge they have acquired in one job, they carry to the next. When they become self-conscious of this continuity, they begin to speak of a "career." What is more, human beings tend to develop social and cultural mechanisms to protect and enhance this continuity. Thus we find a trend toward more formal occupational associations and more formalized occupational codes of behavior in many diverse lines of work. This we describe as a movement toward professionalization.

In the terminology that we shall use here, a "profession" is really an ideal type of occupational institution. The ministry, law, and medicine have been considered to be the traditional and original professions in Western society. However, when we look at a diverse sample of occupational groups, we find that today many are assuming, at least in rudimentary form, some of the characteristics commonly attributed to the traditional professions. Furthermore, we find that many groups usually considered within the context of the traditional professions fall short of the professional model in significant respects. Therefore, it seems more useful to analyze and describe the characteristics of occupational institutions in terms of the concept of *professionalization,* assuming that many, if not all, occupations may be placed somewhere on a continuum between the ideal-type "profession" at one end and completely unorganized occupational categories, or "non-professions," at the other end. Professionalization is a process then, that may affect any occupation to a greater or lesser degree.

* * *

Greenwood's attributes of a profession can be used as criteria to evaluate nursing's progression along the continuum of professionalization described by Vollmer and Mills.

3.
Attributes of a Profession

Ernest Greenwood

The professions occupy a position of great importance on the American scene.[1] In a society such as ours, characterized by minute division of labor based upon technical specialization, many important features of social organization are dependent upon professional functions. Professional activity is coming to play a predominant role in the life patterns of increasing numbers of individuals of both sexes, occupying much of their waking moments, providing life goals, determining behavior, and shaping personality. It is no wonder, therefore, that the phenomenon of professionalism has become an object of observation by sociologists.[2] The sociological approach to professionalism is one that views a profession as an organized group which is constantly interacting with the society that forms its matrix, which performs its social functions through a network of formal and informal relationships, and which creates its own subculture requiring adjustments to it as a prerequisite for career success.[3]

Within the professional category of its occupational classification the United States Census Bureau includes, among others, the following: accountant, architect, artist, attorney, clergyman, college professor, dentist, engineer, journalist, judge, librarian, natural scientist, optometrist, pharmacist, physician, social scientist, social worker, surgeon, and teacher.[4] *The nurse is also included on this list.* What common attributes do these professional occupations possess which distinguish them from the nonprofessional ones? After a careful canvass of the sociological literature on occupations, this writer has been able to distill five elements, upon which there appears to be consensus among the students of the subject, as constituting the distinguishing attributes of a profession.[5] Succinctly put, all professions seem to possess: (1) systematic theory, (2) authority,

---

Modified with permission from Ernest Greenwood, "Attributes of a Profession," *Social Work* 2, no. 3 (National Association of Social Workers, Inc., July 1957): 45–55.

(3) community sanction, (4) ethical codes, and (5) a culture. The purpose of this article is to describe fully these attributes.

Before launching into our description, a preliminary word of caution is due. With respect to each of the above attributes, the true difference between a professional and a nonprofessional occupation is not a qualitative but a quantitative one. Strictly speaking, these attributes are not the exclusive monopoly of the professions; nonprofessional occupations also possess them, but to a lesser degree. *The quantification makes it possible to place an occupation on the professionalization scale.* As is true of most social phenomena, the phenomenon of professionalism cannot be structured in terms of clear-cut classes. Rather, we must think of the occupations in a society as distributing themselves along a continuum.[6] At one end of this continuum are bunched the well-recognized, and undisputed professions (e.g., physician, attorney, professor, scientist); at the opposite end are bunched the least skilled and least attractive occupations (e.g., watchman, truckloader, farm laborer, scrubwoman, busboy). The remaining occupations, less skilled and less prestigeful than the former, but more so than the latter, are distributed between these two poles. The occupations bunched at the professional pole of the continuum possess to a maximum degree the attributes about to be described. As we move away from this pole, the occupations possess these attributes to a decreasing degree. Thus, in the less developed professions (*nursing?*), these attributes appear in moderate degree. When we reach the midregion of the continuum, among the clerical, sales, and crafts occupations, they occur in still lesser degree; while at the unskilled end of the continuum the occupations possess these attributes so minimally that they are virtually nonexistent. If the reader keeps this concept of the continuum in mind, the presentation will less likely appear as a distortion of reality.

SYSTEMATIC BODY OF THEORY[7]

It is often contended that the chief difference between a professional and a nonprofessional occupation lies in the element of superior skill. The performance of a professional service presumably involves a series of unusually complicated operations, mastery of which requires lengthy training. The models referred to in this connection are the performances of a surgeon, a concert pianist, or a research physicist. However, some nonprofessional occupations actually involve a higher order of skill than many professional ones. For example, tool-and-die making, diamond-cutting, monument-engraving, or cabinet-making involve more intricate operations than schoolteaching, nursing, or social work. Therefore, to focus on the element of skill per se in describing the professions is to miss the kernel of their uniqueness.

The crucial distinction is this: the skills that characterize a profession flow from and are supported by a fund of knowledge that has been organized into an internally consistent system, called a *body of theory*. A profession's underlying body of theory is a system of abstract propositions that describe in general terms the classes of phenomena comprising the profession's focus of interest. Theory serves as a base in terms of which the professional rationalizes his operations in concrete situations. Acquisition of the professional skill requires a prior or simultaneous mastery of the theory underlying that skill. Preparation for a profession, therefore, involves considerable preoccupation with systematic theory, a feature virtually absent in the training of the nonprofessional. And so treatises are written on legal theory, musical theory, *nursing theory,* social work theory, the theory of the drama, and so on; but no books appear on the theory of punch-pressing or pipe-fitting or brick-laying.

Because understanding of theory is so important to professional skill, preparation for a profession must be an intellectual as well as a practical experience. On-the-job training through apprenticeship, which suffices for a nonprofessional occupation, becomes inadequate for a profession. Orientation in theory can be achieved best through formal education in an academic setting. Hence the appearance of the professional school, more often than not university affiliated, wherein the milieu is a contrast to that of the trade school.

The American Nurses' Association's Proposal for 1985 indicates that all nursing education should be in institutions of higher learning, with the baccalaureate degree as a basis for beginning practice. This long-term goal is still being fought, even by nurses themselves.

Theoretical knowledge is more difficult to master than operational procedures; it is easier to learn to repair an automobile than to learn the principles of the internal combustion engine. There are, of course, a number of free-lance professional pursuits (e.g., acting, painting, writing, composing, and the like) wherein academic preparation is not mandatory. Nevertheless, even in these fields various "schools" and "institutes" are appearing, although they may not be run along traditional academic lines. We can generalize that as an occupation moves toward professional status, apprenticeship training yields to formalized education, because the function of theory as a groundwork for practice acquires increasing importance.

The importance of theory precipitates a form of activity normally not encountered in a nonprofessional occupation, viz., theory construction via systematic research. To generate valid theory that will provide a solid base for professional techniques requires the application of the scientific method to the service-related problems of the profession. Continued employment of the scientific method is nurtured by and in turn reinforces the element of *rationality*.[8] As an orientation, rationality is the antithesis of traditionalism. The spirit of rationality in a profession encourages a critical, as opposed to a reverential, attitude toward the theoretical system. It implies a perpetual readiness to discard any portion of that system, no matter how time honored it may be, with a formulation demonstrated to be more valid. The spirit of rationality generates group self-criticism and theoretical controversy. Professional members convene regularly in their associations to learn and to evaluate innovations in theory. This produces an intellectually stimulating milieu that is in marked contrast to the milieu of a nonprofessional occupation.

In the evolution of every profession there emerges the researcher-theoretician whose role is that of scientific investigation and theoretical systematization. In technological professions[9] a division of labor thereby evolves, that between the theory-oriented and the practice-oriented person. Witness the physician who prefers to attach himself to a medical research center rather than to enter private practice. This division may also yield to cleavages with repercussions upon intraprofessional relationships. However, if properly integrated, the division of labor produces an accelerated expansion of the body of theory and a sprouting of theoretical branches around which specialties nucleate. The net effect of such developments is to lengthen the preparation deemed desirable for entry into the profession. This accounts for the rise of graduate professional training on top of a basic college education.

Nursing, as are the other health professions, is exposed to the great explosion of knowledge and technology, shortening the half-life of knowledge every year. Social work, physical therapy, speech therapy, and pharmacy are moving to advanced degrees as beginning levels of practice, because of this increased knowledge necessary for practice. Yet nursing continues to support associate degree and diploma school backgrounds of its beginning practitioners.

PROFESSIONAL AUTHORITY

Extensive education in the systematic theory of his discipline imparts to the professional a type of knowledge that highlights the layman's comparative ignorance. This fact is the basis for the professional's authority, which has some interesting features.

A nonprofessional occupation has customers; a professional occupation has clients. What is the difference? A customer determines what services and/or commodities he wants, and he shops around until he finds them. His freedom of decision rests upon the premise that he has the capacity to appraise his own needs and to judge the potential of the service or of the commodity to satisfy them. The infallibility of his decisions is epitomized in the slogan: "The customer is always right!" In a professional relationship, however, the professional dictates what is good or evil for the client, who has no choice but to accede to professional judgment. Here the premise is that, because he lacks the requisite theoretical background, the client cannot diagnose his own needs or discriminate among the range of possibilities for meeting them. Nor is the client considered able to evaluate the caliber of the professional service he receives. In a nonprofessional occupation the customer can criticize the quality of the commodity he has purchased, and even demand a refund. The client lacks this same prerogative, having surrendered it to professional authority. This element of authority is one, although not the sole, reason why a profession frowns on advertising. If a profession were to advertise, it would, in effect, impute to the potential client the discriminating capacity to select from competing forms of service. The client's subordination to professional authority invests the professional with a monopoly of judgment. When an occupation strives toward professionalization, one of its aspirations is to acquire this monopoly.

The client derives a sense of security from the professional's assumption of authority. The authoritative air of the professional is a principal source of the client's faith that the relationship he is about to enter contains the potentials for meeting his needs.

Nurses have questioned whether nursing meets the professionalism requirement of an extensive body of knowledge as basis for legitimate professional authority. One approach to meeting this criterion has been interest in identifying a unique body of knowledge for nursing, "nursing theory." A number of nurses have put forth their "nursing theories" and "conceptual frameworks" to this end. Undergraduate and graduate nursing programs are offering content in "nursing theory" as part of the body of knowledge transmitted to students. Yet there is disagreement among nurses not only as to which nursing theory is appropriate, but even as to whether nursing theory even exists.

Luther Christman sees the professions as applied sciences, and states:

> There is not any theory . . . of applied science. Applied scientists use theory. They are not theories in themselves nor is their work. Thus, one cannot identify a theory of engineering, of medicine, of dentistry, or of nursing. . . .
>
> All clinicians utilize the same theoretical sciences. The range and depth of the utilization are vast, limited only by the boundaries of individual educational training . . . Physiology, for instance, is the same no matter who utilizes it or where it is utilized.*

If we follow Christman's thinking, then, we will judge the professionalism of nursing on this criterion, by whether decisions of nurses are based empirically, rather than by whether or not "nursing theory" exists.

---

*Luther Christman. "There is No Theory of Nursing." Paper presented at Chautauqua '82, Colorado Nurses Association, Vail, CO, August 12, 1982.

The professional's authority, however, is not limitless; its function is confined to those specific spheres within which the professional has been educated. This quality in professional authority Parsons calls *functional specificity*.[10] Functional specificity carries the following implications for the client-professional relationship.

The professional cannot prescribe guides for facets of the client's life where his theoretical competence does not apply. To venture such prescriptions is to invade a province wherein he himself is a layman and, hence, to violate the authority of another professional group. The professional must not use his position of authority to exploit the client for purposes of personal gratification. In any association of superordination-subordination, of which the professional-client relationship is a perfect specimen, the subordinate member—here, the client—can be maneuvered into a dependent role. The psychological advantage which thereby accrues to the professional could constitute a temptation for him. The professional must inhibit his impulses to use the professional relationship for the satisfaction of the sexual need, the need to manipulate others, or the need to live vicariously. In the case of the therapeutic professions it is ideally preferred that client-professional intercourse not overflow the professional setting. Extraprofessional intercourse could be used by both client and professional in a manner such as to impair professional authority, with a consequent diminution of the professional's effectiveness.

Thus far we have discussed that phase of professional authority which expresses itself in the client-professional relationship. Professional authority, however, has professional-community ramifications. To these we now turn.

SANCTION OF THE COMMUNITY

Every profession strives to persuade the community to sanction its authority within certain spheres by conferring upon the profession a series of powers and privileges. Community approval of these powers and privileges may be either informal or formal; formal approval is that reinforced by the community's police power.

Among its powers is the profession's control over its training centers. This is achieved through an accrediting process exercised by one of the associations within the profession. By granting or withholding accreditation, a profession can, ideally, regulate its schools as to their number, location, curriculum content, and caliber of instruction. Comparable control is not to be found in a nonprofessional occupation.[11] The profession also acquires control over admission into the profession. This is achieved via two routes. First, the profession convinces the community that no one should be allowed to wear a professional title who has not been conferred it by an accredited professional school. Anyone can call himself a carpenter, locksmith, or metal-plater if he feels so qualified. But a person who assumes the title of physician or attorney without having earned it conventionally becomes an impostor. Secondly, the profession persuades the community to institute in its behalf a licensing system for screening those qualified to practice the professional skill. A sine qua non for the receipt of the license is, of course, a duly granted professional title. Another prerequisite may be an examination before a board of inquiry whose personnel have been drawn from the ranks of the profession.

State boards for nursing are charged with the licensing function for nursing. They determine the examination, requirements for recertification, and disciplinary action. Yet control is not completely by the profession. State boards of many states have non-nurses as voting members. Physicians, licensed practical nurses, and consumers help make these important decisions about nurses.

Police power enforces the licensing system; persons practicing the professional skill without a license are liable to punishment by public authority.[12]

Among the professional privileges, one of the most important is that of confidentiality. To facilitate efficient performance, the professional encourages the client to volunteer information he otherwise would not divulge. The community regards this as privileged communication, shared solely between client and professional, and protects the latter legally from encroachments upon such confidentiality. To be sure, only a select few of the professions, notably medicine and law, enjoy this immunity. Its very rarity makes it the ultimate in professionalization. Another one of the professional privileges is a relative immunity from community judgment on technical matters. Standards for professional performance are reached by consensus within the profession and are based on the existing body of theory. The lay community is presumed incapable of comprehending these standards and, hence, of using them to identify malpractice. It is generally conceded that a professional's performance can be evaluated only by his peers.

Some institutional nursing staffs are fighting for control of the nursing standards in their institutions. By definition the standards should be their prerogative, and not a collective bargaining issue. Nurse practitioners, too, have their work supervised by others. In Idaho, for example, physicians regularly audit the records of nurse practitioners.

The powers and privileges described above constitute a monopoly granted by the community to the professional group. Therefore, when an occupation strives toward professional status, one of its prime objectives is to acquire this monopoly. But this is difficult to achieve, because counter forces within the community resist strongly the profession's claims to authority. Through its associations the profession wages an organized campaign to persuade the community that it will benefit greatly by granting the monopoly. Specifically the profession seeks to prove: that the performance of the occupational skill requires specialized education; that those who possess this education, in contrast to those who do not, deliver a superior service; and that the human need being served is of sufficient social importance to justify the superior performance.

Nursing has a great deal of "PR" yet to do, to establish itself as an independent profession before the public. One wonders if this is possible when so few nurses are available for an "organized campaign" through the single banner of the American Nurses Association.

REGULATIVE CODE OF ETHICS

The monopoly enjoyed by a profession vis-à-vis clients and community is fraught with hazards. A monopoly can be abused; powers and privileges can be used to protect vested interests against the public weal.[13] The professional group could peg the price of its services at an unreasonably high level; it could restrict the numbers entering the occupation to create a scarcity of personnel; it could dilute the caliber of its performance without community awareness; and it could frustrate forces within the occupation pushing for socially beneficial changes in practices.[14] Were such abuses to become conspicuous, widespread, and permanent, the community would, of course, revoke the profession's monopoly. This extreme measure is normally unnecessary, because every profession has a built-in regulative code which compels ethical behavior on the part of its members.

The profession's ethical code is part formal and part informal. The formal is the written code to which the professional usually swears upon being admitted to practice; this is best exemplified by the Hippocratic Oath of the medical profession. The informal is the unwritten code, which nonetheless carries the weight of formal prescriptions. Through its ethical code the profession's commitment to the social welfare becomes a matter of public record, thereby ensuring for itself the continued confidence of the community. Without such confidence the profession could not retain its monopoly. To be sure, self-regulative codes are characteristic of all occupations, nonprofessional as well as professional. However, a professional code is perhaps more explicit, systematic, and binding; it certainly possesses more altruistic overtones and is more public service-oriented.[15] These account for the frequent synonymous use of the terms "professional" and "ethical" when applied to occupational behavior.

While the specifics of their ethical codes vary among the professions, the essentials are uniform. These may be described in terms of client-professional and colleague-colleague relations.

Toward the client the professional must assume an emotional neutrality. He must provide service to whoever requests it, irrespective of the requesting client's age, income, kinship, politics, race, religion, sex, and social status. A nonprofessional may withhold his services on such grounds without, or with minor, censure; a professional cannot. Parsons calls this element in professional conduct *universalism*. In other words, only in his extraoccupational contacts can the professional relate to others on particularistic terms, i.e., as particular individuals with concrete personalities attractive or unattractive to him. In his client contacts particularistic considerations are out of place. Parsons also calls attention to the element of *disinterestedness* in the professional-client relationship.[16] In contrast to the nonprofessional, the professional is motivated less by self-interest and more by the impulse to perform maximally. The behavior corollaries of this service orientation are many. For one, the professional must, under all circumstances, give maximum caliber service. The nonprofessional can dilute the quality of his commodity or service to fit the size of the client's fee; not so the professional. Again, the professional must be prepared to render his services upon request, even at the sacrifice of personal convenience.

The ethics governing colleague relationships demand behavior that is co-operative, equalitarian, and supportive. Members of a profession share technical knowledge with each other. Any advance in theory and practice made by one professional is quickly disseminated to colleagues through the professional associations.[17] The proprietary and quasi-secretive attitudes toward discovery and invention prevalent in the industrial and commercial world are out of place in the professional. Also out of place is the blatant competition for clients which is the norm in so many nonprofessional pursuits. This is not to gainsay the existence of intraprofessional competition; but it is a highly regulated competition, diluted with co-operative ingredients which impart to it its characteristically restrained quality. Colleague relations must be equalitarian; intraprofessional recognition should ideally be based solely upon performance in practice and/or contribution to theory.[18] Here, too, particularistic considerations must not be allowed to operate. Finally, professional colleagues must support each other vis-à-vis clientele and community. The professional must refrain from acts which jeopardize the authority of colleagues, and must sustain those whose authority is threatened.[19]

Nurses frequently comment about how doctors "stick together" and defend the actions of one another. Yet little of this behavior is emulated by nurse colleagues. Brooten, Hayman, and Naylor explain this behavior of nurses as an aspect of their powerlessness, both as nurses and as members of a "women's profession:"

> *When people lack power and control over much of their lives, they often exercise a sense of power by controlling the behavior of others in their same position. In nursing this is often done by controlling the dress and behavior of the peer group. As a group we are competitive, but unlike other groups that compete in the outside world for money, status, and power, we compete with each other and tend to withhold support from those within our ranks who show signs of succeeding.**

---

*Dorothy A. Brooten, Laura Lucia Hayman, and Mary Duffin Naylor. *Leadership for Change: A Guide for the Frustrated Nurse* (Philadelphia: J.B. Lippincott Company, 1978), p. 56.

The ways and means whereby a profession enforces the observance of its ethical code constitute a case study in social control. Self-discipline is achieved informally and formally.

Informal discipline consists of the subtle and the not-so-subtle pressures that colleagues exert upon one another. An example in this connection is the phenomenon of consultation and referral.[20] Consultation is the practice of inviting a colleague to participate in the appraisal of the client's need and/or in the planning of the service to be rendered. Referral is the practice of affording colleagues access to a client or an appointment. Thus, one colleague may refer his client to another, because lack of time or skill prevents his rendering the needed service; or he may recommend another for appointment by a prospective employer. Since professional ethics precludes aggressive competition and advertising, consultation and referral constitute the principal source of work to a professional. The consultation-referral custom involves professional colleagues in a system of reciprocity which fosters mutual interdependence. Interdependence facilitates social control; chronic violation of professional etiquette arouses colleague resentment, resulting in the cessation of consultation requests and referrals.

The interdependence of physicians provides a model for nursing. Physicians specialize, and rely on the expertise of colleagues to provide the comprehensive care that individual patients require. Nurses have functioned chiefly as generalists, expecting of themselves ability to function in all settings and under all conditions. The job enrichment benefits of specializing will be discussed later. In the context of this section, specialization of nurses can offer the interdependence and social support characteristic of professionalism.

A more formal discipline is exercised by the professional associations, which possess the power to criticize or to censure, and in extreme cases to bar recalcitrants. Since membership in good standing in the professional associations is a sine qua non of professional success, the prospect of formal disciplinary action operates as a potent force toward conformity.

THE PROFESSIONAL CULTURE

Every profession operates through a network of formal and informal groups. Among the formal groups, first there are the organizations through which the profession performs its services; these provide the institutionalized setting where professional and client meet. Examples of such organizations are hospital, clinic, university, law office, engineering firm, or social agency. Secondly, there are the organizations whose functions are to replenish the profession's supply of talent and to expand its fund of knowledge. These include the educational and the research centers. Third among the formal groups are the organizations which emerge as an expression of the growing consciousness-of-kind on the part of the profession's members, and which promote so-called group interests and aims. These are the professional associations. Within and around these formal organizations extends a filigree of informal groupings: the multitude of small, closely knit clusters of colleagues. Membership in these cliques is based on a variety of affinities: specialties within the profession; affiliations with select professional societies; residential and work propinquity; family, religious, or ethnic background; and personality attractions.

The interactions of social roles required by these formal and informal groups generate a social configuration unique to the profession, viz., a professional culture. All occupations are characterized by formal and informal groupings; in this respect the professions are not unique. What is unique is the culture thus begotten. If one were to single out the attribute that most effectively differentiates the professions from other occupations, this is it. Thus we can talk of a professional culture as distinct from a nonprofessional culture. Within the professions as a logical class each profession develops its own subculture, a variant of the professional culture; the engineering subculture, for example, differs from the subcultures of medicine and social work. In the subsequent discussion, however, we will treat the culture of the professions as a generic phenomenon. The culture of a profession consists of its *values, norms,* and *symbols.*

The social values of a professional group are its basic and fundamental beliefs, the unquestioned premises upon which its very existence rests. Foremost among these values is the essential worth of the service which the professional group extends to the community. The profession considers that the service is a social good and that community welfare would be immeasurably impaired by its absence. The twin concepts of professional authority and monopoly also possess the force of a group value. Thus, the proposition that in all service-related matters the professional group is infinitely wiser than the laity is regarded as beyond argument. Likewise nonarguable is the proposition that acquisition by the professional group of a service monopoly would inevitably produce social progress. And then there is the value of rationality; that is, the commitment to objectivity in the realm of theory and technique. By virtue of this orientation, nothing of a theoretical or technical nature is regarded as sacred and unchallengeable simply because it has a history of acceptance and use.

The norms of a professional group are the guides to behavior in social situations. Every profession develops an elaborate system of these role definitions. There is a range of appropriate behaviors for seeking admittance into the profession, for gaining entry into its formal and informal groups, and for progressing within the occupation's hierarchy. There are appropriate modes of securing appointments, of conducting referrals, and of handling consultation. There are proper ways of acquiring clients, of receiving and dismissing them, of questioning and treating them, of accepting and rejecting them. There are correct ways of grooming a protégé, of recompensing a sponsor, and of relating to peers, superiors, or subordinates. There are even group-approved ways of challenging an outmoded theory, of introducing a new technique, and of conducting an intraprofessional controversy. In short, there is a behavior norm covering every standard interpersonal situation likely to recur in professional life.

The symbols of a profession are its meaning-laden items. These may include such things as: its insignias, emblems, and distinctive dress; its history, folklore, and argot; its heroes and its villains; and its stereotypes of the professional, the client, and the layman.

Comparatively clear and controlling group values, behavior norms, and symbols, which characterize the professions, are not to be encountered in nonprofessional occupations.

Our discussion of the professional culture would be incomplete without brief mention of one of its central concepts, the *career* concept. The term career is, as a rule, employed only in reference to a professional occupation. Thus, we do not talk about the career of a bricklayer or of a mechanic; but we do talk about the career of an architect or of a clergyman. At the heart of the career concept is a certain attitude toward work which is peculiarly professional. A career is essentially a *calling,* a life devoted to "good works."[21] Professional work is never viewed solely as a means to an end; it is the end itself. Curing the ill, educating the young, advancing science are values in themselves. The professional performs his services primarily for the psychic satisfactions and secondarily for the monetary compensations.[22] Self-seeking motives feature minimally in the choice of a profession; of maximal importance is affinity for the work. It is this devotion to the work itself which imparts to professional activity the service orientation and the element of disinterestedness. Furthermore, the absorption in the work is not partial, but complete; it results in a total personal involvement. The work life invades the after-work life, and the sharp demarcation between the work hours and the leisure hours disappears. To the professional person his work becomes his life.[23] Hence the act of embarking upon a professional career is similar in some respects to entering a religious order. The same cannot be said of a nonprofessional occupation.

To succeed in his chosen profession, the neophyte must make an effective adjustment to the professional culture.[24] Mastery of the underlying body of theory and acquisition of the technical skills are in themselves insufficient guarantees of professional success. The recruit must also become familiar with and learn to weave his way through the labyrinth of the professional culture. Therefore, the transformation of a neophyte into a professional is essentially an acculturation process wherein he internalizes the social values, the behavior norms, and the symbols of the occupational group.[25] In its frustrations and rewards it is fundamentally no different from the acculturation of an immigrant to a relatively strange culture. Every profession entertains a stereotype of the ideal colleague; and, of course, it is always one who is thoroughly adjusted to the professional culture.[26]

Part I: The Professional and the Institution 25

The poorly acculturated colleague is a deviant; he is regarded as "peculiar," "unorthodox," "antisocial," and in extreme cases a "troublemaker." Whereas the professional group encourages innovation in theory and technique, it tends to discourage deviation from its social values and norms. In this internal contradiction, however, the professional culture is no different from the larger culture of society.

NOTES

1. Talcott Parsons, "The Professions and Social Structure," *Social Forces*, Vol. 17 (May 1939), pp. 457–467.
2. Theodore Caplow, *The Sociology of Work* (Minneapolis: University of Minnesota Press, 1954).
3. Oswald Hall, "The Stages of a Medical Career," *American Journal of Sociology*, Vol. 53 (March 1948), pp. 327–336; "Types of Medical Careers," *American Journal of Sociology*, Vol. 55 (November 1949), pp. 243–253; "Sociological Research in the Field of Medicine: Progress and Prospects," *American Sociological Review*, Vol. 16 (October 1951), pp. 639–644.
4. U.S. Bureau of the Census, *1950 Census of Population: Classified Index of Occupations and Industries* (Washington, D.C.: Government Printing Office, 1950).
5. The writer acknowledges his debt to his former students at the School of Social Welfare, University of California, Berkeley, who, as members of his research seminars, assisted him in identifying and abstracting the sociological literature on occupations. Their conscientious assistance made possible the formulation presented in this paper.
6. The occupational classification employed by the U.S. Census Bureau is precisely such a continuum. The categories of this classification are: (a) professionals and semiprofessional technical workers; (b) proprietors and managers, both farm and nonfarm, and officials; (c) clerical, sales, and kindred workers; (d) craftsmen, skilled workers, and foremen; (e) operatives and semiskilled workers; and (f) laborers, unskilled, service, and domestic workers. (U.S. Bureau of the Census, *op. cit.*).
7. The sequence in which the five attributes are discussed in this paper does not reflect upon their relative importance. The order selected has been dictated by logical considerations.
8. Parsons, *op. cit.*
9. A technology is a profession whose aim is to achieve controlled changes in natural relationships. Convention makes a distinction between technologists who shape nonhuman materials and those who deal with human beings. The former are called engineers; the latter practitioners.
10. Parsons, *op. cit.*
11. To set up and run a school for floral decorating requires no approval from the national florists' association, but no school of nursing could even open without approval of the state board of nursing.
12. Many nonprofessional occupations have also succeeded in obtaining licensing legislation in their behalf. Witness the plumbers, radio operators, and barbers, to mention a few. However, the sanctions applied against a person practicing a nonprofessional occupation are much less severe than is the case when a professional occupation is similarly involved.
13. Abraham Flexner, "Is Social Work a Profession?" in *Proceedings of the National Conference of Charities and Corrections* (Chicago: 1915), pp. 576–590.
14. Robert K. Merton, "Bureaucratic Structure and Personality," in Alvin Gouldner, ed., *Studies in Leadership* (New York: Harper & Brothers, 1950), pp. 67–79.
15. Flexner, *op. cit.* Parsons, *op. cit.*

16. Parsons, *op. cit.*
17. Arlien Johnson, "Professional Standards and How They Are Attained," *Journal of American Dental Association*, Vol. 31 (September 1944), pp. 1181–1189.
18. Flexner, *op. cit.*
19. This partly explains why physicians do not testify against each other in malpractice suits.
20. Hall, *op. cit.*
21. The term *calling* literally means a divine summons to undertake a course of action. Originally, it was employed to refer to religious activity. The Protestant Reformation widened its meaning to include economic activity as well. Henceforth divinely inspired "good works" were to be both secular and sacred in nature. Presumably, then, any occupational choice may be a response to divine summons. In this connection, it is interesting to note that the German word for vocation is *Beruf*, a noun derived from the verb *berufen*, to call.
22. Johnson, *op. cit.*
23. The all-pervading influence of work upon the lives of professionals results in interesting byproducts. The members of a profession tend to associate with one another outside the work setting (Oswald Hall, "The Stages of a Medical Career," *op. cit.*). Their families mingle socially; leisure time is spent together; "shop talk" permeates social discourse; and a consensus develops. The profession thus becomes a whole social environment, nurturing characteristic social and political attitudes, patterns of consumption and recreation, and decorum and *Weltanschauung* (Caplow, *op. cit.*; and William H. Form, "Toward an Occupational Social Psychology," *Journal of Social Psychology*, Vol. 24, February 1946, pp. 85–99).
24. Oswald Hall, "The Stages of a Medical Career" and "Types of Medical Careers," *op. cit.*
25. R. Clyde White, "'Social Workers in Society': Some Further Evidence," *Social Work Journal*, Vol. 34 (October 1953), pp. 161–164.
26. The laity also entertain a stereotypic image of the professional group. Needless to say, the layman's conception and the professional's self-conception diverge widely, because they are fabricated out of very different experiences. The layman's stereotype is frequently a distortion of reality, being either an idealization or a caricature of the professional type.

* * * *

Greenwood described the professionals' view of their work—as an end in itself, as psychic satisfaction, as something for which they have an affinity, as total person involvement, as their life. RNs must find this satisfaction in their work. As a medical sociologist, Freidson looks at the future of nursing and sees little hope that nursing can become a profession, because of its relation to medicine.

4.
Professions and Professionalism

Eliot Freidson

While it is dangerous to assume too much fixity in organization since, in the United States in particular, many occupations are aggressively seeking to improve their prestige and position, nonetheless the comprehensiveness of its scope and the strategic importance of its focus virtually guarantees medicine's superiority over others. An aggressive occupation like nursing can have its own schools for training, can control licensing boards in many instances, and can have its own "service" in hospital, in this way giving the appearance of formal, state-supported, and departmental autonomy, but the work which its members perform remains subject to the order of another occupation. Legally and otherwise the physician's right to diagnose, cut and prescribe is the center around which the work of many other occupations swings, and the physician's authority and responsibility in that constellation of work are primary. As the case of nursing shows, those paramedical occupations which are ranged around the physician cannot fail to be subordinate in authority and responsibility and, so long as their work remains medical in character, cannot gain occupational autonomy no matter how intelligent and aggressive its leadership. To attain the autonomy of a profession, the paramedical occupation must control a fairly discrete area of work that can be separated from the main body of medicine and that can be practiced without routine contact with or dependence on medicine. Few if any of the present paramedical occupations deal with such potentially autonomous areas.

* * * *

As department heads in institutions for delivery of health care, nursing administrators feel heavily the responsibility for bringing their own field to recognition as a profession. Abrahamson offers further insight into the obstacles that institutional nursing must overcome before it can be recognized as a profession.

Excerpted from Eliot Freidson, *Profession of Medicine* (New York: Dodd, Mead, 1970), p. 69.

5.
Role Specialization in a Formal Organization

Mark Abrahamson

While "red tape" is the feature of bureaucratic organization which stands out in most peoples' minds, role specialization is probably a much more important characteristic.

Saint-Simon, writing during the middle nineteenth century, was greatly impressed with a new form of social organization which he saw developing. He felt that the new, formal, rational structure would be the organizational model of the future. To Saint-Simon, the main difference between administration in the Middle Ages and that which was to be in the future, lay in the justification of authority. Religion and coercion were once the foundation and cement of organizations. In the future, Saint-Simon felt, authority would not be legitimated on the basis of either religion or coercion, but rather on the basis of expertise, particularly in science.[1] This more limited type of authority, based upon specialized knowledge, necessarily creates a system of elaborate role specialization.

Max Weber's "ideal type" conceptualization of bureaucracy, the point of departure for most modern theories, stresses rationalization, routinization, and impersonalization as the primary characteristics of bureaucracy.[2] All three of these features result in, and are crystallized in terms of, role specialization.

The rational characteristic of bureaucracy, to Weber, was intimately related to the "de-mystification" of the world. Weber, like numerous sociologists before him, viewed simple or primitive societies as being "traditional" in orientation. That is, in making decisions, most members of the society reflexively used the decisions of past generations as their criteria. This orientation to the past precludes a self-conscious deliberation of alternatives, weighted according to a set of values that are also amenable to the same type of deliberate scrutiny.

Modified with permission from Mark Abrahamson, *The Professional in the Organization* (Chicago: Rand McNally, 1967), pp. 4–8.

Modern man, as Weber saw him during the early twentieth century, carried a rational orientation. He was a deliberate weigher of means and ends. Scientific and technological developments encouraged this trend as man sought to utilize these developments within an organizational framework. The primary source of the bureaucratic administration's superiority, to Weber, was its ability to utilize technical knowledge. In fact, it was this superiority of bureaucratic administration which, in part, led Weber to view bureaucracy as "indispensable." Thus, even in the event of revolution, the bureaucratic apparatus would continue to function because of its indispensability. And, in protest movements short of a revolution, newly formed organizations were seen as equally subject to the bureaucratization process.[3]

As the result of rationalization, bureaucratic organizations are characterized by an elaborate division of labor. Technically competent participants, selected by objective (usually written) demonstrations of their competence, are placed in specialized positions. Thus the organization employs specialists. Because their competence is limited and specific, rather than general, the authority of the incumbents is correspondingly limited to their specialty. *In hospitals, for example, more and more specialization is occurring. New practitioners, such as respiratory, physical, occupational, and recreational therapists, as well as various technicians who help monitor the new technology in nursing areas, are taking over functions that formerly fell under the general "nursing umbrella."*

Within a clearly differentiated hierarchy of authority, specialists are oriented to a system of rules. The rules governing behavior are ideally internalized by members of the bureaucracy to whom advancement in the organization constitutes a career. The officials do not own their positions; neither do they have the right to expropriate them. All ownership is separate from administration. As a result, advancement along known career lines is dependent upon strict adherence to the rules. (This is a voluntary contractual relationship which they may leave at any time; however, the officials are protected from arbitrary dismissal in return for their "career commitment.")

Because decisions in a bureaucracy are made by placing specific problems, or situations, in a general rubric—under which courses of action are explicated—the normal operations of a bureaucracy are geared to proceed in a routine fashion. Ideally, then, technically competent participants who are oriented to a governing system of rules will perform their duties in a routine manner.

The separation of ownership and the rules of selection and advancement both function to create a situation in which authority within the hierarchy is directly related to competence. Prompt obedience to superiors is demanded not only because they hold positions of direct authority, but, presumably, because their authority reflects competence as well.[4] Purely personal considerations are irrelevant in such a system; in fact, the entire structure is designed to eliminate them. Impersonal contact between officials and between officials and clients of the organization is required. One of the clearest indications of this appears in the written communication, the preferred form in a bureaucracy, which identifies information or direction as coming from a position rather than an individual (e.g., "From the Desk of the Personnel Director:" rather than, "From John Smith:").

In summary, role specialization is the hallmark of a bureaucracy. Individuals occupy positions because of their specialized knowledge, which must be objectified; their authority is correspondingly restricted, and the ties which exist between officials are based upon structural positions, exclusive of interpersonal affect.

The characteristics of a bureaucracy are definitely intended to maximize the stability of an organization. This stability is enhanced not only in routine, day-to-day affairs but over long periods of time as well. The orientation to rules, relations between positions, impersonality, etc. are all designed to overcome the "mortal" nature of man. In an ideal bureaucracy, most officials are highly dispensable. The whole orientation of the organization pushes incumbents to adjust to the organization rather than the other way around. Thus, it is the need of the *organization* for durability and stability which is maximized by a bureaucratic administration, and not the needs of its human elements.

This view of the ideal bureaucracy clarifies the conflict edge of the Getzels-Guba model, for the individual is expected to subordinate need-dispositions to the institution's goals. The more closely the health care institution conforms to the bureaucratic model, the more conflict will arise between the nomothetic and idiographic dimensions of organizational behavior.

THE PROFESSIONS: SPECIALIZATION AND BUREAUCRATIZATION

The proliferation of role specialization, which characterizes both society and bureaucratic administration, also typifies recent developments in most professions. Within the past few decades, the majority of the professions have greatly multiplied their number of practicing specialties.[5] Of perhaps even greater importance is the fact that professional knowledge now largely emanates from a bureaucratic organization; an organization which sifts clients or problems and sets the conditions under which the professional works.

Historically, the professions, consisting primarily of physicians, attorneys, and the clergy, were regarded as the "free professions." They were free in at least two respects. First, they were bound by special types of occupational norms developed within the professional body. While these special norms were somewhat restrictive, they freed the practitioner from a variety of external client pressures to which most non-professionals had to be highly sensitive. Second, the free professionals tended to be free from organizational restraints. For the most part, they worked alone with individual clients, were oriented to their own set of norms and were free from responsibility to an immediate employing organization.

This second characteristic of free professionals has been changing rapidly. More physicians are being employed by hospitals and medical research institutions, for example; and newly licensed attorneys are turning increasingly to large law firms rather than to private practice. These changes reflect the interdependence of the two characteristics of the free professionals. Strains upon autonomous professional norms have grown as organizational restraints have come into the picture. This problem is seen even more clearly in some of the recently growing professions, particularly in the sciences, whose practitioners are almost never "free" in the organizational sense.

Functioning as a "free" professional is especially difficult for nurses, as most nurses never had that privilege. Nurses do not have to regain a lost professional characteristic as much as they have to achieve it—without the historical advantage of experience to help them identify and win the position.

Professional training produces a strong identification with a professional role. A man's sense of identity—his entire conception of who he is—is intimately tied to his professional role. This was once true for the practitioners of many trades which would not ordinarily be considered professional. The cabinet-maker, for example, tended to be so involved in his work that his occupational role strongly entered into his self-concept. In mass production, however, the great bulk of wage-earners no longer work at a trade which functions as their "calling card." Present-day workers, when asked to identify themselves occupationally, are probably more apt to name their employer than their specific job. This change has not occurred for professionals, though, since theirs is an "unstandardized product." The problems of each client are ideally considered to have unique characteristics, requiring custom-tailored applications of knowledge. This is probably one of the reasons for the high prestige accorded to professionals, and one of the explanations for their having maintained their occupational roles as integral parts of their self-conceptions.

The sense of obligation to, and involvement with, one's work characterizes professionals, but it often runs counter to the type of career commitment demanded by a bureaucracy. So too does the sense of public service, infused into the training of most professionals, unless the practitioner is employed by a welfare organization. But perhaps most incompatible with the tenets of a bureaucratic organization is the professional's occupational identification, because it carries with it an emotional commitment to one's colleagues. Professional training produces, in Hughes' words, "A professional conscience and solidarity. The profession claims and aims to become a moral unit."[6] This produces an orientation to horizontal, collegial authority which is directly antithetical to the bureaucratic conception of strict, vertical, unilateral authority.

NOTES

1. See Alvin W. Gouldner, "Organizational Analysis," in Robert K. Merton, et al. (Eds.), *Sociology Today* (New York: Basic Books, 1959).
2. Max Weber, *The Theory of Social and Economic Organization* (trans. by A.M. Henderson and Talcott Parsons; Glencoe, Ill.: Free Press, 1947).
3. The inevitability of bureaucracy is one of the most hotly contested of Weber's assertions. The interested reader should see the discussions by Friedrich Burin and others in Robert K. Merton, et al. (Eds.), *Reader in Bureaucracy* (Glencoe, Ill.: Free Press, 1952).
4. William M. Evan and Morris Zelditch, Jr. report a series of interesting findings as a consequence of the "artificial" separation of authority and competence. See "A Laboratory Experiment on Bureaucratic Authority," *American Sociological Review*, 6, 1961.
5. One of the neglected problems created by this expansion is the potential for conflict which it produces. The range of areas over which a given profession can lay claim to competence has increased. Internal expansion results in overlapping, which is apt to produce conflict, at least in the minds of potential clients. Consider for example, the American Sociological Association Committee on Medical Sociology and the American Medical Association Committee on Socio-Economic Affairs. Does either association possess more legitimacy in this overlapping area?
6. Everett C. Hughes, "Dilemmas and Contradictions of Status," *American Journal of Sociology*, 50, 1945.

* * * *

And so the setting for the problem: an organizational framework that is based on the establishment and continuation of routines is an appropriate structure for the production of identical units of merchandise, but not for an "unstandardized product," such as a patient. Nor is the bureaucratic organization functional as a setting for the practice of a professional, whose role is to individualize care of patients based on their unique nonroutine needs.

Part II

Motivation of the Professional

Motivation theorists do not differentiate between the motivation of professionals and that of nonprofessionals. Their theories are intended to show that their motivation techniques apply to all persons in the work world. Literature on professionalism, however, often refers to the drive of all workers toward professional status, which becomes a motivator in itself. An analysis of common motivation theories can reveal the aspects of professionalism that have become identified motivators in the world of work.

In "The Esteem Needs" and "The Self-Actualization Needs," Goble comments on Maslow's work on motivation. Maslow identified man's needs as a hierarchy, with the lower needs of health, safety and security, and love and belongingness identified as at least partially met in the work force. Those less completely met are the esteem needs and the self-actualization (growth) needs.

Douglas McGregor discusses two approaches to leadership, labeling them Theory X and Theory Y. The Theory Y manager takes the approach which forms the climate that Herzberg will describe under job enrichment.

Gouldner identifies a concept of motivation based on direct versus indirect supervision in "The Problem of 'Close Supervision.'" This concept relates directly to the professional's autonomy, as well as to two of the identified leadership styles that affect the work environment of the professional: direct versus indirect supervision.

The organization's nomothetic needs will not be met by the professionals hired to do so unless the professionals' own idiographic needs are met. In "From Motivation Theory to Principles of Job Design," Walters and his associates reinforce the dangers of close supervision, and suggest putting responsibility for performance on the worker rather than on the supervisor. Gouldner's suggestion is to use bureaucratic rules instead of close supervision for direction of the worker.

Fuszard discusses in "Job Rotation, Job Purity, and Job Enlargement" the precursors to job enrichment. Aspects of these approaches to motivation are still in use in institutional nursing. They are an evolutionary step to the final approach to motivation of the professional—job enrichment.

6.
The Esteem Needs
Frank Goble

Maslow found that people have two categories of esteem needs—self-respect and esteem from other people. 1. Self-esteem includes such needs as desire for confidence, competence, mastery, adequacy, achievement, independence, and freedom. 2. Respect from others includes such concepts as prestige, recognition, acceptance, attention, status, reputation, and appreciation. Esteem needs were generally ignored by Sigmund Freud, but were stressed by Alfred Adler. A person who has adequate self-esteem is more confident and capable and, thus, more productive. However, when the self-esteem is inadequate the individual has feelings of inferiority and helplessness, which may result in discouragement and possible neurotic behavior. "The most stable and, therefore, the most healthy self-esteem is based on *deserved* respect from others rather than on external fame or celebrity and unwarranted adulation."[1]

NOTE

1. Abraham Maslow, *Motivation and Personality* (New York: Harper & Row, 1954).

* * * *

Both esteem needs are important in the work setting. The greatest dissatisfaction reported by nurses in one survey[1] *was that chronic poor staffing made it impossible for them to "feel good" (have self-esteem) about the care they gave patients. Correct placement in and orientation to a job can help the employee achieve mastery, independence, and freedom. Herzberg adds to these "worth-*

Excerpted from Frank Goble, *The Third Force* (New York: Grossman, 1970), pp. 40–41.

while work." *All are essential for the confidence that will make the worker more satisfied and, therefore, more productive.* Respect from others comes from a job well done, with deserved recognition from co-workers and employers. This respect from society meets one of the characteristics of a profession.

NOTE

1. Marjorie A. Godfrey, "Job Satisfaction—Or Should That Be *Dis*satisfaction? How Nurses Feel about Nursing: II," *Nursing 78* 8 (May 1978): 108.

7.
The Self-Actualization Needs

Frank Goble

"What a man *can* be, he *must* be."[1] The identification of the psychological need for growth, development, and utilization of potential—what Maslow calls self-actualization—is an important aspect of his theory of human motivation. Maslow has also described this need as "the desire to become more and more what one is, to become everything that one is capable of becoming."[2] Maslow finds that the need for self-actualization generally emerges after a reasonable satisfaction of the love and esteem needs.

This need for self-actualization can be met in work as well as in leisure time. Maslow writes that the self-actualized person enjoys play; he enjoys work; his work becomes play; his vocation and avocation become the same. The research indicates that healthy people are most integrated when facing a great creative challenge or some worthwhile goal.

Without exception, Maslow found self-actualizing people to be dedicated to some work, task, duty, or vocation which they considered important. Because they were interested in this work, they worked hard, yet the usual distinction between work and play became blurred. For them work was exciting and pleasurable. It seems that commitment to an important job is a major requirement for growth, self-actualization, and happiness. However, it is not enough to have an important job—the self-actualizing person must be doing it well. If he is a physician, he must be a good physician, not a poor one. This involves hard work, discipline, training, and often postponement of pleasure.

NOTES

1. Abraham Maslow, *Motivation and Personality* (New York: Harper & Row, 1954).
2. Ibid.

Modified from Frank Goble, *The Third Force* (New York: Grossman, 1970), pp. 41, 28, and 26.

* * * *

This description of the self-actualizing person could almost be taken as a description of a professional! Maslow's years of research established the motivation of and need for work in healthy persons. The idiographic needs of the nursing staff must be dealt with by the nursing manager who seeks to meet the nomothetic goals of institutional behavior. A second important philosophical base to Herzberg's work on job enrichment is McGregor's familiar Theory X and Theory Y.

8.
Theory X and Theory Y

Douglas McGregor

The conventional conception of management's task in harnessing human energy to organizational requirements can be stated broadly in terms of three propositions. In order to avoid the complications introduced by a label, I shall call this set of propositions "Theory X":

1. Management is responsible for organizing the elements of productive enterprise—money, materials, equipment, people—in the interest of economic ends.
2. With respect to people, this is a process of directing their efforts, motivating them, controlling their actions, modifying their behavior to fit the needs of the organization.
3. Without this active intervention by management, people would be passive—even resistant—to organizational needs. They must therefore be persuaded, rewarded, punished, controlled—their activities must be directed. This is management's task in managing subordinate managers or workers. We often sum it up by saying that management consists of getting things done through other people.

Proposition "Theory X" involves manipulation, control, reward and punishment as methods for motivating or moving workers. It does not address the meeting of the higher level needs that Maslow addressed.

We recognize readily enough that a man suffering from a severe dietary deficiency is sick. The deprivation of physiological needs has behavioral consequences. The same is true—although less well recognized—of deprivation of

---

Modified with permission from Douglas McGregor, *Leadership and Motivation* (Cambridge, Mass.: M.I.T. Press, 1966), pp. 5, 12, 13, and 15.

higher level needs. The man whose needs for safety, association, independence, or status are thwarted is sick just as surely as is he who has rickets. And his sickness will have behavioral consequences. We will be mistaken if we attribute his resultant passivity, his hostility, his refusal to accept responsibility to his inherent "human nature." These forms of behavior are *symptoms* of illness—of deprivation of his social and egoistic (self-actualization) needs.

The man whose lower level needs are satisfied is not motivated to satisfy those needs any longer. For practical purposes they exist no longer. Management often asks, "Why aren't people more productive? We pay good wages, provide good working conditions, have excellent fringe benefits and steady employment. Yet people do not seem to be willing to put forth more than minimum effort."

The fact that management has provided for these physiological and safety needs has shifted the motivational emphasis to the social and perhaps to the egoistic needs. Unless there are opportunities *at work* to satisfy these higher level needs, people will be deprived; and their behavior will reflect this deprivation. Under such conditions, if management continues to focus its attention on physiological needs, its efforts are bound to be ineffective.

Nursing management must pay attention to the idiographic needs of esteem and self-actualization, Maslow's identified "higher needs." Management cannot provide a man with self-respect, or with the respect of his fellows, or with the satisfaction of needs for self-fulfillment. It can create conditions such that he is encouraged and enabled to seek such satisfactions *for himself,* or it can thwart him by failing to create those conditions.

The working conditions that help professional nurses to meet their needs of esteem and self-actualization and, in so doing, to reach for professionalization are based upon a management philosophy that can be called "Theory Y" and contains the following components:

1. Management is responsible for organizing the elements of productive enterprise—money, materials, equipment, people—in the interest of economic ends.
2. People are *not* by nature passive or resistant to organizational needs. They have become so as a result of experience in organizations.
3. The motivation, the potential for development, the capacity for assuming responsibility, the readiness to direct behavior toward organizational goals are all present in people. Management does not put them there. It is a responsibility of management to make it possible for people to recognize and develop these human characteristics for themselves.
4. The essential task of management is to arrange organizational conditions and methods of operation so that people can achieve their own goals *best* by directing *their own* efforts toward organizational objectives.

This is a process primarily of creating opportunities, releasing potential, removing obstacles, encouraging growth, and providing guidance.

* * * *

McGregor goes on to give examples of management practices that are consistent with Theory Y and are available to nursing administrators today, such as decentralization, delegation, job enlargement, participative management, consultative management, and performance appraisal. In his Theory Y philosophy for management, McGregor addresses the higher idiographic needs identified by Maslow and offers a leadership approach that will permit professional functioning in the work setting.

Gouldner has developed a concept of direct versus indirect supervision that further elaborates a leadership style for meeting a professional nurse's idiographic needs. In order to determine why certain leadership styles were or were not effective, he studied workers in a gypsum mine, both those who worked on the surface under close supervision and those who worked deep in the mines under only indirect supervision. His findings give surprising support to a very strong bureaucratic approach—supervision by impersonal rules. Studying close supervision, Gouldner found a vicious circle between employees and their supervisor.

9.

The Problem of "Close Supervision"

Alvin Gouldner

> *If you ride a horse, sit close and tight.*
> *If you ride a man, sit easy and light.*
>   *Poor Richard*

If a supervisor viewed a worker as unmotivated, as unwilling to "do a job," how did the supervisor respond; how did he attempt to solve this problem? He usually attempted to handle this by directing the worker more closely, by watching him carefully, and explicitly outlining his work obligations. As one foreman said: "If I catch a man goofing off, I tell him in an a,b,c, way exactly what he has to do, and I watch him like a hawk 'til he's done it."

At first glance this might appear to be a stable solution; it might seem as if "close supervision" would allow the supervisor to bring the problem under control. Actually, however, there were commanding reasons why supervisors could not rest content to supervise their workers closely and to remind them endlessly of what had to be done. One motive was fairly obvious: The supervisor could not watch all of his men all of the time. As a foreman remarked, "As soon as I turn my back on some of these guys, they slip me the knife."

There is, however, another consideration that made "close supervision" a dangerous solution to the problem of the unmotivated worker. Specifically, workers viewed close supervision as a kind of "strictness" and punishment. In consequence, the more a supervisor watched his subordinates, the more hostile they became to him. Workers shared standardized conceptions of what a "good" or legitimate foreman should be like, and almost universally, these insisted that the good foreman was one who "doesn't look over your shoulder." From the workers' standpoint a "driving" foreman was "bad," and they would retaliate by withholding work effort. As a worker asserted:

Modified with permission from Alvin Gouldner, *Patterns of Industrial Bureaucracy* (Glencoe, Ill.: The Free Press, 1954), pp. 159–162.

"If the foreman doesn't work well with us, we don't give him as good work as we can . . . I just don't care, I let things slide."

In other words, close supervision enmeshed management in a vicious cycle: the supervisor perceived the worker as unmotivated; he then carefully watched and directed him; this aroused the worker's ire and accentuated his apathy, and now the supervisor was back where he began. Close supervision did not solve his problem. In fact, it might make the worker's performance, in the super's absence, even less reliable than it had been.

Differences in philosophical bases make the difference in effectiveness of a leadership style. Close supervision entails an intensification of *face-to-face* direction of the worker. In such a context, it becomes very *evident* exactly "who is boss." This, in turn, suggests one of the distinctive conditions which underpin the strains induced by close supervision; for ours is a culture in which great stress is placed upon the *equality* of persons, and in such a cultural context *visible* differences in power and privilege readily become sources of tension, particularly so if status differences do not correspond with traditionally prized attributes such as skill, experience, or seniority.

Close supervision violated norms of equality internalized by workers, and they responded by complaining that the supervisor was "just trying to *show* who is boss." Workers' devotion to this norm was indicated also by their preference for supervisors who did not act as if they were "better than anyone else;" they insisted that supervisors, or for that matter other workers, should not behave like "big shots." In other words, they were hostile to those who put forth claims of personal superiority.

Again, workers expressed the feeling that close supervision violated their culturally prescribed expectations of equality by saying that such a supervisor was "trying to make a *slave* out of us."

* * * *

Walters and associates echo Gouldner's findings in the conclusions of their own studies.

10.
The Hazards of Close Supervision

Roy W. Walters and Associates

The individual who examines jobs for their motivating potential would do well to look very closely at job situations in which there are doers and checkers or verifiers in the same work operation. Wherever some people are on the job solely to catch other people's errors, there are liable to be motivation problems on both sides of the fence.

There is a valuable maxim related to this kind of tightening up: "If you want to *catch* errors, check and double-check the work. If you want to *prevent* errors, place responsibility on those who do the work." The establishment of instant rules for checks and double-checks and verification by supervisors, or the establishment of layers of people for verification of work reduces the job to the very lowest common denominator of performance; it tars everyone with the same brush and makes no distinctions for those who do excel. If management makes no distinction between the competent and the incompetent; if the former have no immunity from checks and double-checks set up for the latter, then usually the highly competent soon cease to excel. Such organizations seem to be saying to everyone alike— "You can't be trusted; sooner or later we know you're going to flop."

* * * *

Gouldner believes that the use of impersonal rules, rather than direct supervision, will relieve the tensions caused by differences in power between supervisor and employee.

Excerpted from Roy W. Walters and Associates, *Job Enrichment for Results: Strategies for Successful Implementation* (Reading, Mass.: Addison-Wesley, 1975), pp. 52–53.

11.
The Screening Functions of Rules

Alvin Gouldner

A function of bureaucratic rules can be observed if we notice that, in part, they provide a substitute for the personal repetition of orders by a supervisor. Once standing rules have been installed, there are fewer things that a supervisor has to direct a worker to do; thus the frequency and duration of worker-foreman interaction in their *official* capacities is somewhat lessened. Moreover, even if the super does intervene in his capacity as a superior, he need not appear to be doing so on his own account; he is not so apt to be seen as "throwing his weight around." He can say, as one foreman said about the no-absenteeism rule: "I can't help laying them off if they're absent. *It's not my idea.* I've got to go along with the rules *like everyone else.* What *I* want has nothing to do with it." In other words, the rules provide the foreman with an impersonal crutch for his authority, screening the superiority of his power which might otherwise violate the norm of equality. Instead, equality presumably prevails because, "like everyone else," he, too, is bound by the rules which the plant manager has sanctioned.

Differences in power which are not justifiable in terms of the group's norms, or which violate them, seem to establish a situation requiring the utilization of impersonal control techniques. Impersonal and general rules serve in part to obscure the existence of power disparities which are not legitimate in terms of the group's norms.

The idea of being subject to supervision is against professionalism. Nursing administrators have no opportunity to use direct supervision; they cannot be with every employee all the time. Their philosophy of management, however, will be evident by the trust they show in their employees. The use of impersonal rules can create an atmosphere without the supervisor/supervised dichotomy.

Modified with permission from Alvin Gouldner, *Patterns of Industrial Bureaucracy* (Glencoe, Ill.: The Free Press, 1954), pp. 164–166.

The screening function of the rules would seem to work in two directions at once. First, it impersonally bolsters a supervisor's claim to authority without compelling him to employ an embarrassing and debatable legitimation in terms of his personal superiority. Conversely, it permits *workers* to accept managerial claims to deference without committing them to a merely personal submission to the supervisor that would betray their self-image as "any man's equal" (Figure 11–1).

Figure 11–1 Gouldner's Model

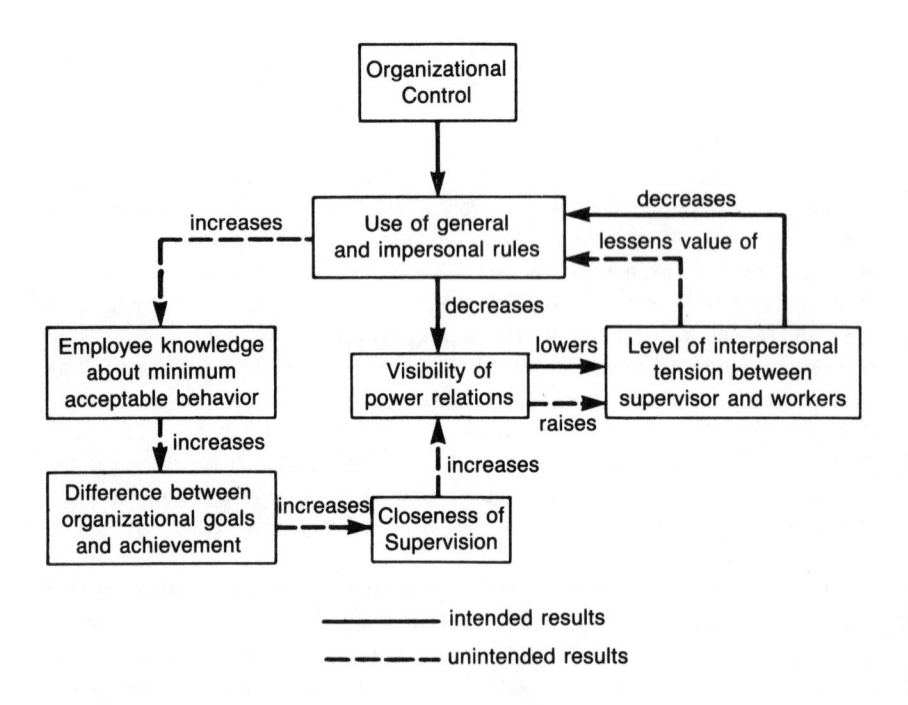

```
                    ┌──────────────┐
                    │Organizational│
                    │   Control    │
                    └──────┬───────┘
                           │
                           ▼
     increases    ┌──────────────────┐    decreases
   ┌─────────────│  Use of general  │◄───────────────┐
   │             │and impersonal rules│ lessens value of│
   │             └────────┬─────────┘◄─ ─ ─ ─ ─ ─ ─ ┐ │
   ▼                      │ decreases                │ │
┌──────────────┐          ▼                          │ │
│  Employee    │   ┌──────────────┐  lowers  ┌──────────────────┐
│  knowledge   │   │ Visibility of├─────────►│ Level of interpersonal│
│about minimum │   │power relations│          │  tension between  │
│acceptable    │   └──────────────┘ ─ ─ ─ ─ ►│supervisor and workers│
│  behavior    │          ▲         raises   └──────────────────┘
└──────┬───────┘          │ increases
       │ increases        │
       ▼                  │
┌──────────────┐ increases ┌──────────────┐
│  Difference  │─ ─ ─ ─ ─ ►│ Closeness of │
│   between    │           │ Supervision  │
│organizational│           └──────────────┘
│goals and     │
│achievement   │
└──────────────┘
```

──────── intended results
─ ─ ─ ─ ─ unintended results

GOULDNER'S MODEL

12.
Job Rotation, Job Purification, and Job Enlargement

Barbara Fuszard

Taylor, the father of scientific management, introduced the concept of work simplification, which is aimed toward fractionalization and specialization of tasks.[1] Time-and-motion studies are conducted to identify the basic components of a task. A worker is assigned to each component, and that worker is expected to develop great skill and speed through repetition. Pure work simplification leads to the typical assembly line production, in which a worker performs one simple task over and over for the entire work day.[2]

The promise of efficiency immediately interested hospital personnel in work simplification, and they hired time-and-motion engineers to analyze the work of the largest hospital department—the department of nursing. Functional nursing (e.g., one nurse taking temperatures, another passing medications) was a natural outgrowth of this concept. The skill level of tasks was also identified, and work simplification gave justification to the development of unskilled and semiskilled positions in nursing. Managers concerned about motivation of employees recognized the nonmotivating factors built into work simplification, however, and tried various approaches to add motivation to work. Some of these precursor concepts to job enrichment are still in use and have met with some success.

Job rotation, for example, was devised to resolve the problem of the monotony that arises when a worker repeats the same functions over and over during the work day. The manager keeps the specific jobs constant, but rotates the workers from one job to another.[3] In nursing, the assignments of nursing personnel may be changed daily or every few days to "keep them from being bored." Nurses on "float pools" often describe their constantly changing job as exciting and express their relief that they are exempt from the boredom of a routine day in one area. Some nursing administrators use job rotation to combat burn-out of nursing personnel in the specialized units; they assign nursing personnel in specialized units to other units for a period of time before reassigning them to the specialized units. In this case, job rotation removes nurses temporarily from high-tension job positions.

Although job purification is related to job rotation, it is more commonly associated with jobs that require a great deal of skill. It involves the analysis of a specific professional's job and the delegation of the more menial duties to a nonprofessional.[4] Its purpose is not only to ensure efficient use of the professional's skills and time, but also to give the professional a greater challenge. Maximizing creative or psychological challenge is congruent with Maslow's concepts of esteem and self-actualization, and it has been found to correlate with high job satisfaction. In Godfrey's study, nurses listed "intellectual challenge" as one of the highest job satisfiers.[5]

Nursing embraced the concept of job purification during World War II, not for the purpose of promoting job satisfaction, but for the purpose of conserving the specialized skills of the limited number of professional nurses available for the functions that only they could perform. This led to the creation of the position of the unskilled nurse's aide, who performed the routine functions of patient care. The need for someone even more skilled to assume even more of the tasks of the professional nurse led quickly to the creation of a position requiring some skills, that of the licensed practical nurse. Job purification has been used successfully to remove the secretarial and nonnursing monitoring functions from the responsibilities of professional nurses, although the decision that direct patient care is a nonskilled function haunts hospitals today. The unit management concept has proved a useful form of job purification for professional nursing in many situations, however. It removes secretarial/clerical functions from nursing without impinging upon nursing's control of direct patient care.

In job enlargement, the manager adds one or more related tasks to the basic job in order to prevent the boredom of repetition. The employee learns to do several steps in making a product or providing a service, instead of doing one task over and over. Since the jobs or tasks added to the worker's assignment are usually of equivalent difficulty and center around the same basic job, this concept is called "horizontal job loading." Much of the early work (1940s and 1950s) in job design for motivation took the form of job enlargement. Proponents of job enlargement have cited reduced fatigue, relief from the boredom of highly repetitive or specialized work, and broadened work skills as motivational factors.[6] Hospital nurses know, however, that job enlargement (to them, team nursing) has not been the answer to their idiographic needs for esteem and self-actualization.

NOTES

1. Arthur G. Bedeian, *Organizations: Theory and Analysis* (Hinsdale, Ill.: The Dryden Press, 1980), pp. 45–46.
2. Harold M.F. Rush, "Motivation through Job Design," *The Conference Board Record* 8 (January 1971): 54–55.

3. Ibid., p. 54.
4. Bonnie Carroll, *Job Satisfaction* (New York: New York State School of Industrial and Labor Relations, Cornell University, 1969), p. 23.
5. Marjorie A. Godfrey, "Job Satisfaction—Or Should That Be *Dis*satisfaction? How Nurses Feel About Nursing: I," *Nursing 78* 8 (April 1978): 92.
6. Rush, "Motivation through Job Design," p. 54.

* * * *

Work simplification, job rotation, job purification, and even job enlargement exist in modern health care facilities, some operating simultaneously and occasionally in conflict. Yet, of all the nurses participating in Godfrey's study, institution-based nurses reported the lowest job satisfaction.[1] Is there an answer? Can a rewarding, fulfilling job be found in institutional nursing? Job enrichment shows promise as a way to fulfill the needs of professional nurses in the work setting.

NOTE

1. Marjorie A. Godfrey, "Job Satisfaction—Or Should That Be *Dis*satisfaction? How Nurses Feel about Nursing: II," *Nursing 78* 8 (May 1978): 107.

Part III
Job Enrichment Defined

Job rotation, job purification, and job enlargement have failed to bring the hoped-for motivation to institutional nursing jobs. Herzberg states that they failed because managers have taken the natural motivation out of work and then tried to restore it by these artificial means. His 30 years of research on motivation have shown that *work itself* is the only true motivator. Herzberg, as do Maslow and McGregor, speaks of pride in one's work, of "loving the product" of one's own efforts. Job enrichment is designed to increase motivation by increasing the satisfaction obtained from the work itself, rather than from working conditions, type of supervision, or pay.

The essence of Herzberg's "orthodox job enrichment theory" is captured in "One More Time: How Do You Motivate Employees?" His approach is acerbic; he attacks the traditional approaches of rule by fear, rule by reward, and rule by brainwashing as motivating managers to push employees, but not motivating employees to push themselves.

This classic article is interrupted by one of Herzberg's more recent writings, "The Human Need for Work," which offers further insight into the philosophy of man that underlies Herzberg's theory. His use of words such as "art" and "love" are refreshing in the midst of the typically unemotional language of business.

All writers of job enrichment theory follow Herzberg's two-factor theory of intrinsic versus extrinsic rewards as motivators. Furthermore, these writers agree that implementation of the premises of the theory requires a change in job descriptions and in management styles. This process is called job design, job redesign, or job development by its proponents; it involves manipulating the job content rather than the employee to achieve motivation.

Not all of the extensive literature on job enrichment involves success stories. Failures of this concept, according to Bagadia and Bakr, are due to misconceptions about job enrichment and to its intrinsic limitations. In "An Update on Job Enrichment," they discuss these misconceptions and limitations, suggesting that the appropriate approach is job redesign. One of their recommendations is that managers develop new jobs, rather than attempt to enrich existing jobs. This is a luxury not often available to the nursing administrator, however.

Herzberg's "orthodox job enrichment" addresses the individual working alone. Bagadia and Bakr cite this aspect of the job enrichment theory in their list of limitations. More recent writings on job enrichment often couple job enrichment principles with semi-autonomous work groups, as is discussed in York's article, "Team Production (Semi-autonomous Work Groups)." As nurses usually work interdependently with other health team members, this combined approach to job enrichment is useful to the nursing administrator.

A new term that has come into management literature in the last few years is *Theory Z*. As described by Fuszard in "Theory Z," it is a synthesis of Theory Y, the precursor to job enrichment and so essential to it; job enrichment; and team production.

13.

One More Time: How Do You Motivate Employees? (Part I)

Frederick Herzberg

How many articles, books, speeches, and workshops have pleaded plaintively, "How do I get an employee to do what I want him to do?"

The psychology of motivation is tremendously complex, and what has been unraveled with any degree of assurance is small indeed. But the dismal ratio of knowledge to speculation has not dampened the enthusiasm for new forms of snake oil that are constantly coming on the market, many of them with academic testimonials. Doubtless this article will have no depressing impact on the market for snake oil, but since the ideas expressed in it have been tested in many corporations and other organizations, it will help—I hope—to redress the imbalance in the aforementioned ratio.

'MOTIVATING' WITH KITA

In lectures to industry on the problem, I have found that the audiences are anxious for quick and practical answers, so I will begin with a straightforward, practical formula for moving people.

What is the simplest, surest, and most direct way of getting someone to do something? Ask him? But if he responds that he does not want to do it, then that calls for a psychological consultation to determine the reason for his obstinacy. Tell him? His response shows that he does not understand you, and now an expert in communication methods has to be brought in to show you how to get through to him. Give him a monetary incentive? I do not need to remind the reader of the complexity and difficulty involved in setting up and administering an incentive system. Show him? This means a costly training program. We need a simple way.

Modified with permission from Frederick Herzberg, "One More Time: How Do You Motivate Employees?" *Harvard Business Review* 46, no. 1 (Jan.-Feb. 1968): 53–56.

Every audience contains the "direct action" manager who shouts, "Kick him!" And this type of manager is right. The surest and least circumlocuted way of getting someone to do something is to kick him in the pants—give him what might be called the KITA.

There are various forms of KITA, and here are some of them:

Negative Physical KITA. This is a literal application of the term and was frequently used in the past. It has, however, three major drawbacks: (1) it is inelegant; (2) it contradicts the precious image of benevolence that most organizations cherish; and (3) since it is a physical attack, it directly stimulates the autonomic nervous system, and this often results in negative feedback—the employee may just kick you in return. These factors give rise to certain taboos against negative physical KITA.

The psychologist has come to the rescue of those who are no longer permitted to use negative physical KITA. He has uncovered infinite sources of psychological vulnerabilities and the appropriate methods to play tunes on them. "He took my rug away;" "I wonder what he meant by that;" "The boss is always going around me"—these symptomatic expressions of ego sores that have been rubbed raw are the result of application of:

Negative Psychological KITA. This has several advantages over negative physical KITA. First, the cruelty is not visible; the bleeding is internal and comes much later. Second, since it affects the higher cortical centers of the brain with its inhibitory powers, it reduces the possibility of physical backlash. Third, since the number of psychological pains that a person can feel is almost infinite, the direction and site possibilities of the KITA are increased many times. Fourth, the person administering the kick can manage to be above it all and let the system accomplish the dirty work. Fifth, those who practice it receive some ego satisfaction (one-upmanship), whereas they would find drawing blood abhorrent. Finally, if the employee does complain, he can always be accused of being paranoid, since there is no tangible evidence of an actual attack.

Now, what does negative KITA accomplish? If I kick you in the rear (physically or psychologically), who is motivated? *I* am motivated; *you* move! Negative KITA does not lead to motivation, but to movement. So:

Positive KITA. Let us consider motivation. If I say to you, "Do this for me or the company, and in return I will give you a reward, an incentive, more status, a promotion, all the quid pro quos that exist in the industrial organization," am I motivating you? The overwhelming opinion I receive from management people is, "Yes, this is motivation."

I have a year-old Schnauzer. When it was a small puppy and I wanted it to move, I kicked it in the rear and it moved. Now that I have finished its obedience training, I hold up a dog biscuit when I want the Schnauzer to move. In this instance, who is motivated—I or the dog? The dog wants the biscuit, but it is I who want it to move. Again, I am the one who is motivated, and the dog is the one who moves. In this

Part III: Job Enrichment Defined   55

instance all I did was apply KITA frontally; I exerted a pull instead of a push. When industry wishes to use such positive KITAs, it has available an incredible number and variety of dog biscuits (jelly beans for humans) to wave in front of the employee to get him to jump.

Why is it that managerial audiences are quick to see that negative KITA is *not* motivation, while they are almost unanimous in their judgment that positive KITA *is* motivation? It is because negative KITA is rape, and positive KITA is seduction. But it is infinitely worse to be seduced than to be raped; the latter is an unfortunate occurrence, while the former signifies that you were a party to your own downfall. This is why positive KITA is so popular: it is a tradition; it is in the American way. The organization does not have to kick you; you kick yourself.

MYTHS ABOUT MOTIVATION

Why is KITA not motivation? If I kick my dog (from the front or the back), he will move. And when I want him to move again, what must I do? I must kick him again. Similarly, I can charge a man's battery, and then recharge it, and recharge it again. But it is only when he has his own generator that we can talk about motivation. He then needs no outside stimulation. He *wants* to do it.

With this in mind, we can review some positive KITA personnel practices that were developed as attempts to instill "motivation:"

1. Reducing time spent at work—This represents a marvelous way of motivating people to work—getting them off the job! We have reduced (formally and informally) the time spent on the job over the last 50 or 60 years until we are finally on the way to the "6½-day weekend." An interesting variant of this approach is the development of off-hour recreation programs. The philosophy here seems to be that those who play together, work together. The fact is that motivated people seek more hours of work, not fewer. *As Maslow has shown that work is play and play is work for the internally motivated, self-actualizing person, it is easy to understand why this approach fails.*
2. Spiraling wages—Have these motivated people? Yes, to seek the next wage increase. Some medievalists still can be heard to say that a good depression will get employees moving. They feel that if rising wages don't or won't do the job, perhaps reducing them will.
3. Fringe benefits—Industry has outdone the most welfare-minded of welfare states in dispensing cradle-to-the-grave succor. One company I know of had an informal "fringe benefit of the month club" going for a while. The cost of fringe benefits in this country has reached approximately 25% of the wage dollar, and we still cry for motivation.

People spend less time working for more money and more security than ever before, and the trend cannot be reversed. These benefits are no longer rewards; they are rights. A 6-day week is inhuman, a 10-hour day is exploitation, extended medical coverage is a basic decency, and stock options are the salvation of American initiative. Unless the ante is continuously raised, the psychological reaction of employees is that the company is turning back the clock.

When industry began to realize that both the economic nerve and the lazy nerve of their employees had insatiable appetites, it started to listen to the behavioral scientists who, more out of a humanist tradition than from scientific study, criticized management for not knowing how to deal with people. The next KITA easily followed.

4. Human relations training—Over 30 years of teaching and, in many instances, of practicing psychological approaches to handling people have resulted in costly human relations programs and, in the end, the same question: How do you motivate workers? Here, too, escalations have taken place. Thirty years ago it was necessary to request, "Please don't spit on the floor." Today the same admonition requires three "please's" before the employee feels that his superior has demonstrated the psychologically proper attitudes toward him.

The failure of human relations training to produce motivation led to the conclusion that the supervisor or manager himself was not psychologically true to himself in his practice of interpersonal decency. So an advanced form of human relations, KITA, sensitivity training, was unfolded.

5. Sensitivity training—Do you really, really understand yourself? Do you really, really, really trust the other man? Do you really, really, really, really cooperate? The failure of sensitivity training is now being explained, by those who have become opportunistic exploiters of the technique, as a failure to really (five times) conduct proper sensitivity training courses.

With the realization that there are only temporary gains from comfort and economic and interpersonal KITA, personnel managers concluded that the fault lay not in what they were doing, but in the employee's failure to appreciate what they were doing. This opened up the field of communications, a whole new area of "scientifically" sanctioned KITA.

6. Communications—The professor of communications was invited to join the faculty of management training programs and help in making employees understand what management was doing for them. House organs, briefing sessions, supervisory instruction on the importance of communication, and all sorts of propaganda have proliferated until today there is even an International Council of Industrial Editors. But no motivation resulted, and the obvious thought occurred that perhaps management was not hearing what the employees were saying. That led to the next KITA.

7. Two-way communication—Management ordered morale surveys, suggestion plans, and group participation programs. Then both employees and management were communicating and listening to each other more than ever, but without much improvement in motivation.

The behavioral scientists began to take another look at their conceptions and their data, and they took human relations one step further. A glimmer of truth was beginning to show through in the writings of the so-called higher-order-need psychologists. People, so they said, want to actualize themselves. Unfortunately, the "actualizing" psychologists got mixed up with the human relations psychologists, and a new KITA emerged.

8. Job participation—Though it may not have been the theoretical intention, job participation often became a "give them the big picture" approach. For example, if a man is tightening 10,000 nuts a day on an assembly line with a torque wrench, tell him he is building a Chevrolet. Another approach had the goal of giving the employee a *feeling* that he is determining, in some measure, what he does on his job. The goal was to provide a *sense* of achievement rather than a substantive achievement in his task. Real achievement, of course, requires a task that makes it possible. *(Another name for job participation is participative management.)* But still there was no motivation. This led to the inevitable conclusion that the employees must be sick, and therefore to the next KITA.

9. Employee counseling—The initial use of this form of KITA in a systematic fashion can be credited to the Hawthorne experiment of the Western Electric Company during the early 1930s. At that time, it was found that the employees harbored irrational feelings that were interfering with the rational operation of the factory. Counseling in this instance was a means of letting the employees unburden themselves by talking to someone about their problems. Although the counseling techniques were primitive, the program was large indeed.

The counseling approach suffered as a result of experiences during World War II, when the programs themselves were found to be interfering with the operation of the organizations; the counselors had forgotten their role of benevolent listeners and were attempting to do something about the problems that they heard about. Psychological counseling, however, has managed to survive the negative impact of World War II experiences and today is beginning to flourish with renewed sophistication. But, alas, many of these programs, like all the others, do not seem to have lessened the pressure of demands to find out how to motivate workers.

Since KITA results only in short-term movement, it is safe to predict that the cost of these programs will increase steadily and new varieties will be developed as old positive KITAs reach their satiation points.

* * * *

KITAs have not worked to motivate workers. Their failure is founded in the basic needs of human beings elucidated by Maslow. The special distinctions between animals and man are the higher needs of self-esteem and self-actualization.

14.
The Human Need for Work

Frederick Herzberg

Men and women are human beings who need to know they are creative. What they seek to create is something that expresses their uniqueness as individuals: a work of art. The underlying dynamic peculiar to human life (in contrast to other animal life) is the growth dynamic that comes from loving something or someone you can learn from. The results of this distinctly human love are ethics and art.

In this sense, psychological growth can be described as the addition of works of art to your life. As you grow psychologically, your life becomes an art collection. Conversely, if there is a lack of art in core aspects of your life, such as your job, there will be a commensurate lack of learning and growth. When learning and growth are no longer central to a population's aspirations, a major result is a society of obsolete people. You have all seen these obsolete people in your own organizations. They are the overeducated, underutilized young; the unskilled worker; the middle manager with no place to go; and the worker nearing retirement who has become a social nuisance rather than the social repository of wisdom.

A man whose work possesses no content in terms of self-fulfillment, but exists exclusively to fulfill the purposes of the enterprise or a social organization, is a man doomed to a life of human frustration, despite a return of animal contentment. You do not inspire employees by giving them higher wages, more benefits, or new status symbols. It is the successful achievement of a challenging task which fulfills the urge to create and adds one more work of art to the collection. The employer's task is not to motivate his people to get them to achieve; he should provide opportunities for people to achieve, so they will become motivated.

There is no way to turn a psychologically empty activity into a work of art. There is no way to produce quality in our work lives with fractionated jobs that have become psychological drudgery to the workers who perform them. Personal

---

Modified with permission from Frederick Herzberg, "The Human Need for Work," *Industry Week* 198, no. 2 (1978): 49–51.

meaning equals what is happening to you. Therefore, if what you are doing lacks intrinsic meaning, your self-appraisal is equally diminished. Quality of life and quality of work life are not separate. We cannot choose one or the other. We must choose both or neither.

Ever since the Industrial Revolution the world has been slowly going through what is called the "modernization process." It is easy to see how we can modernize technology, but how do we modernize people?

'Grotesque' Unity. For centuries before the Industrial Revolution a society evolved in which most people felt that they knew their place in the local community and knew what was expected of them in their work life, in their home life, and in their church. A person's entire existence appeared to be a neatly structured unity.

Then along came the much-commented-on modernization process, with the socio-personal life breaking down. Work was separated from personal life; it was broken away from aesthetics; it was broken away from religion; it was broken away from social responsibility and the family; finally, it was even broken away from personal identity.

Tearing People Apart. The concept underlying the fractionating of human lives in the modernization process was "progress in technology." The simple engineering concept of the best machine was one in which each little component had a particular function to perform. Naturally, when it came to modernizing people, the same design was chosen—that is, individuals were supposed to operate best as separate little components, each performing a separate function in the production process and, more tragic, in their living process.

Over the years, as the fractionated human being was torn apart, pieces began falling off him. So it became necessary to keep gluing him back together. The cement we used in his working environment was pay and fringe benefits, and when these did not hold, we tried another kind of cement: the behavioral sciences and the human relations movement. Soon, the human being was living his life on the basis of slogans and procedures.

The Biggest Joke. The best place to start bringing meaning and substance back to people's lives is in the work place since work (not labor) is special to the human species. How can you relate to other members of a work group if what you are doing is without personal intrinsic value? If you view what you are doing as deficient in intrinsic value, your interpersonal relationships become equally superficial.

A few years ago a rather trite motion picture was produced in America called "Love Story." It achieved instantaneous and phenomenal success wherever it played. It can be summed up in one of the often-quoted lines from the film: "Love means never having to say you're sorry." That simple phrase says quite succinctly much of what I have been trying to say.

You do not have to say you're sorry to those you love because you are never intentionally unfair or unethical with them. The same thing is true with *what* you are in love with. If you love a sport, you play it fairly. Don't you think the concept equally applies to a man's relationship to his work? How can you be fair in a system where there is not love for the work itself? When a worker turns out poor-quality work or demonstrates shoddy craftsmanship, he is actually saying, "I did not love it, so I did not have to be fair with my supervisor, or my employer, or even the customer."

The novelist Galsworthy wrote a short story called "Quality" in which he describes the men who made boots for him in his youth. They spent their time and effort competing with themselves in an attempt to make better and better boots. They truly loved their work. In contrast, the bootmakers who replaced them—ultimately driving them out of business—spent their time competing with each other, chiefly through advertising and human relations technology with their clients, and in the process, making cheaper, shoddier boots. They had ceased to love their work.

A human being needs to love his work, never to have to say he's sorry about something he produces, because he has done his best. Loving is the basis for ethics; unethical behavior stems from the lack of love in work as well as in all other aspects of life.

Work, therefore, requires the opportunity to express the human need to love. If we cannot make our work a source of loving and a place to create art for our personal enjoyment, we will have lost a society that still believes in human illusions. We must reverse the fragmentation process inherent in our post-industrial society and strive to bring a wholeness back to the individual.

Anticipation of the future used to sustain mankind and stabilize the economy as well. The time has come to give the individual back the anticipation of the future that comes only from determining it himself. If the "now generation" is given the opportunity to produce quality, it will do so.

To produce such quality, we do not need to return to the romantic past. We need to create a romantic future.

* * *

With this background of man's needs, we can now look at how these needs become motivators in the work world. Exhibit 14–1 summarizes the following section.

Exhibit 14–1 Major Principles of the Motivation-Hygiene Theory

- Satisfaction and dissatisfaction are not opposite feeling states.
- The experience of satisfaction is qualitatively different from the experience of relief from dissatisfaction. Eliminating the causes of an individual's dissatisfaction does not produce satisfaction because it is determined by different factors.
- The opposite of satisfaction is no satisfaction.
- The opposite of dissatisfaction is no dissatisfaction.
- There is no neutral point within or between each continuum.
- There is no overall concept that combines the two feeling states.

Hygiene principles
- The underlying dynamic of dissatisfaction is pain avoidance.
- The sources of relief from pain are found outside the individual. These sources are called hygiene factors because they serve to prevent dissatisfaction.
- The hygiene factors are based on the needs of man the animal.
- The hygiene needs parallel the primary drives—those that are preprogrammed at birth as automatic life-preserving processes.
- Relief of hygiene needs is short-term and cyclical, returning to physical or psychological zero-states. The zero-point of pain escalates as an individual's expectations rise.
- The activities an individual engages in because of hygiene needs are activities that he is made to engage in and lead to *movement* on his part.

Motivation principles
- The underlying dynamic of satisfaction is individual psychological growth.
- Satisfaction is caused by the richness of the ingredients in the activities the individual performs. Psychological growth is nourished by intrinsic factors called motivators; they lead to performance in activities that the individual personally wants to engage in.
- The motivator needs are based on the potential drives of man residing in the higher brain levels.
- Instilling the desire to engage in excelling performance is called the motivating process.
- The motivator needs are long-term and are not cyclical. They are limited in source because they must be created; they do not occur naturally, as hygiene pain does.
- The ingredients of activities that the individual pursues for psychological growth—to fulfill his motivator needs—lead not to movement but to *motivation*.

15.
One More Time: How Do You Motivate Employees? (Part II)

Frederick Herzberg

HYGIENE VS. MOTIVATORS

Let me rephrase the perennial question this way: How do you install a generator in an employee? A brief review of my motivation-hygiene theory of job attitudes is required before theoretical and practical suggestions can be offered. The theory was first drawn from an examination of events in the lives of engineers and accountants. At least 16 other investigations, using a wide variety of populations (including some in the Communist countries), have since been completed, making the original research one of the most replicated studies in the field of job attitudes.

The findings of these studies, along with corroboration from many other investigations using different procedures, suggest that the factors involved in producing job satisfaction (and motivation) are separate and distinct from the factors that lead to job dissatisfaction. Since separate factors need to be considered, depending on whether job satisfaction or job dissatisfaction is being examined, it follows that these two feelings are not opposites of each other. The opposite of job satisfaction is not job dissatisfaction but, rather, *no* job satisfaction; and, similarly, the opposite of job dissatisfaction is not job satisfaction, but *no* job dissatisfaction.

Stating the concept presents a problem in semantics, for we normally think of satisfaction and dissatisfaction as opposites—i.e., what is not satisfying must be dissatisfying, and vice versa. But when it comes to understanding the behavior of people in their jobs, more than a play on words is involved.

Two different needs of man are involved here. One set of needs can be thought of as stemming from his animal nature—the built-in drive to avoid pain from the environment, plus all the learned drives which become conditioned to the basic

---

Modified with permission from Frederick Herzberg, "One More Time: How Do You Motivate Employees?" *Harvard Business Review* 46, no. 1 (Jan.-Feb. 1968): 56–63.

biological needs. For example, hunger, a basic biological drive, makes it necessary to earn money, and then money becomes a specific drive. The other set of needs relates to that unique human characteristic, the ability to achieve and, through achievement, to experience psychological growth. The stimuli for the growth needs are tasks that induce growth; in the industrial setting, they are the *job content*. Contrariwise, the stimuli inducing pain-avoidance behavior are found in the *job environment*.

The growth or *motivator* factors that are intrinsic to the job are: achievement, recognition for achievement, the work itself, responsibility, and growth or advancement. The dissatisfaction-avoidance or *hygiene* (KITA) factors that are extrinsic to the job include: company policy and administration, supervision, interpersonal relationships, working conditions, salary, status, and security.

A correlation can be seen between Maslow's basic needs and these hygiene and motivation factors:

Maslow	Herzberg
Self-actualization	
Self-esteem	Motivators
Belonging (love)	
Safety/security	Hygiene Factors
Physiology	

A composite of the factors that are involved in causing job satisfaction and job dissatisfaction, drawn from samples of 1,685 employees, is shown in Exhibit 15–1. The results indicate that motivators were the primary cause of satisfaction, and hygiene factors the primary cause of unhappiness on the job. The employees, studied in 12 different investigations, included lower-level supervisors, professional women, agricultural administrators, men about to retire from management positions, hospital maintenance personnel, manufacturing supervisors, nurses, food handlers, military officers, engineers, scientists, housekeepers, teachers, technicians, female assemblers, accountants, Finnish foremen, and Hungarian engineers.

They were asked what job events had occurred in their work that had led to extreme satisfaction or extreme dissatisfaction on their part. Their responses are broken down in the exhibit into percentages of total "positive" job events and of total "negative" job events. (The figures total more than 100% on both the "hygiene" and "motivators" sides because often at least two factors can be attributed to a single event; advancement, for instance, often accompanies assumption of responsibility.)

To illustrate, a typical response involving achievement that had a negative effect for the employee was, "I was unhappy because I didn't do the job

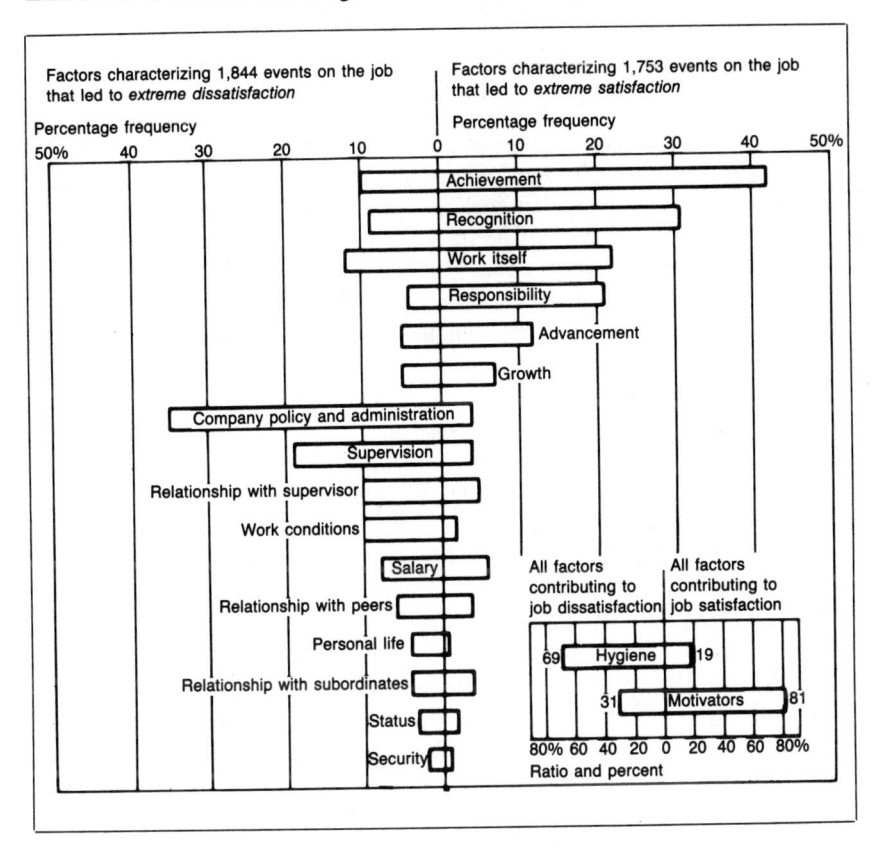

Exhibit 15–1 Factors Affecting Job Attitudes, as Reported in 12 Investigations

Factors characterizing 1,844 events on the job that led to *extreme dissatisfaction*	Factors characterizing 1,753 events on the job that led to *extreme satisfaction*

Percentage frequency
50% 40 30 20 10 0 10 20 30 40 50%

- Achievement
- Recognition
- Work itself
- Responsibility
- Advancement
- Growth
- Company policy and administration
- Supervision
- Relationship with supervisor
- Work conditions
- Salary
- Relationship with peers
- Personal life
- Relationship with subordinates
- Status
- Security

All factors contributing to job dissatisfaction | All factors contributing to job satisfaction

69 | Hygiene | 19
31 | Motivators | 81

80% 60 40 20 0 20 40 60 80%
Ratio and percent

successfully." A typical response in the small number of positive job events in the Company Policy and Administration grouping was, "I was happy because the company reorganized the section so that I didn't report any longer to the guy I didn't get along with."

As the lower right-hand part of the exhibit shows, of all the factors contributing to job satisfaction, 81% were motivators. And of all the factors contributing to the employees' dissatisfaction over their work, 69% involved hygiene elements.

Eternal Triangle

There are three general philosophies of personnel management. The first is based on organizational theory, the second on industrial engineering, and the third on behavioral science.

The organizational theorist believes that human needs are either so irrational or so varied and adjustable to specific situations that the major function of personnel management is to be as pragmatic as the occasion demands. If jobs are organized in a proper manner, he reasons, the result will be the most efficient job structure, and the most favorable job attitudes will follow as a matter of course.

The industrial engineer holds that man is mechanistically oriented and economically motivated and his needs are best met by attuning the individual to the most efficient work process. The goal of personnel management therefore should be to concoct the most appropriate incentive system and to design the specific working conditions in a way that facilitates the most efficient use of the human machine. By structuring jobs in a manner that leads to the most efficient operation, the engineer believes that he can obtain the optimal organization of work and the proper work attitudes.

The behavioral scientist focuses on group sentiments, attitudes of individual employees, and the organization's social and psychological climate. According to his persuasion, he emphasizes one or more of the various hygiene and motivator needs. His approach to personnel management generally emphasizes some form of human relations education, in the hope of instilling healthy employee attitudes and an organizational climate which he considers to be felicitous to human values. He believes that proper attitudes will lead to efficient job and organizational structure.

There is always a lively debate as to the overall effectiveness of the approaches of the organizational theorist and the industrial engineer. Manifestly they have achieved much. But the nagging question for the behavioral scientist has been: What is the cost in human problems that eventually cause more expense to the organization—for instance, turnover, absenteeism, errors, violation of safety rules, strikes, restriction of output, higher wages, and greater fringe benefits? On the other hand, the behavioral scientist is hard put to document much manifest improvement in personnel management, using his approach.

The three philosophies can be depicted as a triangle, as is done in Figure 15–1, with each persuasion claiming the apex angle. The motivation-hygiene theory claims the same angle as industrial engineering, but for opposite goals. Rather than rationalizing the work to increase efficiency, the theory suggests that work be *enriched* to bring about effective utilization of personnel. Such a systematic attempt to motivate employees by manipulating the motivator factors is just beginning.

The term *job enrichment* describes this embryonic movement. An older term, job enlargement, should be avoided because it is associated with past failures stemming from a misunderstanding of the problem. Job enrichment provides the opportunity for the employee's psychological growth, while job enlargement merely makes a job structurally bigger. Since scientific job enrichment is very new, this article only suggests the principles and practical steps that have recently emerged from several successful experiments in industry.

Part III: Job Enrichment Defined 67

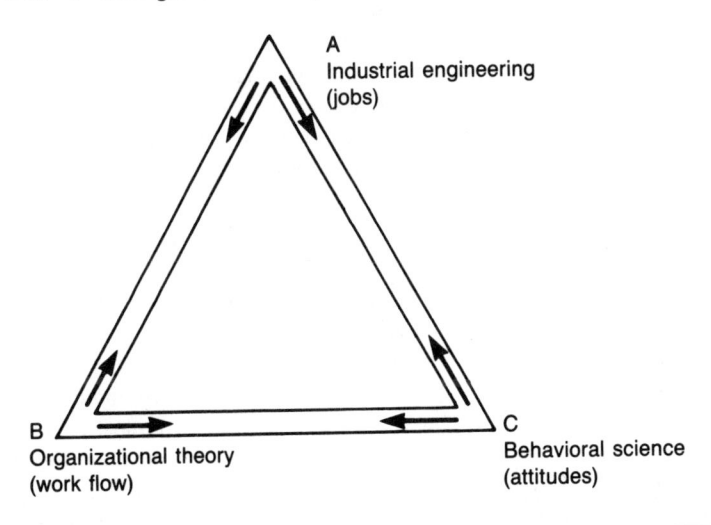

Figure 15–1 'Triangle' of Philosophies of Personnel Management

A
Industrial engineering
(jobs)

B
Organizational theory
(work flow)

C
Behavioral science
(attitudes)

Job Loading

In attempting to enrich an employee's job, management often succeeds in reducing the man's personal contribution, rather than giving him an opportunity for growth in his accustomed job. Such an endeavor, which I shall call horizontal job loading (as opposed to vertical loading, or providing motivator factors), has been the problem of earlier job enlargement programs. This activity merely enlarges the meaninglessness of the job. Some examples of this approach, and their effect, are:

- Challenging the employee by increasing the amount of production expected of him. If he tightens 10,000 bolts a day, see if he can tighten 20,000 bolts a day. The arithmetic involved shows that multiplying zero by zero still equals zero.
- Adding another meaningless task to the existing one, usually some routine clerical activity *(job enlargement)*. The arithmetic here is adding zero to zero.
- Rotating the assignments of a number of jobs that need to be enriched *(job rotation)*. This means washing dishes for a while, then washing silverware. The arithmetic is substituting one zero for another zero.
- Removing the most difficult parts of the assignment in order to free the worker to accomplish more of the less challenging assignments. *(This is a travesty of job purification, removing any of the challenge still existing in a*

job.) This traditional industrial engineering approach amounts to subtraction in the hope of accomplishing addition.

These are common forms of horizontal loading that frequently come up in preliminary brainstorming sessions on job enrichment. The principles of vertical loading have not all been worked out as yet, and they remain rather general, but I have furnished seven useful starting points for consideration in Exhibit 15-2.

A Successful Application

An example from a highly successful job enrichment experiment can illustrate the distinction between horizontal and vertical loading of a job. The subjects of this study were the stockholder correspondents employed by a very large corporation. Seemingly, the task required of these carefully selected and highly trained correspondents was quite complex and challenging. But almost all indexes of performance and job attitudes were low, and exit interviewing confirmed that the challenge of the job existed merely as words.

A job enrichment project *(job redesign or job development)* was initiated in the form of an experiment with one group, designated as an achieving unit, having its job enriched by the principles described in Exhibit 15-2. A control group continued to do its job in the traditional way. (There were also two "uncommitted" groups of correspondents formed to measure the so-called Hawthorne Effect—that is, to gauge whether productivity and attitudes toward the job changed artificially

Exhibit 15-2 Principles of Vertical Job Loading

Principle	Motivators Involved
A. Removing some controls while retaining accountability	Responsibility and personal achievement
B. Increasing the accountability of individuals for own work	Responsibility and recognition
C. Giving a person a complete natural unit of work (module, division, area, and so on)	Responsibility, achievement, and recognition
D. Granting additional authority to an employee in his activity; job freedom	Responsibility, achievement, and recognition
E. Making periodic reports directly available to the worker himself rather than to the supervisor	Internal recognition
F. Introducing new and more difficult tasks not previously handled	Growth and learning
G. Assigning individuals specific or specialized tasks, enabling them to become experts	Responsibility, growth, and advancement

merely because employees sensed that the company was paying more attention to them in doing something different or novel. The results for these groups were substantially the same as for the control group, and for the sake of simplicity I do not deal with them in this summary.) No changes in hygiene were introduced for either group other than those that would have been made anyway, such as normal pay increases.

The changes for the achieving unit were introduced in the first two months, averaging one per week of the seven motivators listed in Exhibit 15–2. At the end of six months the members of the achieving unit were found to be outperforming their counterparts in the control group, and in addition indicated a marked increase in their liking for their jobs. Other results showed that the achieving group had lower absenteeism and, subsequently, a much higher rate of promotion.

Figure 15–2 illustrates the changes in performance, measured in February and March, before the study period began, and at the end of each month of the study period. The shareholder service index represents quality of letters, including

Figure 15–2 Shareholder Service Index in Company Experiment (Three month cumulative average)

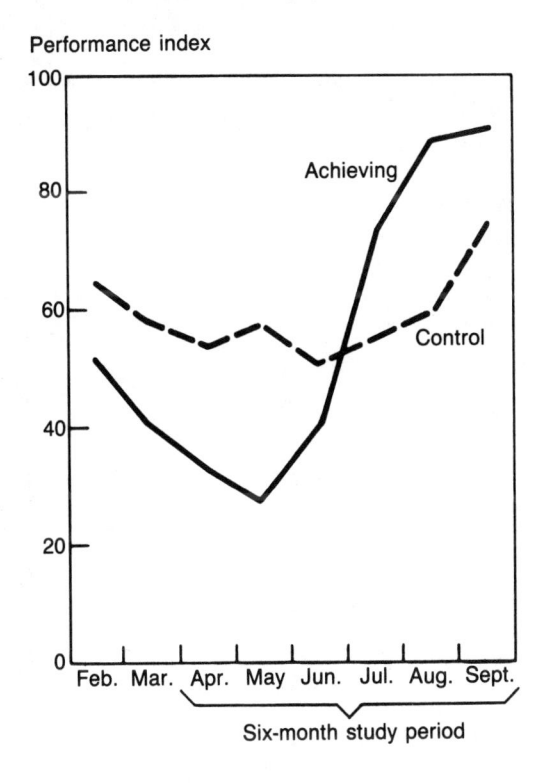

accuracy of information, and speed of response to stockholders' letters of inquiry. The index of a current month was averaged into the average of the two prior months, which means that improvement was harder to obtain if the indexes of the previous months were low. The "achievers" were performing less well before the six-month period started, and their performance service index continued to decline after the introduction of the motivators, evidently because of uncertainty over their newly granted responsibilities. In the third month, however, performance improved, and soon the members of this group had reached a high level of accomplishment.

Figure 15–3 shows the two groups' attitudes toward their job, measured at the end of March, just before the first motivator was introduced, and again at the end of September. The correspondents were asked 16 questions, all involving motivation. A typical one was, "As you see it, how many opportunities do you feel that you have in your job for making worthwhile contributions?" The answers were scaled from 1 to 5, with 80 as the maximum possible score. The achievers became much more positive about their job, while the attitude of the control unit remained about the same (the drop is not statistically significant).

How was the job of these correspondents restructured? Exhibit 15–3 lists the suggestions made that were deemed to be horizontal loading, and the actual

Figure 15–3 Changes in Attitudes toward Tasks in Company Experiment (Changes in mean scores over six month period)

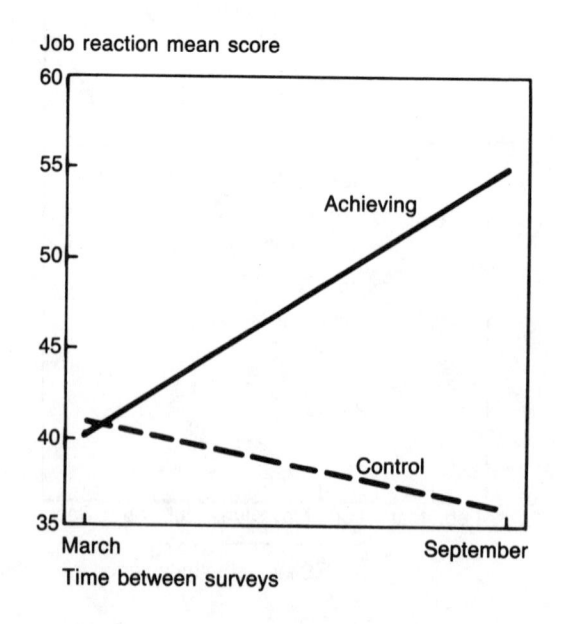

Exhibit 15–3 Enlargement vs. Enrichment of Correspondents' Tasks in Company Experiment

Horizontal Loading Suggestions (Rejected)	Vertical Loading Suggestions (Adopted)	Principle
Firm quotas could be set for letters to be answered each day, using a rate which would be hard to reach.	Subject matter experts were appointed within each unit for other members of the unit to consult with before seeking supervisory help. (The supervisor had been answering all specialized and difficult questions.)	G
The women could type the letters themselves, as well as compose them, or take on any other clerical functions.	Correspondents signed their own names on letters. (The supervisor had been signing all letters.)	B
All difficult or complex inquiries could be channeled to a few women so that the remainder could achieve high rates of output. These jobs could be exchanged from time to time.	The work of the more experienced correspondents was proofread less frequently by supervisors and was done at the correspondents' desks, dropping verification from 100% to 10%. (Previously, all correspondents' letters had been checked by the supervisor.)	A
The women could be rotated through units handling different customers, and then sent back to their own units.	Production was discussed, but only in terms such as "a full day's work is expected." As time went on, this was no longer mentioned. (Before, the group had been constantly reminded of the number of letters that needed to be answered.)	D
	Outgoing mail went directly to the mailroom without going over supervisors' desks. (The letters had always been routed through the supervisors.)	A
	Correspondents were encouraged to answer letters in a more personalized way. (Reliance on the form-letter approach had been standard practice.)	C
	Each correspondent was held personally responsible for the quality and accuracy of letters. (This responsibility had been the province of the supervisor and the verifier.)	B, E

vertical loading changes that were incorporated in the job of the achieving unit. The capital letters under "Principle" after "Vertical loading" refer to the corresponding letters in Exhibit 15–2. The reader will note that the rejected forms of horizontal loading correspond closely to the list of common manifestations of the phenomenon.

STEPS TO JOB ENRICHMENT

Now that the motivator idea has been described in practice, here are the steps that managers should take in instituting the principle with their employees:

1. Select those jobs in which (a) the investment in industrial engineering does not make changes too costly, (b) attitudes are poor, (c) hygiene is becoming very costly, and (d) motivation will make a difference in performance.
2. Approach these jobs with the conviction that they can be changed. Years of tradition had led managers to believe that the content of the jobs is sacrosanct and the only scope of action that they have is in ways of stimulating people.
3. Brainstorm a list of changes that may enrich the jobs, without concern for their practicality.
4. Screen the list to eliminate suggestions that involve hygiene, rather than actual motivation.
5. Screen the list for generalities, such as "give them more responsibility," that are rarely followed in practice. This might seem obvious, but the motivator words have never left industry; the substance has just been rationalized and organized out. Words like "responsibility," "growth," "achievement," and "challenge," for example, have been elevated to the lyrics of the patriotic anthem for all organizations. It is the old problem typified by the pledge of allegiance to the flag being more important than contributions to the country—of following the form, rather than the substance.
6. Screen the list to eliminate any *horizontal* loading suggestions.
7. Avoid direct participation by the employees whose jobs are to be enriched. Ideas they have expressed previously certainly constitute a valuable source for recommended changes, but their direct involvement contaminates the process with human relations hygiene and, more specifically, gives them only a sense of making a contribution. The job is to be changed, and it is the content that will produce the motivation, not attitudes about being involved or the challenge inherent in setting up a job. That process will be over shortly, and it is what the employees will be doing from then on that will determine their motivation. A sense of participation will result only in short-term movement.

8. In the initial attempts at job enrichment, set up a controlled experiment. At least two equivalent groups should be chosen, one an experimental unit in which the motivators are systematically introduced over a period of time, and the other one a control group in which no changes are made. For both groups, hygiene should be allowed to follow its natural course for the duration of the experiment. Pre- and post-installation tests of performance and job attitudes are necessary to evaluate the effectiveness of the job enrichment program. The attitude test must be limited to motivator items in order to divorce the employee's view of the job he is given from all the surrounding hygiene feelings that he might have.
9. Be prepared for a drop in performance in the experimental group the first few weeks. The changeover to a new job may lead to a temporary reduction in efficiency.
10. Expect your first-line supervisors to experience some anxiety and hostility over the changes you are making. The anxiety comes from their fear that the changes will result in poorer performance for their unit. Hostility will arise when the employees start assuming what the supervisors regard as their own responsibility for performance. The supervisor without checking duties to perform may then be left with little to do.

Although job enrichment involves moving decision making, authority, and responsibility down through every level of the organization so that supervisory personnel receive responsibilities to replace those that they delegate, the insecurity of change seems to hit hardest at this level. After a successful experiment, however, the supervisor usually discovers the supervisory and managerial functions he has neglected, or which were never his because all his time was given over to checking the work of his subordinates. For example, in the R&D division of one large chemical company I know of, the supervisors of the laboratory assistants were theoretically responsible for their training and evaluation. These functions, however, had come to be performed in a routine, unsubstantial fashion. After the job enrichment program, during which the supervisors were not merely passive observers of the assistants' performance, the supervisors actually were devoting their time to reviewing performance and administering thorough training.

What has been called an employee-centered style of supervision will come about not through education of supervisors, but by changing the jobs that they do.

CONCLUDING NOTE

Job enrichment will not be a one-time proposition, but a continuous management function. The initial changes, however, should last for a very long period of time. There are a number of reasons for this:

- The changes should bring the job up to the level of challenge commensurate with the skill that was hired.
- Those who have still more ability eventually will be able to demonstrate it better and win promotion to higher-level jobs.
- The very nature of motivators, as opposed to hygiene factors, is that they have a much longer-term effect on employees' attitudes. Perhaps the job will have to be enriched again, but this will not occur as frequently as the need for hygiene.

Not all jobs can be enriched, nor do all jobs need to be enriched. If only a small percentage of the time and money that is now devoted to hygiene, however, were given to job enrichment efforts, the return in human satisfaction and economic gain would be one of the largest dividends that industry and society have ever reaped through their efforts at better personnel management.

The argument for job enrichment can be summed up quite simply: If you have someone on a job, use him. If you can't use him on the job, get rid of him, either via automation or by selecting someone with lesser ability. If you can't use him and you can't get rid of him, you will have a motivation problem.

* * * *

Herzberg's article has become a classic presentation on job enrichment. Bagadia and Bakr summarize more recent writings on job enrichment, concluding with a pragmatic plan for the management approach and a four-step plan to ensure its success.

16.
An Update on Job Enrichment

Kishan Shyamlal Bagadia and M.M. Bakr

Job enrichment is fundamentally the reintroduction of the opportunity for achievement in work, which would lead to employee satisfaction and motivation. This is achieved by giving the employee the following:

a. Greater responsibility
b. Greater autonomy in carrying out his responsibilities
c. Increased "closure" (doing the whole thing)
d. More timely feedback as to how well he has done
e. More recognition for doing a job well.[1-3]

This concept is schematically represented in Figure 16–1.

MISCONCEPTIONS AND LIMITATIONS OF JOB ENRICHMENT

A number of common misconceptions and limitations were cited as a source of failure in many job enrichment programs. One of the misconceptions is the belief that if a man is given more to do, he is motivated (*job enlargement*). This has not proven to be the case. Recently, some interesting experiments were conducted at General Motors, wherein the scope of a number of jobs was increased. The result was *not* that the workers were motivated but that they complained that they had less break time.[4] Another misconception is that addition of the planning, goal setting, and decision-making responsibilities to a job takes care of the situation automatically. It is not necessarily so, because the worker gets more frustrated if he is not given the skills to carry out these responsibilities.[4,5] *These points are*

Modified with permission from Kishan Shyamlal Bagadia and M.M. Bakr, "An Update on Job Enrichment," *Industrial Management* 19, no. 3 (1977): 8–11.

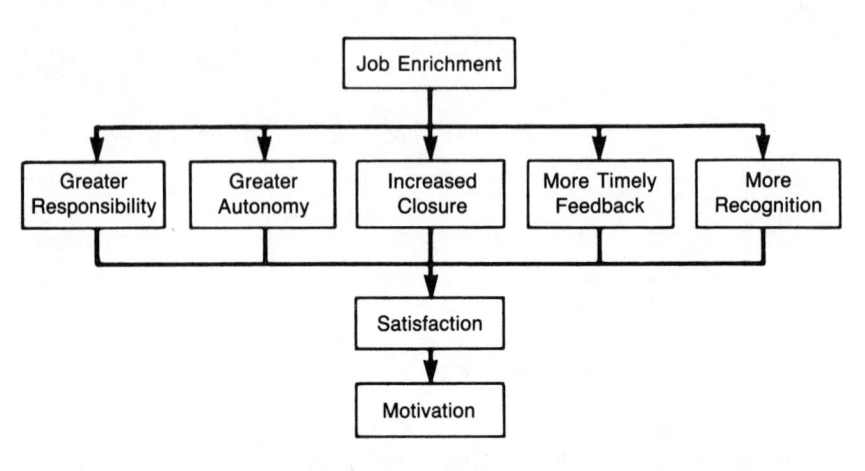

Figure 16–1 Approach to Job Enrichment

```
                    Job Enrichment
    ┌──────┬──────────┬──────┬──────────┐
    ▼      ▼          ▼      ▼          ▼
 Greater  Greater  Increased More Timely More
Responsi- Autonomy  Closure   Feedback  Recognition
 bility
    └──────┴──────┬───┴──────┴──────────┘
                  ▼
              Satisfaction
                  ▼
              Motivation
```

---

raised by Herzberg as he condemns participative management. Focusing the attention on the worker and redesigning his job while the boss is being completely forgotten is another misconception. By giving the worker the opportunity to set all aspects for conducting his work, the supervisor has such a little part left in the problem solving, decision making and goal setting that he can easily become a source of failure in job enrichment programs.[4-6]

Another misconception, and a significant one, is that it is always thought that restructuring the job will accomplish enrichment whereas it can be done without job restructuring.[4,5] Yet another misconception is that job enrichment can be applied to any and all jobs and that there is no need to examine the job and the work situation before implementing job enrichment programs.[7] The final misconception lies in the fact that the job enrichment program is utilized for jobs other than those for which it was designed (where job content is the root of problems) such as those in which attitudes are poor. It can't be assumed that job enrichment solves all corporate ills.[7]

In addition to previous misconceptions, there are many limitations experienced in the job enrichment approach. It is very difficult, for example, to convince all workers to take part in job enrichment programs because some of them have fear stemming from the lack of knowhow. However, exposure to a successful job enrichment program elsewhere will ease those fears.[8]

In the contemporary dynamic organizations, as new managers take charge, they may not opt to continue the job enrichment program as they had not been exposed to the work situation from the beginning. New managers fear that any changes that prove unsuccessful will be assessed as their failure whether it is true or not, while they feel it would be safer if something goes wrong when it is done the way it has always been done. Because of the time consumption of many weeks needed to plan, develop, and implement job enrichment, some managers lose their enthusiasm before the job enrichment program has a chance to work.[3]

When a change in the current method is recommended, the feeling often is that there was fault with that method. Overcoming this kind of management problem is difficult as it means admitting that there was some error. It is often difficult for plant employees to regard a job enrichment program as an essential part of their job, especially when involving technical training for very specific practical goals, or behavior adjustment for broad, elusive goals. This means that job enrichment might be regarded as having low priority, as it is assumed to be something extra. Lower and middle management members often feel powerless to alter job content because they are too far down in the organization while upper management members feel impotent because they are too far removed from the work itself. On the other hand, job interdependency is also a very real and complex problem. The redesign of the job under consideration is not very difficult if it is independent of other jobs. However, when the jobs are highly interdependent and alteration of one job affects all others, job enrichment becomes very difficult.[9]

Increased responsibility is not always seen by the worker as an opportunity for advancement, achievement and recognition. He often regards it as an overburden. Labor must be able to voice their opinion concerning job enrichment of their jobs. Excluding such representation may jeopardize the success of any job enrichment efforts. The scope of job enrichment is often not clear to workers. Rotation through a succession of boring jobs, and/or adding more of the same boring tasks have been called job enrichment. Job enrichment has become a source of confusion and uncertainty to them.[9] Unless top management also participates very sincerely and actively, any long range effect of job enrichment is doubtful.

APPROACH TO THE PROPER APPLICATION OF JOB ENRICHMENT

Job enrichment can successfully be implemented only after a thorough analysis of the organization has been made which shows that job enrichment would be a solution to the existing problems. A survey of studies on the strategy for successful implementation of job enrichment programs has resulted in the identification of the following four steps in implementing the enrichment strategy:

Step (1): Diagnosis of the Job

Job enrichment is more suitable for some jobs than others. The success of job enrichment programs lies in the selection of the right job. A simple and effective method of job evaluation is based upon the analysis of certain work and company related factors. This will be helpful to decision makers in selecting jobs that have the greatest potentiality for enrichment.

The potentiality for enrichment is primarily dependent upon four sets of variables which are the job itself, technology, the workers, and management.

a. The job itself: The nature of the job itself is very significant for the successful application of job enrichment. Cost, quality, flexibility, co-ordination, specialization, wage payment plans, and man-machine relationship, have been found to be the most relevant job related criteria for selection purposes.
b. Technology: It is wise to construct enriched job designs into new facilities as opposed to enriching present jobs. New systems, specialized equipment, and conversion of technology can be costly to integrate into existing plants, which can place limits on the extent of enrichment.
c. The workers: The basic concept of job enrichment assumes that enriched jobs will have more intrinsic satisfaction which will then instigate equal or better performance of job demands. There are several indicators that are useful in predicting how workers will react to job enrichment. Skill level, education, previous work experience, and background have been found to be very useful indicators.[7]
d. Management: It is advantageous in the development and implementation of sound job enrichment projects to have competent management teams committed to the job enrichment concept. With such a group, many hurdles can be overcome that could otherwise spell defeat or cause delays in job enrichment application.

Step (2): Supervisory Coaching

Coaching and training of supervisory personnel in job enrichment concepts is a necessary requirement to the implementation process, because people involved in the enrichment program should be exposed to the fundamental concepts.[10]

Step (3): Implementation

In accord with Herzberg's recommendations, the actual implementation of job enrichment depends on the nature of the job. The following general recommendations should be considered.

Employees should be given an opportunity and additional authority to handle new and different tasks. They should also be allowed to plan and control their job assignments as much as possible, and accountability for their own work should be increased.

Part III: Job Enrichment Defined   79

As adjustments to the enriched job are made, the managers should expect a decrease of short duration in performance of employees, simply because it is a new situation.

Step (4): Feedback and Followup

As disinterest in the newly enriched job can occur, it is necessary to constantly monitor and investigate the employee's performance in order to obtain feedback on enrichment implementation.

In summary, when a job enrichment program has been carefully deliberated, developed, and put into action by organizations ready to commit themselves to job enrichment's inherent changes, work is more meaningful for employees. This results in increased job satisfaction and productivity.

NOTES

1. Penzer, W.N., "After Everyone's Had His Job Enriched, Then What?" *Administrative Management*, Vol. 34, October, 1973.
2. Sirota, D., "Job Enrichment—Another Management Fad?," *Conference Board Report*, Vol. 10, April, 1973.
3. Sirota, D. and Wolfson, A.D., "Job Enrichment: What Are the Obstacles?" *Personnel:* 49,N3, 1972.
4. Benjamin, B. Tregoe, "What's Wrong with Job Enrichment," *Duns Review*, Vol. 102, December, 1973.
5. Benjamin, B.T., "How to Avoid the Pitfalls," *Personnel Journal*, Vol. 53, June, 1974.
6. "How About Enriching the Manager's Job?," *Management Review*, Vol. 61, December, 1972.
7. Reif, W.E., and Tinnel, D.C., "A Diagnostic Approach to Job Enrichment," *M.S.U. Business Topics*, Vol. 21, 1973.
8. "A Spoonful of Job Enrichment Won't Solve All Personnel Problems," *Management Review*, Vol. 61, May, 1972.
9. Schappe, R.H. "Twenty-Two Arguments Against Job Enrichment," *Personnel Journal*, Vol. 53, February, 1974.
10. Archie, B. Carroll, "Conceptual Foundations of Job Enrichment." *Public Personnel Management*, Vol. 3, Jan.-Feb., 1974.

* * * *

One potential problem with job enrichment that is not addressed by Bagadia and Bakr revolves around union acceptance. The scanty literature available on the willingness of unions to accept job enrichment is inconclusive,[1,2] *indicating the need for further research in this area.*

York presents a final adaptation of Herzberg's original concept of job enrichment. He describes the achievement of job enrichment through group, rather than individual, effort.

NOTES

1. Thomas M. Rohan, "A Job Enrichment Experiment Backfires," *Industry Week* 204, no. 2 (1980): 26–28.
2. William F. Giles, and William H. Holley, Jr., "Job Enrichment Versus Traditional Issues at the Bargaining Table: What Union Members Want," *Academy of Management Journal* 21, no. 4 (1978): 725–730.

17.
Team Production (Semi-Autonomous Work Groups)

Lyle York

Some job redesign specialists have opted for a different approach to the design of jobs: the development of a team of workers to carry out the many tasks necessary for a given work unit to meet its production objectives. Under this approach a group of workers is given collective responsibility for a segment of the production process. The group decides which individuals are to perform which tasks; it copes with any problems arising in the production process; it temporarily reassigns tasks to cover for absenteeism, unanticipated problems in the work, or changing priorities; and it selects members to serve on any plant committees which may be formed to deal with problems.

In addition to basic production work, the group performs such support functions as minor maintenance work, quality control, basic industrial engineering, counseling and coaching of team members who are performing below standard, and selecting replacements for departing group members. It receives basic management information such as costs, yields, deadlines, and company procedures. In effect, the group is collectively given an enriched job. Experiments in team production have tended to be more ambitious than job enrichment efforts in attempting to reform the operating structure of the organization.

In practice, aspects of each of the two approaches have been combined at times. Each individual in a work flow may have a job which corresponds to the three-part model of an enriched job: *(1) a complete piece of work, (2) worker control over the way in which the goal will be achieved, and (3) feedback*. A series of client relationships is developed between workers, which in turn provides the groundwork for a production team.

For example, in a small assembly operation, the work of basic assemblers and harness assemblers is channeled to the same subassemblers who, in turn, produce

---

Modified with permission from Lyle York, *Job Enrichment Revisited* (New York: Amacom, 1979), pp. 9–10.

work for a specific final assembler. Each individual in the work flow has as complete a job as possible, including in-process inspection and test work. Each assembler receives a record of the percentage of boards which develop problems traceable to workmanship. In addition, each assembler has a certain amount of autonomy, for example, deciding when to take coffee and lunch breaks.

The explicit interdependencies between each assembler in the process lays the groundwork for a team. As a group, the various assemblers within a work flow (basic, harness, sub, and final assembly) can meet regularly with foreman and engineers to discuss production problems. In those situations where sales requirements are known sufficiently in advance, the group can receive weekly production targets as well as productivity reports for the past week. The emphasis is on individual job enrichment, but characteristics of team production are incorporated in the restructured design as well.

The individual and team approaches share an emphasis on restructuring the employees' responsibilities to provide them with increased control over their work experiences. Under the proper circumstances, each can result in significant benefits for an organization.

* * *

An administration with a Theory Y philosophy of man takes a job enrichment approach that permits the work itself to motivate the employees. Theory Z, a relative newcomer, has caught the attention and interest of American management because it includes all the components of Theory Y and gives specific behaviors of management that can make job enrichment possible. Fuszard compares the "American business philosophy" with the new approach in accordance with Theory Z.

18.
Theory Z

Barbara Fuszard

What is happening in America? We've always been tops—made the best products, were biggest and best. How can Japan and Europe, and even small countries in Asia, produce more cheaply, perhaps even better products? The early immigrants' image of American streets being paved in gold was not far from reality. It seemed all American industry had the Midas touch—no matter what they did, what management philosophy they had, American businessmen were successful.

Suddenly big is not best, and other countries are offering stiff competition. We are beginning to question if there is a better way than the "American way" for doing business.

THE AMERICAN WAY

Beliefs in the American way that are beginning to be questioned are:

- Massive capital investments are necessary for efficient production.
- Large factories promote efficiency.
- High quality comes from more testing.
- Decision making by consensus results in camels when we want horses.
- High specialization leads to high production.
- Creativity comes from individual maverick genius.
- Turnover rates of 26 percent annually and absenteeism of 8 percent are irreducible minima.
- Only high pay and rapid promotion will spur the most talented to achieve.

Modified with permission from Barbara Fuszard, "Management Concepts That Work—Theory Z," *The Facilitator* 8, no. 4 (1982): 2–3.

Among companies questioning the above beliefs are General Motors, Hewlett-Packard, General Electric, IBM, Eli Lilly, Honeywell, Pillsbury, Lockheed, Ford, Chrysler, and Westinghouse. All have undertaken attempts recently to move from the "Company A" philosophy given above, to a "Company Z" philosophy. And what is this Z philosophy?

THEORY Z

What Theory Z is not, is a simple package that can be imposed upon an existing organization with dispatch and efficiency, producing magical results. Its major components are alternatives to some of the philosophy statements listed above as the "American way."

Theory Z managers want the smallest plants possible so that change is possible to keep up with new technologies. Rather than more testing, Theory Z managers believe that high quality comes from inviting workers themselves to work to continually refine design and manufacturing processes.

Rather than distrusting decision making by consensus, Theory Z plants have achieved "superlative levels of quality and efficiency through participation." Lower specialization is used, with the most creative companies in America spearheading the introduction of Theory Z into American enterprise.

Turnover in Theory Z companies are between six and twelve percent, with lower absenteeism rates as well. And instead of high pay and rapid promotion, the companies are using commitment and participation for motivation.

Theory Z companies have adopted this new approach to management because they see a difference in their employees and all of society: employees are better educated, more interested in job security, want to be convinced rather than commanded, include increasing female and minority representation, want to be heard, desire ownership, and share decision making. Employees are considered the most valued commodity of an organization, and therefore organizations must change as to beliefs, traditions, values, and the management systems.

All the literature on Theory Z emphasizes that this philosophy will not work in an organization unless it is the philosophy of top management. Nursing administrators will have to use their positions as members of top management to win the other members of the management team to this approach in order for it to be successful. Even after top administration makes a total commitment to Theory Z, it will take years for the philosophy to impact every level of the organization.

Quality Circles are a real part of Theory Z on the operating level, and efforts of these groups do show rapid benefits. A total change of philosophy and management style is less easily achieved.

Management styles based upon Taylorism, or even Theory Y, are not adequate for today's workers. For American health care institutions to continue to meet the demands of the American people, they too will have to adopt management styles appropriate to the 1980s health care workers. Marketing of health care will have no material to market if the health care workers are not motivated to produce quality care.

* * * *

Herzberg identifies work itself as the great motivator. His seven types of vertical job loading permit the employee to experience this motivation of work:

1. *removal of controls*
2. *increased accountability*
3. *a total job*
4. *increased authority*
5. *direct feedback*
6. *new and more difficult tasks*
7. *specialization leading to expertise*

Job redesign can be added to Herzberg's concept as a method of vertical job loading. Job redesign is appropriate to Herzberg's definition of job enrichment and merely offers a structural approach to implementation of it. Team or interdisciplinary functioning is not part of Herzberg's definition of job enrichment. Yet, it is a necessary component of professional functioning of the future and, therefore, must be integrated into his basic model. Theory Z is based on participative management, which requires structural and functional changes in order to make job enrichment a reality.

Part IV

Restructuring Work for Job Enrichment

The concept of job enrichment sounds exciting, but is it workable? Nursing administrators have a responsibility to take advantage of all the methods and structures available to create "a climate for growth" in their institutions. For example, an adhocracy organizational structure, as discussed by Fuszard and Bishop in " 'Adhocracy' in Health Care Institutions?" offers the institutional nurse all the motivators: responsibility and personal achievement, recognition (esteem from others), internal recognition (self-esteem), growth and learning, and advancement. Adhocracy places control in the hands of the bedside nurse, who is recognized by the patient, other staff members, the administration, and other members of the health team as a competent professional. The nurse has an opportunity to learn and grow through added responsibility, specialization, and interprofessional problem solving.

The operating adhocracy organizational structure is new to health care institutions. One of the concepts inherent in an adhocracy is participative management. In "Participative Management," Herzberg expresses his view of this approach as merely a part of the human relations movement to offer employees hygiene factors. In "Participative Decision Making: An Experimental Study in a Hospital," however, Bragg and Andrews describe a study in which the effects of this approach compare favorably to those of Theory Z organizations.

Professional nurses are members of the patient project teams in an adhocracy. As members of the project teams work right at the bedside, primary nursing is the appropriate patient care delivery system. The value of primary nursing for the individual nurse is discussed by Tobin in "Primary Nursing's Effect on Professional Development." Primary nursing offers the nurse increased accountability, a complete natural unit of work, additional authority, instant feedback on decisions, a chance to gain expertise in one's area, and interdisciplinary functioning. Not all nurses are equally prepared for this responsible role, however. Professional nurses do not wish to be treated as interchangeable cogs in a machine. They prize differences in experience, expertise, and interests. These differences in "readiness" for the responsibility of primary nursing must be addressed before this type of nursing care delivery can be effective.

A clinical nurse specialist (CNS) may have many roles in an adhocracy. In "Extending the Influence of the Clinical Nurse Specialist," the authors describe a teaching/modeling role that the CNS can play to help primary nurses reach the level of competence required for their position.

Job enrichment through vertical job loading can also be accomplished by offering the professional nurse an opportunity to specialize, to become expert in one area. Faulconer and Reeves, in "Clinical Ladders and Specialty Teams," address the motivators associated with specialization: responsibility, growth, and advancement. Nurses on each specialty team are given responsibility for all patients of their specialty, including equipment, supplies, budget, goals, and objectives. An opportunity for growth is offered through in-depth study of the specialty, in leadership and other special courses, and in participative management. Advancement is provided through peer review and evaluations, with the ladder concept giving credit for level of expertise and education.

The articles mentioned thus far deal with Herzberg's principles of vertical job loading for job enrichment. The final two articles in this part are included to respond to York's approach to job enrichment, which adds team functioning to individual endeavor.

A changing world implies changes in the professional role and necessitates a new look at job enrichment for professional nurses. Harris' work "Professional Synergy," provides such a new look at professionalism. Harris believes that traditional "learned" professions stand in danger of extinction because of the public's level of education. Although professionals in the past have been exclusive repositors of specialized knowledge, it is expected that this information will be increasingly available to ever larger numbers of the population through new information media. True professionals, Harris believes, must meet the future in conscious cooperation for the mutual benefit of all. He quotes Alvin Toffler's "The Third Wave Culture" as demanding such collaboration. Although professional colleagues in each discipline have long shared and collaborated, the future calls for multidisciplinary sharing based upon mutual interests rather than on previous education or training. The future holds such complex problems that intellectual or professional ethnocentrism will be ineffectual in solving them.

Harris warns of the difficulties of multidisciplinary functioning. Interdisciplinary work brings together persons with differing value systems, professional cultures, approaches, and goals. He offers a list of characteristics that each interdisciplinary team member should have. The nursing administrator needs such criteria to select professional nurses who will be able to work effectively in professional synergy.

That the difficulties described by Harris are a reality is borne out by Riley and Moses in "Coordinated Care: Making It a Reality." They discuss the formation of an interdisciplinary team to work with patients with catastrophic disease. The team has the physician as leader for the initial phases of the patient's illness, with more and more responsibility given to other team members as the patient progresses through rehabilitation. Guidelines presented in this article can serve as a model for institutions that do not yet have an adhocracy structure.

19.
"Adhocracy" in Health Care Institutions?

Barbara Fuszard and Janet K. Bishop

Nursing administrators, who are well aware of their responsibilities to their employing institutions, are expected to provide professional nursing care to patients. Patient care can, however, be less than complete to meet all the patient needs in the organizational structure of a health care institution. The institution can also impinge on the functioning of institutional professionals, such as nurses.

Toffler had a dream of an organizational structure that would be built around the task to be accomplished, rather than around a hierarchy. It would be adaptable to the specific task, would use the persons most qualified to perform the task, and would self-destruct the moment the task was completed. He called it "adhocracy."[1]

THE BUREAUCRATIC STRUCTURE

Our large health care institutions have long been labeled bureaucracies. They do, in fact, bear many of the trappings of the "closed-systems thinking" that characterizes the bureaucratic structure. Hospitals and other large health care agencies have rules, division of labor, hierarchy, specialists, line and staff positions, a separately designated administrative staff, and records. These contribute to bureaucratic stability, but stability also causes paralysis.

Even more fatal to a bureaucracy's functioning in a large organization is the false assumption on which bureaucratic structure is based: that management can make all decisions intelligently. At one time, perhaps the manager could be the expert in all areas of the company's endeavor,[2] but today, rapidly changing health

---

Modified with permission from Barbara Fuszard, " 'Adhocracy' in Health Care Institutions?" *Journal of Nursing Administration* 13, no. 1 (1983): 14–19, and Janet K. Bishop, "Adhocracy as an Organizational Structure in a Psychiatric Institution," *Journal of Nursing Administration* 13, no. 1 (1983): 20–24.

care technology and the many facets of our complex organizations make it impossible for the management team to maintain the current level of knowledge required for sound decision making. The persons most knowledgeable in specialty areas, and therefore most appropriately the decision makers, are the technical specialists who carry out the functions of the bureaucratically structured health care institutions. Yet, in most bureaucracies, specialists are not permitted to use their expert knowledge for decision making. Thus, bureaucracy fails to offer the vertical job loading motivators of responsibility, growth, achievement, and recognition.

THE COLLEGIAL STRUCTURE

Rice and Bishoprick[3] describe hospitals as collegial, rather than bureaucratic models of organization. This collegial, or professional, model of organization is more sensitive to the changing needs of the environment than the bureaucratic model, yet it retains enough components of the bureaucratic model to provide organizational stability. For example, the housekeeping or support personnel are arranged hierarchically as in the typical bureaucracy and are directed by the administrative staff. The unique component of the collegial model is the group of professional specialists who function completely independently of the bureaucratic structure and are responsible for decisions affecting patients. Because of their special knowledge, decision making at this level is the right of professional specialists.

Within this collegial model, Rice and Bishoprick see hospital administrators functioning only to maintain institutional facilities and to ensure that decisions of the professional specialists, the physicians, are implemented. This view puts the nurse and other health care professionals in the support or housekeeping hierarchy. Their role is merely to carry out the physicians' decisions. The collegial model is much like the bureaucratic model, in that the knowledge of health care professionals, with the exception of that of the physicians, is not tapped for decision making. As in the case of the bureaucracy, the vertical job loading motivators are lost to the professional nursing staff.

OPEN-SYSTEMS STRUCTURE

The search for the organizational form that is most receptive to the rapid changes occurring in the health care field and that uses all resources for its functioning leads to a more open system, an organizational structure sensitive to the environment. Large organizations cannot fully adapt to rapid changes in their environments. They require some stable structure along with flexibility. Robbins suggests that the appropriate approach for health care institutions is "open-systems thinking" rather than "open systems" in its pure form. The flexibility plus structure Robbins calls "adhocracy."[4]

ADHOCRACY

In the nursing literature, the term *adhocracy* refers to the use of ad hoc committees.[5] Toffler, originator of the term, defined it more broadly.[6] He writes of throw-away organizations, autonomous and semi-attached units, task forces, and project teams. In Toffler's adhocracy, an organizational chart over three months old is out of date. In the proliferating business organizations that have adopted the open-systems thinking of adhocracy, people from different parts of the organization are available for specific problem solving and stay together as a group to implement their ideas. When the task is finished, the temporary group of specialists dissolves, its membership moving to different problems, and the process is repeated with different groups and other problems. The organizational arrangement at any one time is based solely on the specific tasks at that time.

Along with an organizational structure open to change, adhocracy also brings a new locus of control for decision making. Adhocracy requires and gives power to experts, professionals whose knowledge and skills have been highly developed in formal training programs.[7] This organizational structure demands that the different specialists join forces in multidisciplinary teams, each formed around a specific project or innovation.[8]

The benefits of adhocracy to nursing are clear. Such an organizational structure would provide nurses with recognition for their special expertise and the responsibility to act as autonomous professionals within the health care institution.

ADHOCRACY IN A HEALTH CARE INSTITUTION

What would adhocracy look like in a health care facility? Around each patient in the facility a project team would form, each member chosen for special expertise relevant to the patient's unique needs. The team would exist as a group only for a single patient. Its members would solve problems, share expertise, make decisions, implement these decisions, and evaluate their effectiveness, using the open-systems feedback to monitor and modify the treatment plan. Once the project is completed and the patient discharged, the group of experts would disband to assume roles in other projects needing such expertise.

Does this organizational structure appear possible for large health care institutions? Mintzberg[9] would say no. He states that adhocracy is prevalent in almost every industry that has grown since World War II. No existing adhocracy that he can think of was established before that time. Health care institutions existed over a century before World War II. With this reasoning, we must ask, are these institutions then to be frozen into bureaucracies (traditional or professional), sluggish to respond to change, and treating patients on an "assembly line"? The Idaho State Hospital South in Blackfoot, Idaho went through the evolution from bureaucracy to collegial organization to adhocracy. Before June 1979, the philosophy of care and consequently the organizational structure reflected the closed-systems thinking of a traditional bureaucratic structure. The administrative director was deemed the only person in the system who possessed all the knowledge for decision making.[10] Top management made decisions and funneled them downward. Similarly, any problems, clinical or managerial, were "kicked upstairs" for the appropriate all-knowing administrator to solve. For example, clinical decisions that affected the budget were made by the fiscal officer.

Periodically, the administration introduced the collegial, or professional, model of organizational structure in an effort to involve professional staff in decision making. However, the decision making process did not truly change; it merely shifted from the administrative director to the clinical director, or physician. This collegial model also fell short of fully using the abilities of the highly trained and qualified health care professionals who were directly involved with patients.

In June 1979, the hospital began a slow process of reorganization based on the philosophy and leadership style of the newly appointed administrative director. It became, and is now, the philosophy of the institution that decision making should occur at the level closest to the patient. Specifically, patients and their immediate caregivers are involved in treatment planning and decisions affecting patient care and well-being. Concern for the institution's efficiency had helped force the adoption of the concept of open-systems thinking.[11,12] The administration found, for example, that they could contain costs by using professionals more appropriately. The open-systems concept of adhocracy allowed creativity in providing quality health care, and it allowed professional development.

Adhocracy can work in other institutions, too. A courageous and politically astute nursing administrator can help win the benefits of adhocracy for patients and nursing staff. Evidence of some components of operating adhocracy already appear in the nursing literature. These components include group decision making, use of experts, communication and coordination, fluid organizational structure, and decentralization.

Group Decision Making

In an adhocracy, decisions are made by the team or group of persons most appropriate, as determined by their expertise. Hospital and nursing literature is replete with descriptions of matrix organizations that exist in many rehabilitation and teaching hospitals.[13] In these organizations health care professionals work as teams in the process of delivering health care. The decision makers are "on the scene" and, therefore, are the people most knowledgeable about the individual patient. They are in the best position to continually modify the patient's plan of care, based upon the patient's observed response to it.

Nursing administrators could modify two aspects of existing matrix structures to give nursing the full benefits of adhocracy. First, they must make all members of the patient care team equal contributors to decision making. This criterion is not met by the physician matrix model, in which the patient care team is hierarchical, so that the physician specifies orders that are followed by nurses and technicians.[14] This centralization of decision making makes this matrix model no more effective than the professional bureaucracy, for decisions are made by only one member of the "team."

Second, nursing administrators must allow the membership of patient care teams to be fluid. Matrix organizations often have predetermined members from each health care specialty. For example, the team on a patient care unit in a rehabilitation hospital might be composed of a physical therapist, dietitian, occupational therapist, and rehabilitation nurse under the direction of a physician. With open-systems thinking, we see the need to open the membership of patient care teams to any specialist in the institution who can meet the special needs of the individual patient. This would preclude the use of professionals such as RNs as interchangeable parts with identical abilities.

Idaho State Hospital South's treatment divisions are now organized as a form of an adhocracy; the matrix model has been adapted for more individualized care of patients and professional decision making. Each treatment division is a matrix organization in that it is comprised of a fixed group of professionals and paraprofessionals from which project teams are formed around individual patients. It differs from the usual matrix organization in that its leadership is not fixed. Any member of the group can be selected as a project leader. The decision as to leadership depends on the patient's area of greatest need. The professionals who make up the project teams are on the treatment unit and are the most knowledgeable about the patient and his or her progress in treatment. The project or treatment team is not hierarchical, with the patient's primary therapist giving the orders and the nurse carrying out those orders. Instead, all team members are equal contributors in patient care decision making.

Each matrix group brings specialists into the project team as needed to meet the needs of the individual patient. For example, a regressed and withdrawn psychotic 43-year-old man was admitted to the general adult psychiatric unit. After his psychosis cleared, the treatment team recognized that the patient had deficits for which team members were unable to provide services. Therefore, a specialist within the institution was brought into the project team. The specialist, an occupational therapist, provided the sensory integration therapies that this patient needed. In yet another example, a 73-year-old man was admitted to the medium security unit (a treatment unit for the criminally insane). After evaluation by the treatment team, the man was deemed not dangerous and was transferred to the geriatric unit, as appropriate to his age and mental status at that time. As his sensorium cleared, it became apparent that placement on the geriatric unit was inappropriate. The patient's intellectual functioning was higher than that of the other patients. He was then transferred to a general adult psychiatric unit where his specific needs could be met. As a function of the operating adhocracy, he was placed with the treatment team deemed appropriate by professionals and not placed according to his age, as would have been the case in a bureaucratic structure.

Use of Experts

In transferring patients from one treatment unit to another or by bringing in other resources within the hospital structure when needed, experts with particular skills are used to treat patients. Power to make these decisions lies with the professionals, the experts. Experts from different parts of the organization are able to share ideas, problem solve, and implement their ideas. When the task is completed, the temporary group of specialists dissolves. Patients are treated as individuals with unique needs. The structure never allows patients to be treated on an "assembly line."

The experts also work together to create and execute new treatment programs and treatment designs. They are no longer limited to working apart to perfect their individual skills. In the closed-systems thinking of a traditional bureaucracy, the administrator or the physician makes such decisions. The group decision-making process inherent in an adhocracy allows all professionals the opportunity to make and implement their decisions and to evaluate the results.

One expert on the collegial decision-making team is the nurse. For nurses to function collegially with the other members of the interdisciplinary team, they must be educationally equal to other members of the team. This means that RNs must give patient care, and the model requires an all-RN nursing staff.

An all-RN staff is not a new concept in nursing literature. Alfano[15] documents numerous cases of hospitals that function with all-RN nursing staffs and offer high-quality care at a cost less than or equal to traditionally staffed hospitals. Where an all-RN staff is not possible, health care institutions can meet the need for specialists in nursing in another way, through the use of clinical specialists. Nurses with expertise and education at the graduate level are already available to many health care institutions and are prepared to assume collegial relationships with the well-prepared specialists in other disciplines. To function in an adhocracy, they need to be free to use their expertise in collegial decision making at the patient level. Clinical specialists freed from administrative responsibilities can increase the numbers of RNs at the bedside. Further, they can assist staff nurses to grow and to learn the responsibility for collegial decision making.

Communication and Coordination

A third characteristic of adhocracy is an extensive system for communication and coordination. In an adhocracy, every member shares responsibility for communication and coordination. This is a clear departure from Likert's "linking pin" concept of overlapping responsibilities and roles and the managerial hierarchy, which are the formal tools presently used in health care institutions.[16]

Rather than a large number of formal committees, the adhocracy has ad hoc committees with membership, goals, and functions to meet each committee's single, emergent need. When its work is done, the ad hoc committee disappears, just like the project teams formed around patient needs. Because of the constantly changing membership of committees and project teams, each member becomes aware of the functioning of the entire institution. In this way, each can become a linking pin of communication and coordination for the organization.

Idaho State Hospital South has several liaison devices, including a multidisciplinary hospital evaluation team composed of professionals from each of the three treatment divisions. The team meets weekly to review patients who are nearing discharge or who need special services. Decisions regarding discharges and transfers rest with this group.

Another liaison device is the twice monthly meeting of division managers and department heads with the members of the executive module. The department heads are directors of support services (dietary, pharmacy, maintenance, housekeeping, and so forth). They may become project managers, depending on the task undertaken and their particular areas of expertise. The committee's purpose is communication and coordination of policy development, budget planning, recruitment of professionals, and long-range planning. Participation on this committee allows department heads and division managers to be knowledgeable about the hospital's overall goals and plans and to coordinate their efforts accordingly.

Fluid Organizational Structure

A fourth component for an adhocracy is a fluid organization, one that cannot be represented by a diagram like the organizational charts of the bureaucratic or collegial structures. Rapid, continual change eliminates the predetermined positions common to the typical administrative organizational chart.

Many nursing administrators have adopted both functional and administrative organizational charts to describe their departments. The functional chart, on which the patient is placed at the top or in the center, is intended to show the relationships among the personnel in the nursing department and between the nurses and the patients. It shows interaction and communication more realistically than does an administrative chart. The nursing department's administrative organizational chart, in contrast, shows lines of authority and accountability in the employer-employee hierarchy.

At Idaho State Hospital South, the *administrative* organizational chart demonstrates lines of authority and accountability in relation to the administrator of community rehabilitation, the director of the Department of Health and Welfare, and the governor. It demonstrates fixed positions to which defined responsibilities are attached. Unfortunately, this diagram does not adequately describe hospital functioning. The *functional* organizational chart, on the other hand, shows functional interrelationships, but does not show responsibility or accountability to a hierarchy. The functional chart representing the operating adhocracy demonstrates that each individual is personally accountable and also accountable to the patient or project group, rather than to the administrative hierarchy. This chart is diagrammatically represented in Figure 19–1, which demonstrates line managers, staff, and experts all working together in ever changing relationships. Experts are distributed unevenly throughout the system.

Decentralization

A final component of adhocracy is decentralization of the organization. Many nursing administrators are already functioning within decentralized nursing departments and have found that decentralization requires an increased number of management personnel. An adhocracy is more decentralized than any other decentralized nursing department. Administrative and managerial positions are defined accordingly.

Top administration remains in place in an operating adhocracy. Administrators' overall responsibilities are twofold: to interface with the public to determine new,

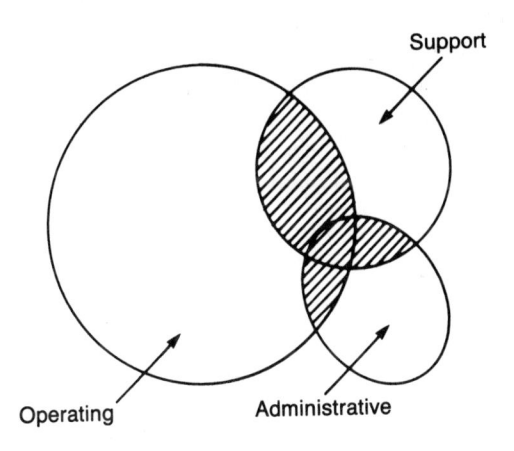

Figure 19–1 Diagrammatic Representation of the Functional Organization

unmet needs and to follow through to ensure that projects are completed in the quality and time predetermined by the joint project and administration groups. Three different types of managers exist in the operating adhocracy; they are functional, integrating, and project managers. The presence of managers does not, however, imply supervision or direction of work. Managers in an adhocracy are liaisons and negotiators coordinating the work laterally among the different project teams and between the project and the concerned functional units. The system needs a large number of managers because of the small size and large number of project teams. Project managers are the most numerous. In fact, a project manager is required for *every project*. In the health care setting, this implies a project manager for *every patient*!

Project managers are the leaders of the project teams, but again, their leadership has nothing to do with control, giving orders, or providing direct supervision. In addition to acting as liaison to coordinate the work of the project team with other teams and with the functional units (nursing, physical therapy, and so forth), the project manager will also be an expert in one of the fields needed on that particular project and will function as an equal team member in the work of that interdisciplinary project as well as others. For example, a project manager for a rehabilitation patient could well be an occupational therapist. This therapist would function as project manager and team member for the patient whose most pressing need is the regaining of skills required for the activities of daily living. At the same time, this occupational therapist would function as a team member for other patients who have some need for occupational therapy, but for whom this is not the primary need. The individual occupational therapist's caseload of patients would be determined by patient need, number of occupational therapists available, and the limitations of time. The same occupational therapist could also be functioning on one or the other of the teams as liaison manager or functional manager, joining the team to other teams or to the administrative hierarchy for coordination and communication.

The designation *manager* is one of immediate function, rather than a permanent designation that limits some professionals to management functions only. The number of personnel needed is only slightly increased, because most management work is completed by health care professionals already in the organization. The health care professional incorporates activities of coordination, communication, and liaison into the professional role, while working with other professionals on the needs of individual patients.

VALUE OF THE ADHOCRACY

The politically astute nursing administrator, especially one who is an active member of the institutional administrative team, has an opportunity to change the

Part IV: Restructuring Work for Job Enrichment 99

nursing department, and perhaps the institution, to an operating adhocracy. Is it worth the work this change entails? The operating adhocracy will meet the needs of individual patients and will also benefit professional employees. The nurse will be accountable to the patient, the project team, and the profession and will see the whole effect of professional accountability in assessment, planning, implementation, and evaluation. Nurses will perform nursing functions, rather than secretarial or supervisory functions. Using their professional expertise in interdisciplinary decision making and practicing as equals with other professionals, theirs will be a true professional role. The nursing administrator is in a unique position to help effect this change for the patients, nurses, and the institution.

NOTES

1. Alvin Toffler, *Future Shock* (New York: Random House, 1970), pp. 112–113.
2. Alvin W. Gouldner, *Patterns of Industrial Bureaucracy* (Glencoe, Illinois: The Free Press, 1954), p. 21.
3. George H. Rice, Jr. and Dean W. Bishoprick, *Conceptual Models of Organization* (New York: Appleton-Century-Crofts, 1971), pp. 91–99.
4. Stephen P. Robbins, *The Administrative Process: Integrating Theory and Practice* (Englewood Cliffs, New Jersey: Prentice-Hall, 1976), p. 271.
5. Kathleen G. Wolff, "Change: Implementation of Primary Nursing through Adhocracy," *The Journal of Nursing Administration* 7(12):24–27, 1977.
6. Alvin Toffler, "Organization: the Coming Ad-hocracy," in *Future Shock* (New York: Random House, 1970), pp. 112–135.
7. Henry Mintzberg, *The Structuring of Organizations* (Englewood Cliffs, New Jersey: Prentice-Hall, 1979), p. 434.
8. Henry Mintzberg, *The Structuring of Organizations*, p. 115.
9. Henry Mintzberg, "Organization Design: Fashion or Fit?" *Harvard Business Review* 59(1):113, 1981.
10. Alvin Toffler, *Future Shock* (New York: Random House, 1970), pp. 112–115.
11. Ibid., pp. 112–135.
12. Stephen P. Rogers, *The Administrative Process: Integrating Theory and Practice* (Englewood Cliffs, New Jersey): Prentice-Hall, 1970), pp. 432–443.
13. Organization Nurses in Action. *Nursing Administration Quarterly*, 3(2):29, 1979.
14. Terence F. Moore and Earl Simendinger, "The Matrix Organization: Its Significance to Nursing," *Nursing Administration Quarterly* 3(2):29, 1979.
15. Genrose Alfano, ed. *All-RN Nursing Staff* (Wakefield, Massachusetts: Nursing Resources, 1980).
16. Rensis Likert, *New Ways of Managing Conflict* (New York: McGraw-Hill, 1976), p. 187.

* * * *

The combined article on adhocracy implies participative decision making. Herzberg speaks strongly against the concept of participative management as a ploy of the human relations movement.

20.
Participative Management

Frederick Herzberg

One outgrowth of the human relations movement, participative management, is a contemporary approach used to improve work. Supporters of participative management assume that the overriding need of the worker is to be involved in decisions affecting his work. This primary need for personal involvement can be attained through worker participation and will provide the commitment necessary to motivate him.

Thus giving the worker more meaningful job content is seen as secondary to his legitimate needs for being consulted and involved in decisions that affect him. Naturally, some decisions in which he participates will concern his job content, and only in these cases can concrete job design changes happen through participation. Most often, however, the manager is in effect saying to the subordinate, "Since you don't have a responsible, meaningful job, I'll let you visit my job, but you will have to return to yours."

Donnelly Mirrors Company declares that its well-publicized change to participative management is so successful that it now markets a workshop on how this was done. The company claims to have raised its profits 20% annually in recent years and lowered prices 25% since 1952 as a result of its change to participative management policies.[1]

Participative policies usually begin with a form of the well-known Scanlon Plan,[2] a perfect example of participation in hygiene matters. The employees establish compensation packages and make commitments to pay for them by reducing waste, eliminating redundant jobs, or improving work methods or equipment.

Employees do, however, also participate in more substantive job decisions. For example, workers are involved in setting their own work standards (note that they

---

Modified with permission from Frederick Herzberg, "The Wise Old Turk," *Harvard Business Review* 52, no. 5 (1974):77.

do not *set* the standards, but are involved in the setting of standards). Also, in some cases machine operators may travel with purchasing agents to inspect new equipment. The purpose of this is to get operator commitment to the proper use of the machinery at a later time. The participation here effectively involves the operator in management decisions, but it does not change his job. When the machine arrives, the job will continue to be that of an operator. His opportunity for future influence and decision making remains at the convenience of management.[3]

So the difference between participation and enrichment is a difference in kind. Consultation does not give a subordinate the chance for personal achievement that he can recognize as his own, and denies him the chance of self-development to the point where he might become an executive himself.

NOTES

1. *Time*, November 9, 1970, p. 74.
2. See Fred G. Lesieur and Elbridge S. Puckett, "The Scanlon Plan Has Proved Itself," HBR September-October 1969, p. 109.
3. William J. Paul, Jr., Keith B. Robertson, and Frederick Herzberg, "Job Enrichment Pays Off," HBR March-April 1969, p. 61.

* * * *

Bragg and Andrews, in their examination of participative decision making in a hospital laundry, take participative management from Herzberg's concept of its use to meet hygiene needs to its use to meet higher level needs.

21.
Participative Decision Making: An Experimental Study in a Hospital

J.E. Bragg and I. Robert Andrews

Since several excellent summaries of previous work on participative decision making (PDM) are already available (see, for example, Bucklow, 1966; Campbell and others, 1970; Lowin, 1968), this report will not include the usual literature survey. In general, the experimental design and analyses in this study were most influenced by Lowin's (1968) theoretical model, which defines PDM as "a mode of organizational operation in which decisions as to activities are arrived at by the very persons who are to execute those decisions," and by his prescriptions for PDM research.

This definition differs considerably from that of Herzberg (see Article 20, "Participative Management"). Stated quite simply, our hypotheses predicted that the introduction of participative decision making into a particular hospital laundry would improve employee attitudes, reduce absenteeism, and increase productivity.

METHOD

In his section on "Experimental Studies in Organizations," Lowin (1968) specified six standards which such an experiment must meet. In addition, his theoretical definition of participative decision making implies a seventh standard. Each of these standards will be considered in turn as they apply to the present study.

Modified with permission from J.E. Bragg and I. Robert Andrews, "Participative Decision Making: An Experimental Study in a Hospital," in D. Katz, R.L. Kahn, and J.S. Adams, Eds., *The Study of Organizations* (San Francisco: Jossey-Bass Publishers, 1982), pp. 531–536.

STANDARDS

1. "A determined effort must be made to unfreeze the system in preparation for the PDM program." In the present study, the attitudes and values of the chief nonmedical administrator were modified by three behavioral science courses in an executive M.B.A. program. According to the administrator, his experiences in the courses sharpened and intensified an already favorable feeling about a participative management style.

Another key figure, the foreman in charge of the laundry, had already established himself as a highly effective supervisor, with a driving, authoritarian style of management. When first approached by the chief administrator about the possibility of trying a participative management style, the foreman was dubious and negative. It was not until six months after the first discussion that the foreman elected to accept the challenge of trying a new management style. A key factor in his acceptance of the challenge was his own very positive response to the high degree of decision-making autonomy which he had been given by the chief administrator. Another important factor was his participation in a weekend sensitivity-training workshop with nonmedical management personnel.

In anticipation of PDM, the foreman prepared a list of eighteen problems that might be encountered during the changeover. He also restated the goals of his department to make them consistent with the PDM philosophy.

When PDM was introduced to the thirty-two laundry workers, the foreman was able to state in all honesty that the basic purpose of the program was to make jobs more interesting. The workers were told that PDM sometimes does result in higher productivity but that this was unimportant to top management because their current level of productivity was already excellent. They were also told that they would have the right to discontinue PDM if they found it unsatisfactory.

One other important factor in the total system was the union leadership. Because of previously established trust and respect (without love, it might be added) for top management, it was fairly easy to obtain union approval for the tentative introduction of PDM. Active support for the program, however, was not offered.

Finally, the unfreezing process was greatly expedited by the results of the first two PDM meetings. One of the key employee suggestions in these early meetings was the revision of work hours to begin and end two hours earlier. Because the laundry unit was completely isolated from other subsystems in the hospital, there was no reason for not acting immediately upon that suggestion. In the following week the work hours were changed, and PDM was off to a good start.

2. "Attitudinal data should be collected to document the adaptation to PDM or its rejection." At the end of every two-month period in our study, a seven-item questionnaire was completed by all thirty-two laundry workers.

Included were such questions as "Should we continue with PDM?" and "Do suggestions get a fair trial?" The data from these questionnaire responses are reported in the Results section.
3. "Similar changes in organization behavior should be recorded." Most closely related to the attitudinal data would be the data on absenteeism, which are reported in the Results section. Less closely related to the attitudinal data are changes in rate of productivity, also reported in the Results section.
4. "Appropriate control groups must be utilized." Two other hospital laundries in the same city were used as comparison groups for evaluating changes in productivity. Strictly speaking, these were not "control groups," since the workers in the comparison laundries were not aware that their performance data were of interest to persons outside their own organization. It is also true, however, that postexperimental interviews with PDM employees showed that they were not aware that they were subjects in an experiment. They knew only that, for the first three months of PDM, the chief administrator seemed to be interested in what they were doing.

During the period studied, there was only one technical innovation to confound the productivity data. Fortunately, it was possible to correct the data for this one factor (the introduction of some polyester fabrics into the linen supply).

Since the comparison hospitals were not able to provide suitable data on absenteeism, results for the PDM group were compared with absence data for other nonmedical staff in the PDM hospital. Neither the PDM nor the comparison groups were aware that their absence records were being monitored in other than routine ways.

In the first three or four months of the study, any differences between the experimental and comparison groups could have been confounded by a strong Hawthorne effect (in the usual sense of "increased attention, novelty"). However, it is highly unlikely that such an effect could have lasted over the eighteen months of the study. Active interest and participation by the chief nonmedical administrator ceased after the first three months. As stated above, the PDM workers were not aware at any time that they were subjects in an experiment.

5. "Long-term research is essential." The eighteen-month time period of the study provided ample time for worker adjustment to PDM and reduced the likelihood that any observed differences were due either to random fluctuations or to a Hawthorne effect. Moreover, both attitudinal and behavioral data showed gradual improvement throughout the study period. It is unlikely that some extraneous factor stabilized behavior at an improved level and continued to do so throughout the study.

6. "The validity of organization records should be checked." The basic record-keeping procedures for absenteeism and productivity were constant throughout the study period, and throughout the period preceding. The absentee record-keeping procedures were identical for the PDM group and the comparison group (other nonmedical employees who worked in the same hospital). With regard to productivity data, the inclusion of pre- and postmeasures for the PDM group and the comparison hospital laundries reduced the likelihood that any differences would be an artifact of record-keeping procedures.
7. In defining PDM (as quoted above), Lowin continues: "The PDM process shifts the locus of some decisions downward—from superior to subordinate." In the present study, decision-making power was transferred from the laundry foreman to a committee composed of all the laundry employees. Any and all aspects of managing the laundry could be considered by the committee. It was agreed, however, that union matters and personal gripes would not be discussed in the meetings.

Herzberg saw participative management only as input to decisions. In this study, personnel had the decision-making power. Few decisions required final approval by top administration.

ROLE OF THE FOREMAN

In the initial PDM meeting, the laundry foreman was elected to serve as a discussion moderator. By the fifth meeting, the role of discussion moderator was taken over by several of the laundry employees, with the foreman's main tasks reduced to agenda setting and the scheduling of meetings. During the meetings, the foreman refused to be active as a task expert, even in cases where the group's decision was, in his opinion, incorrect. Once the group reached a decision, the foreman did what he could to assist the particular employees charged with the responsibility of implementing the changes agreed upon. Because the foreman himself was operating with a very high degree of autonomy, there was seldom need to obtain approval from higher management before taking action. This made it possible to implement most of the proposed changes within one or two weeks of the date of the committee's decision.

It was agreed that meetings should be restricted in length to thirty or forty minutes, and that they should be called only when there were specific proposals to discuss. From this it is clear that most of the PDM work was accomplished outside of the formal meetings. Throughout each working day, the foreman tried to make himself easily available to individual employees (or groups of employees) who wanted to discuss new ideas or problems (*an excellent way to tap into the informal organization*). In these informal meetings, the foreman concentrated on being a good listener—on acting as a sounding board so employees could develop their own ideas with a minimal amount of help from him. Also, whenever it seemed appropriate, the foreman attempted to transfer his task expertise to the employees, thereby reducing their dependence on him. Lastly, because the overall climate in the laundry became supportive and cooperative, even shy employees were able to develop, present, and gain acceptance for their ideas.

RESULTS

PDM Group Meetings. The laundry foreman kept a record of the twenty-eight meetings which occurred during the first fifteen months of PDM. An analysis of his minutes revealed that 147 employee suggestions were discussed. Of these, eleven involved hours of work and working conditions, ninety had to do with the work flow (process and methods), forty-four involved minor equipment modifications, and two were concerned with safety. No record was kept of the innumerable additional ideas discussed on the shop floor between meetings. *Only thirteen of the fifty-seven topics were related to working conditions or safety—the others were motivators*.

Attitudes toward PDM. It was anticipated that some of the older workers would react negatively to PDM, while younger workers would be more receptive. As it turned out, however, the only strong negative reactions came from three younger workers, who objected to the transfer of decision-making power from the foreman to the laundry committee. Fortunately, their attempts to sabotage participative decision making were overcome by the enthusiastic supporters of it; eventually their resistance changed to active support.

For each of the seven items on the employee attitude questionnaire, an employee could write in "yes," "no," or "?" For scoring purposes, the "?" responses were added to the "no" responses, and this total was compared with the number of "yes" responses. The following percentages of "yes" responses are reported by two-month intervals for the first fourteen months of the study: 62, 64, 75, 71, 79, 84, 90. As is apparent from these data, the employees' initial uncertainty about PDM gave way to a positive attitude by the end of the first two months. From that point, there was almost a steady climb to a highly favorable attitude toward PDM.

Absenteeism. In the thirty-eight reporting periods which immediately *preceded* the introduction of PDM, the absence rate for the laundry group was less than the overall hospital absence rate twenty-three out of thirty-eight times. In the thirty-eight reporting periods *after* the introduction of PDM, the absence rate for the laundry group was less than the overall hospital absence rate thirty-two out of thirty-eight times. This shift in proportions, from .61 to .80, was highly significant

Part IV: Restructuring Work for Job Enrichment   107

($Z = 1.9, p < .03$). Thus, an already superior absence record became substantially better after the introduction of PDM. It is of possible interest that, immediately after PDM began, the absence rate for the laundry group was worse than the overall hospital rate in five out of eight reporting periods. After that unimpressive beginning, the absence rate for the laundry group was lower than the overall hospital rate in twenty-nine out of thirty reporting periods. Expressing that remarkable record in different terms, the absence rate for the laundry group averaged 2.95 percent before PDM versus 1.77 percent with PDM. For other nonmedical staff, the rates were 2.80 percent before the study began versus 3.07 percent during the study. Expressed in yet another way, the 1,791 hours of sick time in the laundry group in the year before PDM fell to 1,194 hours in the first year of PDM. There were no long- or short-term trends in the hospital at large to account for this drop in absenteeism.

Productivity. In the year prior to the introduction of PDM, productivity in the experimental group averaged approximately 50 pounds of laundry processed per paid employee hour. In the first six months of PDM, production rose gradually to an average of approximately 61 pounds. In the second six-month period, production surged to 78 pounds, but this was followed by a slight drop in the third six-month period to 73 pounds per paid employee hour. As shown in Table 21-1, the productivity rate in the two comparison hospitals remained constant or perhaps even declined slightly during the year-and-a-half study period.

Since the rate of productivity in the experimental group was already higher than the rates for the two comparison hospitals, these initial differences in favor of the experimental group had to be discounted before testing for the significance of mean differences during the study period. After this adjustment, the mean difference between the experimental group and each of the comparison groups was 23 pounds per paid employee hour. For each of the two comparisons, this difference in mean productivity was significant ($t = 8.43$ for comparisons A and B respectively, $df = 34, p < .01$, two-tailed).

Table 21-1 Productivity Rates[a] for the PDM Laundry and for Two Comparison Laundries

	PDM Laundry[b]	Comparison A	Comparison B
12 months before study	50	47	39
18 months during study	71	45	37

[a]Pounds of laundry processed per paid employee hour, rounded to the nearest whole number.
[b]Figures corrected to allow for the introduction of some polyester fabrics into the linen supply.

Though cost savings through increased productivity was not an important objective of the PDM program, significant economic benefits to the hospital were realized, equal to approximately $1,000 per employee per year.

DISCUSSION

In this study, which attempted to adhere closely to Lowin's (1968) recommendations for PDM experiments in ongoing organizations, it was found that attitudes improved, absence declined, and productivity increased. No such changes were observed in the comparison groups. The differences between the experimental and comparison groups were statistically significant and in the direction hypothesized. Because of the long duration of the study and because the more substantial performance improvements were not realized in the early months of the PDM program, it seems highly improbable that the reported results can be explained in terms of a Hawthorne effect.

There were several factors in the subsystem studied which favored a successful PDM effort: the program was initiated and actively encouraged for three months by the hospital's chief nonmedical administrator; an already successful laundry foreman existed who felt secure enough in his position to experiment with a radical change in his management style and was able to effect PDM; the foreman had been given a high degree of decision-making autonomy well in advance of the PDM program; previously established trust and an already high level of productivity made it easier for the union leaders to believe management when they said that the primary objective of the PDM program was job improvement for the workers; the isolation of the laundry subsystem made it easier for management to comply with some of the initial employee suggestions about such things as hours of work, choice of holidays, and self-control over work breaks; and, lastly, the middle-class work values of several foreign-born immigrants in the work group might have facilitated the establishment of a group norm in favor of PDM.

PDM has been in effect in the hospital laundry for over three years. Neither the foreman nor the workers have expressed any desire to return to the old style of management. The foreman has said that it would be easy for him to revert to his old style of autocratic management, but he would "miss the satisfactions he derives from PDM." He has also mentioned that he has not had to reprimand a worker since PDM began. *It can be concluded that job enrichment, its institutional structural supports, and leadership behaviors, are not only compatible but symbiotic.*

The success of PDM in the laundry has encouraged other subsystems in the hospital to follow suit. In a medical records section where there was an adequate unfreezing of the system and strong support (but no involvement) by the chief nonmedical administrator, a serious turnover problem has been eliminated through PDM, and a high level of union grievances has been reduced to zero. With the nursing staff, on the other hand, a deficiency of unfreezing activities and substantial resistance by the head nurse caused PDM to flounder badly for the first six months. In fact, PDM was a dismal failure until the introduction of a new head nurse with a favorable attitude toward PDM, and until the chief nonmedical administrator found time for some involvement in the program. With these changes, the tide was turned, and after a year and a half the PDM program for nurses is still alive. However, continued resistance by some of the administrative medical personnel has kept PDM from flourishing in the nursing group. *Clearly, nursing administrators have power to change the negative conditions that prevent PDM—and the responsibility to make these changes.*

In closing, it might be of value to ask why production increased when top management's main concern was job improvement for the laundry workers. Looking back at the foreman's record of PDM meetings, it can be seen that 90 percent of all employee suggestions involved technological modifications in the laundry subsystem. This suggests quite convincingly that the creation of a genuine PDM atmosphere led employees to adopt organizational goals as their own. *The Getzels-Guba model helps clarify this phenomenon. Before PDM, the institutional (nomothetic) role expectations for employees differed from their individual (idiographic) need-dispositions. Through PDM, institutional and individual goals became the same, and barriers to full accomplishment of these mutual goals disappeared. PDM was effective in this instance, even though administration and employee continued to relate through union intermediaries.*

Since there was no economic gain for employees' contribution of ideas for technological improvements, it is safe to assume that the underlying motivational force was higher-order need fulfillment. We thus believe that releasing this rich vein of heretofore untapped energy led to technological and attitudinal changes which substantially increased productivity. The relative impact of these two sources of productivity improvement should be tested in future research. For example, one group might experience PDM, and the technological changes they develop might be introduced into other groups by conventional managerial methods. This would enable distinguishing the productivity-raising effects of methods improvement as such from the attitudinal changes occurring in PDM.

NOTES

Bucklow, M. "A New Role for the Work Group." *Administrative Science Quarterly*, 1966, *11*, 59–78.

Campbell, J.P., and others. *Managerial Behavior, Performance, and Effectiveness.* New York: McGraw-Hill, 1970.

Lowin, A. "Participative Decision Making: A Model, Literature Critique, and Prescriptions for Research." *Organizational Behavior and Human Performance*, 1968, *3*, 68–106.

* * * *

An adhocracy calls for experts, i.e., professional nurses, at the bedside. An ideal organizational structure for this approach is the primary nursing system. The term primary nursing *is used in various ways. Here, the definition of primary nursing is that of Holy Cross Hospital, Salt Lake City, Utah:*

> Primary nursing is a system of providing nursing care. Under primary nursing the nursing care of each patient is under the continuous guidance of one RN from admission to discharge, and considers the 24-hour needs of the patient. The primary nurse is responsible for planning, implementing, changing and communicating the patient's plan of care and will be held accountable for the outcome of that care. Planning the care entails collaborating and coordinating with the physician, other hospital departments, other staff members, patients and their families. The plan must include patient care needs, a teaching plan and discharge planning. When on duty the primary nurse should personally give patients total care according to his or her abilities and refer needs beyond or out of the scope of that ability to other staff members or departments.[1]

Primary nursing places a highly skilled nurse on the patient project team, but what does it do for the nurse? Tobin believes that primary nursing meets Herzberg's requirement of worthwhile work. It enhances self-esteem, as well as the esteem of others. Primary nursing offers the nurse a complete function, the satisfaction of seeing the results of personal endeavors, and the collegial and collaborative relationships that are the essence of an adhocracy.

NOTE

1. Tanna Ferrin, "One Hospital's Successful Implementation of Primary Nursing," *Nursing Administration Quarterly* 5, no. 4 (1981): 2.

22.
Primary Nursing's Effect on Professional Development

Marie Tobin

Nursing has long been involved in a struggle to define itself and to clearly delineate its function from that of other health professionals. In recent years there appear to have been great strides made in the establishment of nursing as a profession. Primary nursing creates an environment within which nursing can effectively establish and develop its unique contribution to health care and thus has helped others to understand and acknowledge the professional role of nursing.

The process through which nursing care is delivered to patients separates primary nursing from other nursing care delivery systems. Essential to the optimal functioning of a primary nursing system is the commitment of primary nurses to provide patients with comprehensive care. Using the nursing process, primary nurses design care plans that reflect the needs and individuality of each patient. The problem list, goals and approaches are derived from a nursing assessment rather than a medical history and physical.

When nurses assume the role of care planner as well as care provider, a greater level of accountability appears to occur. The care plan provides a written record of goals to be achieved; goals the primary nurse has made a commitment to facilitate on behalf of the patient and family. As a consequence the public's image of nursing is changed. The continuity of a primary nurse provider enhances the individualized comprehensive approach to care and the nurse is seen as offering a service that is distinct from that offered by other health professionals. Primary nurses are viewed as health professionals who assume their own initiative to plan and provide consistent and personalized nursing care.

Since primary nursing is patient centered rather than task oriented, there is a direct change in the focus of the nursing care delivered. The attention of the primary nurse is focused on the patient and the care received. In my past

---

Reprinted with permission from Marie Tobin, "Primary Nursing's Effect on Professional Development," *Nursing Administration Quarterly* 5, no. 4 (1981): 68–69.

experience as a team leader, a great deal of my time was spent organizing the members of my team and offering bits and pieces of nursing care to a large group of patients as time would allow. Nursing care in such a system is at best fragmented. The focus of care planning changed with each new team leader. In contrast, primary nursing allows continuity of care planning and provides, therefore, comprehensive approaches to care delivery.

Another facet of primary nursing that promotes professional development is the integral role primary nurses play in decisions made about their primary patients. Increased knowledge of the patient provides the primary nurse with the data needed to make nursing care decisions and to enter into collegial and collaborative relationships with other professionals who also provide care or services to patients. Primary nursing also promotes the development of colleagueship among staff nurses. A philosophy is shared and mutual commitments are made. Nurses work collaboratively with each other strengthening their intraprofessional communication and identity.

In summary, primary nursing has become a vehicle through which nursing is provided the opportunity to broaden its scope of practice and fulfill its commitments as a profession.

* * *

One criticism of primary nursing is that not all nurses are sufficiently knowledgeable and skilled to handle the independence of the primary nurse role. For example, the new graduate needs assistance to grow into this responsibility. Therefore, the clinical nurse specialist has a unique role in an adhocracy. As teacher, role model, and professional developer, this nurse ensures the success of the primary nurse as a full team member of the project team. The formal teaching role of the clinical nurse specialist includes orientation and in-service work with groups of nurses. The following section contains additional suggestions for primary nurse development on a more individual basis.

23.
Extending the Influence of the Clinical Nurse Specialist

Mary Blount, Suzanne Burge, Lee Crigler, Betty A. Finkelmeier, and Cindi Sanborn

The clinical expertise of the clinical nurse specialist (CNS) enables him or her to help nurses apply their knowledge and skills as they give patient care. Clinical nurse specialists work with individual nurses to provide guidance in applying the nursing process: enhancing patient assessment, refining problem definition, selecting from among various nursing interventions and evaluating the effectiveness of the care provided. It is equally important for nurses to know when to seek help from other members of the health care team. The CNS can often provide advice on the utilization of the interdisciplinary resources and services available.

INTERACTION WITH THE HEALTH CARE TEAM

There are many ways for the CNS to support staff nurses in learning how to communicate effectively with other professionals. Although CNSs work closely with other professionals, particularly physicians, they establish that their professional identification and alignment are with nursing.

Frequently, staff nurses use the CNS as a sounding board to verify clinical assessments and management suggestions before communicating them to nonnurses. The CNS can endorse the nurse's clinical opinion or provide guidance in considering other relevant options or in gathering additional information. Confirmation from the CNS increases the staff nurse's confidence in communicating these opinions to others.

The physician is the health care team member in closest contact with the unit nursing staff. Both nursing staff and house staff work under a great deal of stress

---

Modified with permission from Mary Blount, Suzanne Burge, Lee Crigler, Betty A. Finkelmeier, and Cindi Sanborn, "Extending the Influence of the Clinical Nurse Specialist," *Nursing Administration Quarterly* 6, no. 1 (1981): 53–63.

because so much is expected of them in providing high-quality care to patients with complex and often catastrophic problems. Frustration tolerances can be reached very quickly when there are divergent views on a patient care situation or when there is disagreement on what each can or should expect of the other. By their own example, CNSs can demonstrate productive methods of discussing areas of disagreement in a professional manner. Because of the liaison nature of the position, the CNS can help keep lines of communication open by interpreting the concerns of each group to the other.

INTERACTION WITH NURSING ADMINISTRATION

Because of their staff position and noninvolvement in the performance evaluation process, CNSs are often approached as a "safe" resource for assistance in problem resolution.

The CNS can be very effective in helping the nurse clarify the situation, identify available options and plan and implement a course of action. When work-related problems are involved, the CNS can provide information about where to get help within the department and reassurance that support will be given. With interpersonal problems, referrals can be made to a variety of departmental resources. *Using their staff position status, the CNSs can take greater problems facing primary nurses directly to the nursing administrator for resolution.*

FACILITATING PROFESSIONAL DEVELOPMENT

Another important component of an environment that fosters clinical excellence is the promotion of professional development in the nursing staff. Many staff nurses are relatively inexperienced and only recently removed from the structured learning environment of their basic educational programs. In addition, they are in a work situation that is physically and emotionally demanding and where job responsibilities must be met in eight-hour blocks. There is a tendency, because of these factors, for nurses to limit their professional activities to what occurs on their unit during working hours. The CNS strives to motivate nurses to assume responsibility for their own professional growth.

Many nurses do not keep abreast of the professional literature. This may be the result of failure to appreciate the importance of supplementing first-hand experience with knowledge available from others, lack of information about how to obtain relevant information or a sense of being overwhelmed by job responsibilities. The CNSs are in a good position to assist staff in this area of development by demonstrating ways in which information from the literature can be relevant to their scope of practice. They do more than provide ready answers;

Part IV: Restructuring Work for Job Enrichment 115

when situations occur where more information is needed for resolution of a clinical problem, they use the opportunity to help nurses explore available resources.

A closely related area in which nursing staff members need assistance with professional development is in the acquisition of the skills and motivation required to contribute to the professional literature and knowledge base. Each CNS devotes a portion of time to research and publication efforts. The nursing administration supports these efforts and encourages other nurses to engage in similar endeavors. The CNSs frequently invite individual nurses to collaborate with them in publication and research efforts. *This provides primary nurses with the opportunity for growth and learning through the vertical loading of new and more difficult tasks.*

The CNSs also encourage nursing staff members to become involved in professional issues, through membership on departmental committees or in nursing organizations. Nursing administrators are flexible in providing staff members with time away from their regular duties to participate in these activities.

Nurses are often asked to participate in the planning and presentation of educational programs for other nurses, *another example of vertical job loading*. The CNSs play an active role in working with staff members to share principles of adult education, foster good teaching techniques, assist with the development of program content and help with the preparation of audiovisual and written resource material.

Individual CNSs work closely with the clinical head nurses on units in their specialty area. The CNSs are committed to provide guidance, role clarification and other support for these nurses, who are at the first level of the clinical career ladder. To date, this type of interaction has been done by the CNSs on an individual basis. The CNS group is now investigating ways that it can work more formally with the clinical head nurse group to foster CNS role development.

RESULTS

The CNS interaction with staff that has been described has a significant positive influence on the nursing staff. It improves the quality of nursing care and limits staff frustration and stress. These extremely important outcomes are certainly not solely the result of the activities of the CNSs; they are the product of the combined efforts of nurses in all of the administrative and clinical career ladder positions.

* * * *

A final aspect of vertical job loading is specialization, i.e., the development of expertise. Nurses are rewarded for expertise not only by increased self-esteem as a result of their increased competence, but also by advancement through the career ladder, as discussed by Faulconer and Reeves.

24.
Clinical Ladders and Specialty Teams

Diane Ramy Faulconer and Diane M. Reeves

Seeking an objective means for evaluating nurses' expertise, Mount Sinai Medical Center of Greater Miami, Miami Beach, Fla., decided to develop career ladders for all professional members of the nursing department regardless of the type of position—clinical, administrative, education, or specialist. This ladder system was adapted to meet the needs of nurses working in the operating room (OR). At the same time, the assistant director of nursing for the operating room and postanesthesia recovery room developed a team approach to intraoperative practice. A team is a group of RNs and OR technicians assigned to a surgical specialty. Both of these changes were seen as ways to improve morale and job satisfaction.

The OR Department had a number of vacancies, compounded by high absenteeism, which added to the frustration of the entire staff. Before the team concept was introduced, nurses did not consistently work in any one specialty area. A nurse was expected to perform with an orthopedic surgeon on one case, a neurosurgeon on another case, and perhaps with an ophthalmologist on a third case, all in one day. Case turnover time was long, and instrument repair was frequent, causing inefficiency.

This staffing pattern did not promote interprofessional recognition. Surgeons did not develop professional rapport with nurses because they did not work with any one nurse or group of nurses consistently. Residents were unable to identify key nurses in their services. This created confusion and frustration among the residents, attending surgeons, and nurses.

Nurses had little staffing flexibility. In June 1980, before the new system was introduced, only 48% of the RNs scrubbed on operative procedures. As of June

---

Modified with permission from Diane Ramy Faulconer and Diane M. Reeves, "Clinical Ladders and Specialty Teams," *AORN Journal* 35, no. 4 (1982): 669–678. Copyright ©, all rights reserved by the Association of Operating Room Nurses, Inc.

1981, under the new system, 97% of all professional OR staff were proficient in scrub procedures for their specialty area.

The system did not encourage development of clinical or managerial expertise. Before the career ladder and team approach were implemented, only one charge nurse had taken a leadership development course offered by the nursing education department. The need for managerial and leadership development was apparent.

After administrative approval was secured, position descriptions for the levels of professional practice were developed, consistent with the guidelines set for all professional nursing staff. Clinical ladders were developed for four levels of professional nurses, licensed practical nurses, and certified and noncertified operating room technicians. All job descriptions have a defined scope of practice and specific qualifications and requirements based on educational and clinical expertise. As the nurses achieve greater expertise through education and/or experience, they assume greater responsibilities. The responsibilities are divided into five areas: clinical, managerial, educational, research, and specific.

Simultaneously with the development of the new position descriptions, several other organizational changes took place. The qualified charge nurses were reclassified as operating room clinicians I, the highest clinical level. To ensure a standard of management, the charge nurses attended appropriate management courses. All successfully completed the leadership development program within one year. The OR clinicians II have completed their basic leadership training to prepare them for charge responsibilities.

Concurrently, the team concept was discussed with the staff. Formal meetings were held with discussions regarding its pros and cons. Generally, the reaction was positive, and the staff agreed to try the team approach. Staff members requested the team they wanted to be a member of:

1. eye, ear, nose, throat, oral, and plastic surgery
2. general surgery
3. genitourinary and gynecologic surgery
4. thoracocardiovascular and open heart surgery
5. orthopedics
6. neurosurgery

There was constant communication among the OR leadership group to develop and approve the job descriptions. The leadership group comprised the assistant director of nursing, OR/PAR coordinators, and OR clinicians I. Each of the six teams were assigned an OR clinician II, an OR clinician III, a licensed practical nurse or certified OR technician, and an OR technician. Six professional associate nurse positions were reserved for entry level nurses. They rotate through all the specialties until they qualify for and receive a promotion.

OR clinicians I are scheduled to work days Monday through Friday. This allows them to be the resource person for their service. They meet with their department chairman and attend conferences that enable them to develop professional rapport with the surgical members of the department. In this way, they become more visible and are seen as integral members of the surgical team. Careful scheduling ensures full coverage, including weekends, of all specialty areas. Two teams assigned to the 3 to 11:30 pm shift are experienced in all specialty emergency procedures. *(On the 3 to 11 pm shift, nurses become experts in emergency procedures.)*

As outlined in the position descriptions, any nurse who begins employment can apply for promotion to OR clinician III in a specialty after six months, assuming he or she has all the qualifications. If a requested position is not available, the nurse is placed on a waiting list. This assures that nursing management positions are not top-heavy.

Nurses are more likely to strive for promotions because they know evaluations will be based on their practice and a documented level of expertise. This stimulates them to increase their productivity and improve the quality of their work.

Each of the specialty teams is responsible for its own inventory, ordering equipment and supplies, recognizing and documenting the needs of its service, submitting proposals for purchasing capital equipment, formulating its own annual budget, and determining goals and objectives. *This provides new tasks, as well as a total piece of work.*

Requests for a transfer to a different service within the OR Department require a letter of recommendation from the clinician I for that team. This accompanies a letter of intent from the person requesting the transfer. Promotions are submitted to the nursing promotion subcommittee, which provides peer review. This is a process all clinical nurses must go through prior to being promoted.

The OR clinicians I are also responsible for completing the yearly performance appraisals for their team members. This is performed in conjunction with the OR coordinator and the assistant director of nursing for the OR/PAR. Thus, evaluation of the OR staff is completed by persons who work consistently and closely with that member. The performance appraisals include a list of objective goals *(an example of management by objectives)*, which are determined and measured by the clinician I and the team member.

A great many benefits have been noted since the clinical ladder and team approach were instituted. The major success is the improved morale of the OR staff. Another is interprofessional recognition. Identifying with a surgical specialty seems to have increased the self-esteem of the team members. This has only been measured indirectly, but we feel morale has improved.

One objective measure of improved relations is better nurse retention. In the year before the new system was implemented, 19 staff members resigned. In the following year, only 5 persons resigned, a reduction of almost 75%.

Professional relationships are better among the nurses as well as between the surgeons and nurses. The OR clinicians II and III are more responsible for their clinical and managerial roles, increasing the effectiveness and efficiency of their service.

An important advantage of the new program was that it did not increase payroll costs, because only a specified number of positions were allocated for each team. With the team structure, care of specialty instruments improved, and time for setting up rooms decreased. The better utilization of personnel and equipment has helped to contain costs.

A quality circle was recently initiated in the operating room, comprising all levels of professional staff from all teams. This is a group of seven or eight members that meets voluntarily on a regular basis and uses problem-solving techniques to identify, analyze, and resolve problems. The quality circle focuses on ways to contain costs and resolve any concerns within the department.

We strongly believe that the team approach and the clinical ladders promote professional growth and recognition. The team approach has enabled members of the nursing staff to develop expertise and receive recognition for their levels of practice. With the improvements resulting from these new programs, the nursing staff is more amenable to implementing new concepts and continually improving intraoperative nursing.

* * * *

Faulconer and Reeves introduce the idea of team functioning that York advocated earlier (see Article 17, "Team Production [Semi-autonomous Work Groups]"). Harris speaks of team functioning not just for job enrichment, but for the very survival of the professions.

25.
Professional Synergy

P.R. Harris

The decades ahead will be years of transition. More and more of humankind will be involved in the process of transforming an industrialized society to a superindustrial system. The emerging "cyberculture" or age of automation and computers will be dominated by a marked increase in knowledge and information processing. Earth peoples are growing in awareness of their basic, collective, *human right* to information and communication. Vocational activity will shift away from blue or white-collar designations to that of knowledge workers. As a result of the ongoing Computer or Cybercultural Revolution, the new "rich" or power class will be those with knowledge skills and access to relevant information.

The term *professional* is used here in the sense of an expert, one who can be characterized as demonstrating the authority of competence in whatever he or she undertakes. It is an attitude of mind, coupled with ability, to work for one's own self-fulfillment and to bring to a task or occupation, a thoroughness or sense of dedication in its execution. In this context, this type of person professes or affirms the quality of his or her thinking, effort, and spirit. The word is not meant in this analysis as membership in the traditional "learned" professions. As Christopher Evans, the late innovator in microprocessors, observed:

> The erosion of the power of the established professions will be a striking feature of the second phase of the Computer Revolution. It will be marked, and perhaps more so, as the intrusion into the work of the skilled and semi-skilled. . . . The vulnerability of the professions is tied up with their special strength—the fact that they have acted as exclusive repositories and disseminators of specialist knowledge. . . . But this

---

Modified with permission from P.R. Harris, "Professional Synergy," *Training and Development Journal* 35, no. 1 (1981): 18–32. Copyright ©, all rights reserved, by the American Society for Training and Development.

state of privilege can only persist as long as the special data and rules for administration remain inaccessible to the general public. Once the barriers which stand between the average person and this knowledge dissolve, the significance of the profession dwindles, the power and the status of its members shrink. Characteristically, the services which the profession originally offered become available at a very low cost.

Thus, to be professional in our discussion, one can be an athlete, technician, or programmer, as well as an attorney, physician, or social scientist. It depends on how one avows self in the development and use of knowledge. It requires expertise in abstract thinking without denying intuition. The new knowledge professionals will be linked together around the planet and beyond by satellites, computers, and videophones.

The issue then arises as to whether this more rapid, enriched knowledge exchange will be used for human and not just technological development. The challenge is to utilize our immense patrimony of scientific, historical, and cultural heritage, as well as our human and natural resources, to improve the human condition. *John Naisbitt, in* Megatrends, *deals with this very issue in his chapter on high tech/high touch.*

Synergy has been described by *The Harper Dictionary of Modern Thought* in this interesting manner:

> The additional benefit accruing to a number of systems should they coalesce to form a larger system. This concept reflects the classical opinion that the "whole is greater than the sum of the part." . . . The word is also frequently used in a much looser way in discussions of corporate strategy to indicate general expectations of collaborative benefit. More generally still, the term is applied to the generation of unplanned social benefits among people who unconsciously cooperate in pursuit of their own interests and goals.

It is my postulate that all peoples, especially those who might be considered "professionals," should consciously cooperate for the mutual benefit of all. The very complexity of what Alvin Toffler has characterized as "The Third Wave Culture" demands such collaboration. (In terms of human development, Toffler describes the First Wave of Change as the Agricultural Revolution, the Second Wave as the Industrial Revolution, and the current transformation of the Third Wave unleashed by the Cybercultural Revolution.)

A panel of professional futurists sought to explain what work is at The First Global Conference on the Future in 1980 at Toronto, Canada. The panelists noted that "work is a way to define one's place (role) in the world; work is vision, vocation, mission, transformation, energy transfer, substantial effort toward results." Finally, one defined work as synergy—energy that is directed toward tasks or problems in cooperation with others, as in "team work." All of the participants in this forum agreed that there was a need in these turbulent times to create situations for synergistic potential to be realized, that is by bringing the right people or team together. *This may be the major way professionals of the future will experience the motivation of achievement.*

Perhaps Figure 25–1 will best illustrate our thinking and the interrelatedness of current terminology. We urge our readers to consult their own dictionaries and thesaurus for the meaning of these words! The designations on the outside of the globe refer to various descriptions of scholars to contemporary world society or culture. The terms inside are somewhat synonymous to the concept of synergy among professionals, descriptions of what happens when peers work together effectively.

Figure 25–1 Synergy for Human Resource Development in the Earth's Global Village

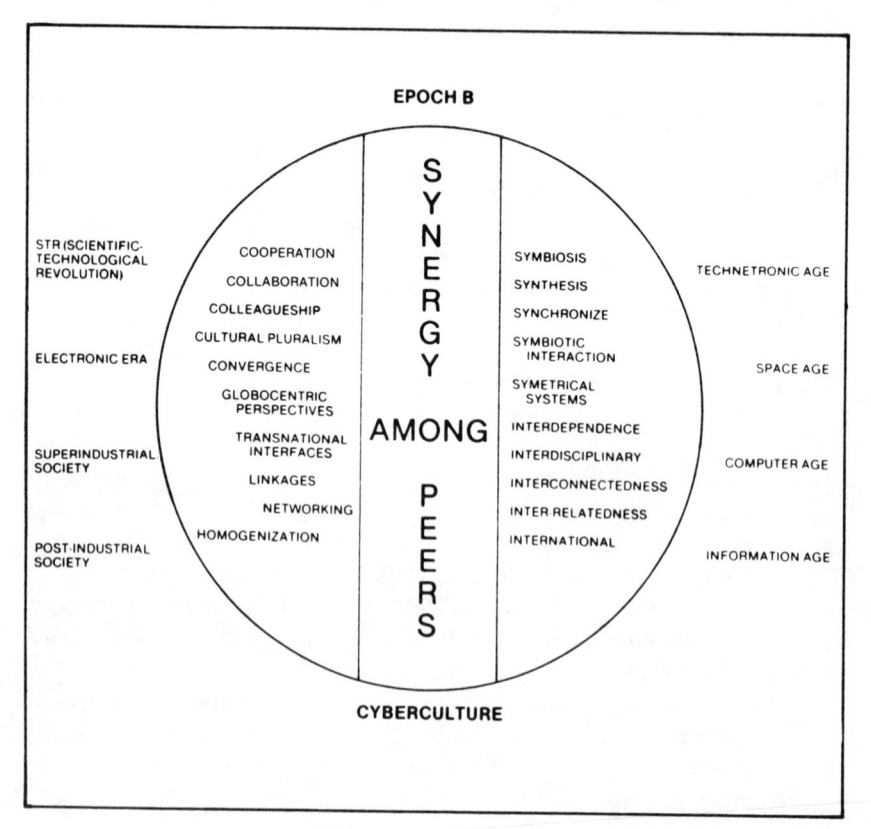

EPOCH B

STR (SCIENTIFIC-TECHNOLOGICAL REVOLUTION)
ELECTRONIC ERA
SUPERINDUSTRIAL SOCIETY
POST-INDUSTRIAL SOCIETY

COOPERATION
COLLABORATION
COLLEAGUESHIP
CULTURAL PLURALISM
CONVERGENCE
GLOBOCENTRIC PERSPECTIVES
TRANSNATIONAL INTERFACES
LINKAGES
NETWORKING
HOMOGENIZATION

SYNERGY AMONG PEERS

SYMBIOSIS
SYNTHESIS
SYNCHRONIZE
SYMBIOTIC INTERACTION
SYMETRICAL SYSTEMS
INTERDEPENDENCE
INTERDISCIPLINARY
INTERCONNECTEDNESS
INTER-RELATEDNESS
INTERNATIONAL

TECHNETRONIC AGE
SPACE AGE
COMPUTER AGE
INFORMATION AGE

CYBERCULTURE

SYNERGISTIC COLLABORATION

For eons of time, humankind has shared information and experience, either formally or informally. Culture itself is an attempt, consciously or unconsciously, by a people to transmit to future generations their acquired wisdom and insight relative to their knowledge, beliefs, customs, traditions, morals, law, art, communication and habits.

Peers in a particular career, trade, or profession have long banded together in pursuit of their common interests. Trade and professional associations, societies and organizations, are formed for this purpose by individuals, institutions, and industries. But many of these social institutions are experiencing "organization shock" in the post-industrial age. They are not perceived as sufficiently relevant and responsive to their constituencies, so they suffer drops in memberships, or attendance at meetings, or support for their various programs. Huge professional associations find that dissidents form splinter groups, and many practitioners do not even bother to join. *Nursing's specialty groups are a good example of this.* Obviously, most labor, trade, and professional associations must go through planned organizational renewal if they are to survive into the 21st century.

Colleagues today are seeking many innovative ways for cooperating. One development for such individuals is to move beyond the narrow confines of one's own discipline or area of activity. Thus, some professionals enter into multi-disciplinary arrangements and new organizational groupings based more on mutual interests, rather than previous education or training. *The Tavistock Institute of Human Relations in London is organized in this way.* Others engage in professional activities that mix public with private sectors, academia with industry. *The increased number of articles in current nursing publications on the integration of nursing education and nursing service indicates that nursing is taking this approach to cope with the rapid changes in society.*

The point is to avoid intellectual or professional ethnocentrism in the sharing of knowledge. This mixing of professional perspectives and skills is so necessary in solving complex contemporary problems. Furthermore, there must be dialogue and a felt need to consult with peers, not just to inform them of one's accomplishment. True professionals confer and seek feedback before making major decisions.

For effective collaboration, certain principles need to be established in the professional relationship. Reciprocity and interdependence are to be encouraged, while imposition and dependency are to be avoided, *advice that is common in current networking articles also.*

There are personality factors involved in maintaining a professional relationship. Furthermore, when the colleague has a different temperament and work style, the interpersonal relations can be a real challenge. But when the collaborator is from a different ethnic, racial, or cultural background, then skills must be practiced for confronting and transcending such differences.

How well does the professional maintain his own and others' self-esteem? Manage anxiety and tension? Maintain meaningful continuity of interpersonal relationships and social supports? Mobilize a sense of autonomy and efficacy in the face of new and complex problematic situations?

Joining others in a new vocational environment requires risk and self-management, as well as human creativity in adaptation. Participants are challenged to create a microculture that accommodates both "doers and thinkers" despite the reality that this mix may produce tension and conflict. As Andre van Dam, director of planning for Corn Products Company-Latin America, asked:

> Can we learn to cooperate in a competitive world? Can cooperation (which thrives on consultation and participation) co-exist with competition (which is deeply engrained in human beings, groups, and nations? . . .
>
> Admittedly, cooperation requires trade-offs between rival ideas or interests—trade-offs imply negotiation. Cooperation hinges upon the recognition of common as well as conflicting interests.

Success in effective teamwork is an added challenge to the professional nurse. This novel experience can offer the vertical loading motivation of growth, which Herzberg identifies as an innate drive.

ENSURING PROFESSIONAL SYNERGY

Social scientists are doing significant research on what people can do in small groups to facilitate a meaningful experience and productive outcome. One exciting example of this is occurring at the East-West Center in Honolulu, Hawaii.

There at the Culture Learning Institute, Dr. Kathleen K. Wilson is spearheading an investigation with 15 other distinguished colleagues on the factors influencing the management of International Cooperative Research and Development Projects (ICRD). Their findings in this five-year project will not be fully available until 1985.

However, their preliminary studies have vital implications now for any professional seeking to improve human performance and collaboration. Although the researchers are examining project team effectiveness, their insights can be extrapolated to other forms of inter- and intra-group behavior, whether it is a matrix organization, a product team, task force, or any work unit. *Their findings would also be applicable to an adhocracy.*

Part IV: Restructuring Work for Job Enrichment   125

Reporting the progress of their research to Australian Commonwealths Scientific and Industrial Research Organizations in June 1980, Dr. Wilson reviewed the varied contexts in which international cooperative groups must operate that affect the environment within the project itself. These include such diverse elements as political, organizational, and cultural factors; the size and scope of the endeavor; the disciplinary background of team members; their individual characteristics; research and development policies; and problems. The East-West Center scholars have identified the following that need to be confronted if synergy on a team is to be ensured:

Situations in which members:

- differed in how they plan project business;
- failed to consider other viewpoints in problem-solving;
- differed on how the work should be organized;
- differed on best individual or team approach to tasks;
- differed because of disciplines on defining problems;
- differed on how to resolve ambiguity in problem formulation;
- differed because of disciplines on methods and procedures;
- differed on decision-making relative to recurring problems;
- differed on the allocation of resources to team members;
- differed on accountability procedures relative to resource use;
- differed on timing and sequencing approaches;
- differed in determining objectives;
- differed on project work organization;
- differed on formal affiliation and liaison with external groups;
- differed on degree of formality in their work relations;
- differed on the quantity and type of project human resources;
- differed on qualifications, recruitment and selection of new members;
- differed on new member orientation and training on the project;
- differed on the management of responsibilities;
- differed on the clarification of roles and relationships;
- felt they were underutilized relative to skill competencies;
- differed in their motivating behavior and reward expectations;
- and soon were concerned over coordination of long/short term members.

(*Vertical job loading principles are clearly identified in this list.*)

Certainly this exhaustive listing points up the need for strategies in managing the many ''cultural'' differences existing between and among professionals attempting to work together effectively. To foster group synergy, these are the suggested team member characteristics to be sought and valued:

The effective team member has the capacity for:

- flexibility and openness to change and other's viewpoints;
- exercising patience, perseverance, and professional security;
- thinking in multidimensional terms and considering different sides of issues;
- dealing with ambiguity, role shifts, and differences in personal and professional styles or social and political systems;
- managing stress and tension well, while scheduling tasks systematically;
- cross-cultural communication, and demonstrates sensitivity for language problems among colleagues;
- anticipating consequences of one's own behavior;
- dealing with unfamiliar situations and lifestyle changes;
- dealing well with different organizational structures and policies;
- gathering useful information related to future projects.

The effective team member described here obviously must be Maslow's self-actualized person, who is able:

- to recognize other member participation in ways they find rewarding;
- to avoid *unnecessary* conflicts among other team members, as well as to resolve unavoidable ones to mutual satisfaction;
- to integrate different team member skills to achieve project goals;
- to negotiate acceptable working arrangements with other team members and their organizations;
- to regard others' feelings and exercise tactfulness;
- to develop equitable benefits for other team members;
- to accept suggestions/feedback to improve his or her participation;
- to provide useful specific suggestions and appropriate feedback;
- to facilitate positive interaction among culturally different members whether in terms of macro differences (nationality/politics), or micro differences (discipline or training); etc.

These insights offer a compendium of the shared leadership skills that professionals should expect to contribute in the course of group collaboration. For those organizations which provide project management training or team building for their members, these are the types of competencies to be sought in the emerging adhocracies. *Clearly, the nursing administrator must consider these factors in selecting and developing professional nurses for this new role.*

* * * *

Harris' concept of the professional of the future differs considerably from Greenwood's concept of the traditional professional (see Article 3, "Attributes of a Profession"). For example, the knowledge base of traditional professionals is identifiable, acquired in a university setting over a long period of time. Harris' professionals include athletes, technicians, and computer programmers, groups whose work is not considered heavily based on theory or research. Harris' criteria, however, exclude traditional professionals only if they insist on monopolies of functioning. The professional for the future demonstrates expertise in the use of theory and utilizes this specialized knowledge not just for technological development, but for human development.

Greenwood's concept of professional authority includes decision making and functional specificity. Harris asks for decision making with professional synergy. Whereas functional specificity changes professionals into laymen outside their specific area of specialty, professional synergy permits the interdisciplinary handling of very complex problems by a group of specialists. In the future, traditional professionals will not have a unique knowledge base, nor will they be capable of handling alone the complex problems that will arise. Harris' definition of professionalism nicely fits nursing's holistic approach, where there can be no simple, one-specialty problems.

Sanction of society for traditional professionals has meant licensure, monopoly, peer-established standards, and confidentiality between professional and client. Harris states that the monopoly of traditional professionals and the licensure that protects the monopoly will disappear and that the standard of excellence required of the future professional will be expertise in abstract thinking and intuition; dedication; and a high quality of thinking, effort, and spirit.

Ethics are closely tied to the protection of society in sanctioning the work of professionals. Greenwood speaks of commitment to the public welfare, universalism, and disinterestedness toward clients. Collegiality with others of the same profession involves cooperation, equality, supportiveness, and sharing of knowledge. Harris' ethical code includes dedication, knowledge used for human development, and self-avowal in work. Harris differs from Greenwood in that future collegiality must be with peers from other professions.

Greenwood states that professional groups form subcultures with their own values, norms, and symbols; that this culture is maintained by existing organizations (e.g., hospitals), fed by the educational institutions that prepare the new members, and bonded by professional associations. Harris lists the differing values, norms, and symbols (e.g., language) as obstacles to multidisciplinary functioning and seeks personal characteristics of the individual professionals to overcome these obstacles. Harris also notes the demise of professional associations that no longer meet the needs of their constituents. Nurses, for example, are reaching out to multidisciplinary associations that include their co-workers, such as the Association of Research Nurses and Dietitians.

To summarize, the traditional professional and the professional of the future will be expected to have the same high ethical standards, and interdisciplinary understanding and functioning will be emphasized. In the health care arena, it can be hoped that, finally, the holistic needs of each patient will be met. Riley and Moses give an example of interdisciplinary functioning under less than ideal conditions.

26.

Coordinated Care: Making It a Reality

Margaret Riley and James A. Moses, Jr.

A Coordinated Care (Co-Care) Program was developed at this hospital in response to the need to improve as well as standardize our medical, nursing, and rehabilitative efforts for patients disabled by stroke or other neurological catastrophes. We found that patients still had fears, anxiety, depression, and gross disability long after acute treatment had been started. Our Co-Care Program was developed from a combination of Regional Medical Programs (RMP) legislation, and national and county guidelines.[1-5]

A survey of health care delivery in our hospital identified four major problems. First, there was significant depersonalization in care delivery. Second, there were gaps in continuity care. Third, there was a serious lack of interdisciplinary communication. The fourth problem, which arose from the others, was a certain amount of provider-user antagonism that lowered quality of care.

On close study we found that these problems were most obvious when patients had catastrophic illnesses, and we therefore elected to start a program for patients with strokes and severely disabling neuromuscular disorders such as amyotrophic lateral sclerosis, multiple sclerosis, and myasthenia gravis. It was recognized that the burden of care might be expected to increase steadily during the hospitalization of some patients. We sought to motivate the hospital staff to accept the concept of long-term, intensive care which might well become increasingly difficult. *The efforts toward staff motivation were in providing structural changes and changes in the work itself, both approaches within Herzberg's concept of vertical job loading.*

Modified with permission from Margaret Riley and James A. Moses, Jr., "Coordinated Care: Making It a Reality," *Journal of Nursing Administration* 7, no. 4 (1977): 21–27.

THE COORDINATED CARE PROGRAM

We sought to create a program that would provide a multidisciplinary approach to the patient with catastrophic disease and would also bridge the treatment gap that so often appeared between inpatient and outpatient care. The name of the Co-Care Program signifies its primary purpose, which is to provide humane, thoughtful, and expert care for the patient as soon as he has been admitted to any primary treatment unit.

The program would be based upon coordinated care provided by the patient's primary physician and nurses in cooperation with a multidisciplinary advisory team. Consultations between the physician and Co-Care team members would occur informally and in formal biweekly conferences. Very early in our planning efforts, it was decided that the team would not superimpose itself on the primary care group as a "visiting advisory panel." The central figures of the Co-Care team for each patient were his primary physician and his nurses. The physician was expected to attend all patient care conferences. Thus, primary medical considerations regulated the management plans, with Co-Care team members contributing their special talents and discussing results with the physician. *This typifies the physician-directed matrix structure, in which the team leader is the patient's physician.*

The Co-Care team consisted of a neurologist (chairman), a physiatrist, a nurse coordinator, a public health nurse, and a social worker. A new staff position had to be created for the nurse coordinator, while other members of the Co-Care team agreed to serve in addition to their regular staff duties.

The Co-Care team developed a protocol specifying basic medical and nursing procedures for all patients in the program. An automatic referral system was included in the protocol to ensure that the patient would be seen by all members of the advisory team. The primary physician was given the responsibility to enroll the patient in the program and to designate the appropriate treatment phase according to the patient's condition. The ward secretary was instructed to send referrals to the various team members, first when the patient was initially enrolled and thereafter whenever his physician requested advancement to the next treatment phase. Team members were given the responsibility to see all patients enrolled in the program, to plan for their care in consultation with their physician, and to follow them throughout their illness.

Team members are expected to assess patient and family needs at the initiation of each phase of treatment. The advisory team is not all-inclusive and can recommend any further consultations approved by the primary physician. Services that are frequently requested include speech and educational therapy, psychological assessment, dietary planning, and spiritual counseling. The Co-Care approach makes it possible to gather far more experience in treatment planning than would ordinarily be available through individual treatment requests.

Co-Care conferences are held every other week to bring together the patient's primary physician, a ward nurse representative, the Co-Care team, and all other therapists involved in the patient's care. The conferences provide a forum for discussion of each patient's care needs, and nurses and therapists are encouraged to discuss patient progress and share their findings about patient reactions to care.

ROLE OF THE NURSE COORDINATOR

The nurse coordinator holds a pivotal position on the Co-Care team. She must 1) bridge communication gaps, 2) focus on *continuity of care problems*, 3) be an information resource person, and 4) be an advisor for patients and their families both in the hospital and after discharge. The nurse coordinator can cross departmental lines to provide each specialist with a fuller understanding of the patient's needs. Her primary identification is with the individual patient and his care needs, and as patient advocate, she complements the other treatment specialists. In this context the term "patient's advocate" also means a person to whom patients can complain without fear of being rejected by the doctor and other team members. The nurse coordinator serves as an advisor to the patient and his family, and as an intermediary between the patient and his family, as well as between the patient and the professional staff. She coordinates the patient's care with the primary treatment team and works directly with the primary social worker and the public health nurse to plan the patient's post-hospital placement and means of financial support.

EXPERIENCES OF THE NURSE COORDINATOR

As a full-time nurse coordinator in a new program, the first author became involved in role development activities. From the start, her role was described as an advisory and collaborative one. She was expected to make herself available as a resource person to the patient and his family throughout the stay in the hospital and even after discharge. It was soon learned that when one becomes accountable to the patient and family rather than to the system, one needs flexibility, autonomy, and support from the hospital management as well as the cooperation of the entire medical staff.

Assuming the role of nurse coordinator required many adjustments and a certain amount of risk-taking. Automatic referrals did not always mean automatic acceptance by the primary teams. Moreover, when the nurse coordinator interviewed patients and/or families to obtain a nursing history, some nurses welcomed it, some viewed it as duplication, and some resented the time spent with the patients. The least resistance came from nurses in specialty units and those who felt more comfortable with collaborative practice. Inviting nurses to the Co-Care conferences and encouraging them to present patients on their units helped decrease resistance. Some feared the presentation, and for these nurses the nurse coordinator provided guidelines on reporting in a multidisciplinary conference.

To ease tension and increase understanding of the Co-Care Program, the nurse coordinator provided orientation conferences for all shifts of personnel about the scope and phased activities of the program. Later, these orientation classes were extended to all new nursing personnel on an ongoing monthly basis. Student nurses and members of other disciplines are now attending these conferences monthly.

Another function that fell to the nurse coordinator was to organize patient and family teaching, which had previously been fragmented, seldom coordinated with the therapists, and often done in haste near discharge time.

Some gaps continue in the discharge planning area. A nurse coordinator can help, but her involvement alone is not enough. Effective discharge planning requires the active participation of the nursing staff assigned to the patient. Head nurses pressured by administrative duties and staff nurses who rotate on team nursing assignments or tours of duty are not able to give patient and family teaching high priority. It continues to be difficult to obtain a designated nurse to plan and follow through with a teaching plan tailored to each patient.

As nurse coordinator, the first author supplements teaching and coordinates learning experiences for patients, families, and staff. In this role, she plans patient and family conferences to identify learning needs. She reinforces instruction given while making patient rounds, discusses patient progress with therapists, and shares this information with the nursing staff. She also participates in home evaluations; engages in patient and family instruction; provides resource materials for the patients, families, and staff; and makes some home visits after discharge.

PHASES OF CO-CARE

We adopted three progressive treatment phases in a protocol in which we included a list of care team people always to be called, some standardized nursing care orders, some rehabilitative measures, and even some discharge planning activities. Progress through the treatment phases is regulated by the patient's physician, usually at a Co-Care meeting.

We found that rotating house staff were often unaware of the program's aims, so the first page of the protocol explained what the Co-Care Program was all about. The remainder of the protocol was concerned with the treatment phases.

Phase I—The Acute Phase

In most cases, the patient is in the acute phase just after admission. He requires detailed observation, appropriate intervention, and prevention of complications.

During this phase, all those involved in the patient's care are asked to attend Co-Care conferences. The patient's doctors are asked to outline the medical problems. Then they hear about the nonmedical aspects of the case, and they are asked to discuss the patient's general situation with the team.

At these conferences the nurses are asked to discuss the patient's reactions to their care activities. These activities supplement rather than supplant the role of the primary physician and his treatment team, and the doctor remains in full control.

Phase II—Post-Acute Phase

When the patient is physiologically stable, the primary physician places him in Phase II. Some patients without severe deficits may be admitted directly to Phase II. It is expected that patients at this level of function can tolerate a more active program directed toward self-care.

Detailed evaluation, testing, and prescribed therapies are intensified by the speech, physical, and occupational therapists, and others as indicated.

Co-Care advisors help provide smooth transition from the acute phase to the later phases, working with some of the old team members and adding new ones according to the patient's needs.

Phase III—The Pre-Discharge Phase

The pre-discharge phase assignment is made by the primary physician when the patient is approaching discharge or transfer from the hospital. With this order the team shifts its attention to discharge planning.

Team efforts are mobilized to define the needs of the patient and his family at the point of discharge or transfer. Necessary training and referrals are made for:

1) Self-care
2) Nursing help in the home
3) Extended care or long-term hospital care
4) Out-patient therapy (medical, nursing, physical therapy, occupational therapy, speech therapy, psychotherapy, vocational counseling)
5) Community agency follow-up
6) Private physician follow-up

Follow-up plans are made to promote coordination with the patient's private physician and community resource agencies.

Family instruction is made available as soon as the continuing needs of the patient are identified. Family members are asked to give assistance in activities of daily living, range of joint motion exercises, and transfer activities.

In all cases, discharge plans are made well in advance. No family, even those competent only in a foreign language, takes the patient home without some fairly explicit information about what has happened and what is to be expected in the follow-up care.

CONCLUSION

At the initiation of the program, we wondered how acceptable it would be in such diverse areas as medical-surgical and psychiatric services. We learned that the program's automatic referrals and a set of basic orders threatened many staff members, especially the rotating house staff and the more experienced nurses. In *Team Practice and the Specialist*, Horowitz refers to the "compartmentalization of services in an ever-increasing number of specialized domains."[6] We had many such specialized domains to deal with and to open to freer communication. First, we had to make the program's protocol simple and direct. Then we explained it to everyone who would listen. Naturally, some would not. We also had to make it clear that we were not going to *supervise or police* the delivery of care. We tried to indicate to the physicians and nursing personnel assigned to the enrolled patients that *together* we would become a Coordinated Care Team.

We eliminated data keeping, insisting only that persons involved in patient care meet with the team at Co-Care conferences. We distributed invitations or reminders to attend the meetings. If the patient's physician was unable to attend, we still discussed the patient's problems and provided the primary physician with feedback as necessary. Specialists such as speech, physical, occupational, and educational therapists, were invited to participate in the conferences and demonstrate their contribution to the total management of any given patient. This has promoted greater utilization of such team members.

We believe we are making significant strides toward providing coordinated care for patients and assistance for their families. We believe that the approach described herein can serve as a model for all patient care delivery systems.

NOTES

1. Margalies, H. *Fact Book on Regional Medical Programs.* Rockville, Md.: Health Services and Mental Health Administration, 1971.
2. Pszcynski, M. et al. *Abstract II Stroke Rehabilitation.* Washington, D.C.: Joint Committee for Stroke Facilities.
3. Schutte, H. *Management of Stroke Patients. A Suggested Outline for Hospitals.* San Jose, Cal.: Santa Clara Heart Association and Regional Medical Programs.
4. Memorial Hospital of Long Beach. *Comprehensive Stroke Program.* Long Beach, Cal.
5. The Association for the North Carolina Regional Medical Program. *Comprehensive Stroke Program.* Winston-Salem, N.C.

6. Horowitz, J.J. *Team Practice and the Specialist. An Introduction to Interdisciplinary Teamwork.* Springfield, Ill.: Charles C Thomas, 1970.

* * * *

Each of this unit's structural arrangements for institutions complies with one or more of Herzberg's vertical job loading principles, with their concomitant motivators. A personal-structural approach can be taken to job enrichment by the use of evaluation, especially Herzberg's concept of feedback. Because this feedback is from leaders and peers, rather than from patients and the work itself, it is associated with the two sources of esteem identified by Maslow. This personal-structural approach is the subject of Part V.

Part V

A Perfect Tool of Job Enrichment: Evaluation

Lefton, Buzzotta, Sherberg, and Karraker, in their book *Effective Motivation through Performance Appraisal*,[1] trace the practice of appraisal as far back as the Sumerians who lived 6,000 years ago. These residents of the Tigris and Euphrates Valleys appraised what was of value to them—the material objects of their great prosperity. Although we in modern society also value material goods, more and more we are coming to value the most precious resource of our prosperity—people. We can count people, as the Sumerians counted bowls; we can assess the worth of the performance of people, as the Sumerians assessed the worth of the performance of their beasts of burden. The performance appraisal of people is unique, however, in that the technique itself can *increase* the value of their performance! This is the basic philosophy that McGregor presents in his classic article, "An Uneasy Look at Performance Appraisal."

When McGregor's article first appeared in 1957, he had not yet presented his famous concepts of Theory X and Theory Y (see Article 8, "Theory X and Theory Y"). Yet the philosophy underlying his approach to performance appraisal is clearly a Theory Y management approach. Instead of treating people like objects to be judged, McGregor advocated a bold new approach in which employees are responsible for their own performance appraisals. This approach is based on the assumption that employees know, or can learn, more about their own capabilities than anyone else. It also indicates management's trust and confidence in employees. Perhaps McGregor has the key to the reason that managers have so often resisted evaluating employees, putting a qualitative amount such as average or above average on a person's work. He says managers are reluctant to "play God" with their employees, and he feels that the whole system of performance appraisal has to change, has to respond to a different philosophy.

As McGregor implies a need for a change in the underlying philosophy regarding employees, so Patten recommends a change in the underlying philosophy regarding job evaluation. In "Job Evaluation and Job Enrichment: A Collision

Course?" Patten describes the bureaucratic model as an inappropriate basis for job evaluation for job enrichment. Umstot, Mitchell, and Bell, in "Goal Setting and Job Enrichment: An Integrated Approach to Job Design," also refer to a topic introduced by McGregor. They suggest that goal setting be added to traditional job evaluations as an added incentive for increased productivity and job enrichment.

"The Evaluation Process" includes the policies and procedures for job evaluation used at Bishop Clarkson Memorial Hospital in Omaha, Nebraska. This hospital's plan for evaluation clearly rises from an overall management philosophy and offers both high productivity for the hospital and job enrichment for employees.

Finally, O'Laughlin and Kaulbach, in "Peer Review: A Perspective for Performance Appraisal," examine the benefits and drawbacks of peer review, its basis in professionalism, its initiation as a process, and its actual implementation. Depending on the composition of the peer review team, it can be offered as part of the evaluation process or as an overall process in which the views of peers with varying perspectives and expertise are obtained.

In accordance with Herzberg's principles of vertical job loading, performance appraisal can offer nurses a removal of some employer control through their participation in the evaluation process. It also can increase their accountability for meeting the mutually established goals. Finally, performance appraisal can provide feedback on the work done.

NOTE

1. Robert Lefton, V.R. Buzzotta, Manuel Sherberg, and Dean L. Karraker, *Effective Motivation through Performance Appraisal* (New York: John Wiley, 1977), pp. 1–2.

27.

An Uneasy Look at Performance Appraisal

Douglas McGregor

Performance appraisal within management ranks has become standard practice in many companies during the past 20 years and is currently being adopted by many others, often as an important feature of management development programs. The more the method is used, the more uneasy I grow over the unstated assumptions which lie behind it. Moreover, with some searching, I find that a number of people both in education and in industry share my misgivings. This article, therefore, has two purposes:

1. To examine the conventional performance appraisal plan which requires the manager to pass judgment on the personal worth of subordinates.
2. To describe an alternative which places on the subordinate the primary responsibility for establishing performance goals and appraising progress toward them.

CURRENT PROGRAMS

Formal performance appraisal plans are designed to meet three needs, one for the organization and two for the individual:

1. They provide systematic judgments to back up salary increases, promotions, transfers, and sometimes demotions or terminations.
2. They are a means of telling a subordinate how he is doing, and suggesting needed changes in his behavior, attitudes, skills, or job knowledge; they let him know "where he stands" with the boss.

Modified with permission from Douglas McGregor, "An Uneasy Look at Performance Appraisal," *Harvard Business Review* 50, no. 5 (1972): 133–138.

3. They also are being increasingly used as a basis for the coaching and counseling of the individual by the superior.

Problem of Resistance

Personnel administrators are aware that appraisal programs tend to run into resistance from the managers who are expected to administer them. Even managers who admit the necessity of such programs frequently balk at the process—especially the interview part. As a result, some companies do not communicate appraisal results to the individual, despite the general conviction that the subordinate has a right to know his superior's opinion so he can correct his weaknesses.

The boss's resistance is usually attributed to the following causes:

- A normal dislike of criticizing a subordinate (and perhaps having to argue about it).
- Lack of skill needed to handle the interviews.
- Dislike of a new procedure with its accompanying changes in ways of operating.
- Mistrust of the validity of the appraisal instrument.

The Underlying Cause

What should we think about a method—however valuable for meeting organizational needs—which produces such results in a wide range of companies with a variety of appraisal plans? The problem is one that cannot be dismissed lightly.

Perhaps this intuitive managerial reaction to conventional performance appraisal plans shows a deep but unrecognized wisdom. In my view, it does not reflect anything so simple as resistance to change, or dislike for personnel technique, or lack of skill, or mistrust for rating scales. Rather, managers seem to be expressing real misgivings, which they find difficult to put into words. This could be the underlying cause:

The conventional approach, unless handled with consummate skill and delicacy, constitutes something dangerously close to a violation of the integrity of the personality, *through an attack on self-esteem*. Managers are uncomfortable when they are put in the position of "playing God." The respect we hold for the inherent value of the individual leaves us distressed when we must take responsibility for judging the personal worth of a fellow man. Yet the conventional approach to performance appraisal forces us not only to make such judgments and to see them acted upon but also to communicate them to those we have judged. Small wonder we resist!

Part V: A Perfect Tool: Evaluation   141

The modern emphasis upon the manager as a leader who strives to *help* his subordinates achieve both their own and the company's objectives is hardly consistent with the judicial role demanded by most appraisal plans. If the manager must put on his judicial hat occasionally, he does it reluctantly and with understandable qualms. Under such conditions, it is unlikely that the subordinate will be any happier with the results than will the boss.

Of course, managers cannot escape making judgments about subordinates. Without such evaluations, salary and promotion policies cannot be administered sensibly. But are subordinates like products on an assembly line, to be accepted or rejected as a result of an inspection process? The inspection process may be made more objective or more accurate through research on the appraisal instrument, through training of the "inspectors," or through introducing group appraisal; the subordinate may be "reworked" by coaching or counseling before the final decision to accept or reject him; but as far as the assumptions of the conventional appraisal process are concerned, we still have what is practically identical with a program for product inspection.

On this interpretation, then, resistance to conventional appraisal programs is eminently sound. It reflects an unwillingness to treat human beings like physical objects. The needs of the organization are obviously important, but when they come into conflict with our convictions about the worth and the dignity of the human personality, one or the other must give. Indeed, by the fact of their resistance, managers are saying that the organization must yield in the face of this fundamental human value.

A NEW APPROACH

If this analysis is correct, the task before us is clear. We must find a new plan—not a compromise to hide the dilemma, but a bold move to resolve the issue.

A number of writers are beginning to approach the whole subject of management from the point of view of basic social values. Peter Drucker's concept of "management by objectives"[1] offers an unusually promising framework within which we can seek a solution.

Responsibility on Subordinate

This approach calls on the subordinate to establish short-term performance goals *for himself*. The superior enters the process actively only *after* the subordinate has (a) done a good deal of thinking about his job, (b) made a careful assessment of his own strengths and weaknesses, and (c) formulated some specific plans to accomplish his goals. The superior's role is to help the man relate his self-appraisal, his "targets," and his plans for the ensuing period to the realities of the organization.

The first step in this process is to arrive at a clear statement of the major features of the job. Rather than a formal job description, this is a document drawn up *by the subordinate* after studying the company-approved statement. It defines the broad areas of his responsibility as they actually work out in practice. The boss and employee discuss the draft jointly and modify it as may be necessary until both of them agree that it is adequate.

Working from this statement of responsibilities, the subordinate then establishes his goals or "targets" for a period of, say, six months. These targets are *specific* actions which the man proposes to take, i.e., setting up regular staff meetings to improve communication, reorganizing the office, completing or undertaking a certain study. Thus they are explicitly stated and accompanied by a detailed account of the actions he proposes to take to reach them. This document is, in turn, discussed with the superior and modified until both are satisfied with it.

At the conclusion of the six-month period, the subordinate makes *his own* appraisal of what he has accomplished relative to the targets he had set earlier. He substantiates it with factual data wherever possible. The "interview" is an examination by superior and subordinate together of the subordinate's self-appraisal, and it culminates in a resetting of targets for the next six months.

Of course, the superior has veto power at each step of this process; in an organizational hierarchy anything else would be unacceptable. However, in practice he rarely needs to exercise it. Most subordinates tend to underestimate both their potentialities and their achievements. Moreover, subordinates normally have an understandable wish to satisfy their boss, and are quite willing to adjust their targets or appraisals if the superior feels they are unrealistic. Actually, a much more common problem is to resist the subordinates' tendency to want the boss to tell them what to write down.

Analysis vs. Appraisal

This approach to performance appraisal differs profoundly from the conventional one, for it shifts the emphasis from *appraisal* to *analysis*. This implies a more positive approach. No longer is the subordinate being examined by the superior so that his weaknesses may be determined; rather, he is examining himself, in order to define not only his weaknesses but also his strengths and potentials. The importance of this shift of emphasis should not be underestimated. It is basic to each of the specific differences which distinguish this approach from the conventional one.

The first of these differences arises from the subordinate's new role in the process. He becomes an active agent, not a passive "object." He is no longer a pawn in a chess game called management development.

Effective development of managers does not include coercing them (no matter how benevolently) into acceptance of the goals of the enterprise, nor does it mean manipulating their behavior to suit organizational needs. Rather, it calls for creating a relationship within which a man can take responsibility for developing his own potentialities, plan for himself, and learn from putting his plans into action. In the process, he can gain a genuine sense of satisfaction, for he is utilizing his own capabilities to achieve simultaneously both his objectives and those of the organization (*idiographic and nomothetic goals*). Unless this is the nature of the relationship, "development" becomes a euphemism.

Who Knows Best?

One of the main differences of this approach is that it rests on the assumption that the individual knows—or can learn—more than anyone else about his own capabilities, needs, strengths and weaknesses, and goals. In the end, only he can determine what is best for his development. The conventional approach, on the other hand, makes the assumption that the superior can know enough about the subordinate to decide what is best for him.

The proper role for the superior, then, is the one that falls naturally to him under the suggested plan: helping the subordinate relate his career planning to the needs and realities of the organization. In the discussions, the boss can use his knowledge of the organization to help the subordinate establish targets and methods for achieving them which will (a) lead to increased knowledge and skill, (b) contribute to organizational objectives, and (c) test the subordinate's appraisal of himself.

This is help which the subordinate wants. He knows well that the rewards and satisfactions he seeks from his career as a manager depend on his contribution to organizational objectives. He is also aware that the superior knows more completely than he what is required for success in this organization and *under this boss*. The superior, then, is the person who can help him test the soundness of his goals and his plans for achieving them. Quite clearly the knowledge and active participation of *both* superior and subordinate are necessary components of this approach.

If the superior accepts this role, he need not become a judge of the subordinate's personal worth. He is not telling, deciding, criticizing, or praising—not "playing God." He finds himself listening, using his own knowledge of the organization as a basis for advising, guiding, encouraging his subordinates to develop their own potentialities. Incidentally, this often leads the superior to important insights about himself and his impact on others.

Looking to the Future

Another significant difference is that the emphasis is on the future rather than the past. The purpose of the plan is to establish realistic targets and to seek the most effective ways of reaching them. Appraisal thus becomes a means to a *constructive end*. The 60-year-old "coaster" can be encouraged to set performance goals for himself and to make a fair appraisal of his progress toward them. Even the subordinate who has failed can be helped to consider what moves will be best for himself. The superior rarely finds himself facing the uncomfortable prospect of denying a subordinate's personal worth. A transfer or even a demotion can be worked out without the connotation of a "sentence by the judge."

Performance vs. Personality

Finally, the accent is on *performance*, on actions relative to goals. There is less tendency for the personality of the subordinate to become an issue. The superior, instead of finding himself in the position of a psychologist or a therapist, can become a coach helping the subordinate to reach his own decisions on the specific steps that will enable him to reach his targets. Such counseling as may be required demands no deep analysis of the personal motivations or basic adjustment of the subordinate.

A NEW ATTITUDE

As a consequence of these differences we may expect the growth of a different attitude toward appraisal on the part of superior and subordinate alike.

The superior will gain real satisfaction as he learns to help his subordinates integrate their personal goals with the needs of the organization so that both are served. Once the subordinate has worked out a mutually satisfactory plan of action, the superior can delegate to him the responsibility for putting it into effect. He will see himself in a consistent managerial role rather than being forced to adopt the basically incompatible role of either the judge or the psychologist.

Problems of Judgment

Of course, managerial skill is required. No method will eliminate that. *The managerial skill of appraising is a specialized skill, founded in the philosophy of Theory Y*. This method can fail as readily as any other in the clumsy hands of insensitive or indifferent or power-seeking managers. But even the limited experience of a few companies with this approach indicates that managerial *resistance* is substantially reduced. As a consequence, it is easier to gain the collaboration of managers in developing the necessary skills.

Cost in Time

There is one unavoidable cost: the manager must spend considerably more time in implementing a program of this kind. It is not unusual to take a couple of days to work through the initial establishment of responsibilities and goals with each individual. And a periodic appraisal may require several hours rather than the typical 20 minutes.

Reaction to this cost will undoubtedly vary. The management that considers the development of its human resources to be the primary means of achieving the economic objectives of the organization will not be disturbed. It will regard the necessary guidance and coaching as among the most important functions of every superior.

CONCLUSION

I have sought to show that the conventional approach to performance appraisal stands condemned as a personnel method. It places the manager in the untenable position of judging the personal worth of his subordinates, and of acting on these judgments. No manager possesses, nor could he acquire, the skill necessary to carry out this responsibility effectively. Few would even be willing to accept it if they were fully aware of the implications involved.

It is this unrecognized aspect of conventional appraisal programs which produces the widespread uneasiness and even open resistance of management to appraisals and especially to the appraisal interview.

A sounder approach, which places the major responsibility on the subordinate for establishing performance goals and appraising progress toward them, avoids the major weaknesses of the old plan and benefits the organization by stimulating the development of the subordinate. It is true that more managerial skill and the investment of a considerable amount of time are required, but the greater motivation and the more effective development of subordinates can justify these added costs.

NOTE

1. See *The Practice of Management* (New York, Harper & Brothers, 1954).

* * * *

McGregor defines the problem with performance appraisal as managers' resistance to "playing God" with employees. Patten feels performance appraisal fails because of its roots in bureaucratic job analysis. Although other aspects of jobs have changed in response to developments in behavioral science and organizational theory, the evaluation of an employee against an inflexible job description has not. Job enrichment, according to Patten, requires a break with bureaucratic rigidity. He prescribes an approach in which the organizational position and the individual in the position are assessed in relation to multidimensional organization. Because Patten sees an organizational position as directly affected by the employee incumbent, he believes that the emphasis of performance appraisal should be on that employee's skills, experiences, attitudes, knowledge, and performance, rather than on those of the ideal incumbent. Thus, the evaluation would be personalized, and the job enrichment would be greater than that offered in a bureaucracy.

28.
Job Evaluation and Job Enrichment: A Collision Course?

Thomas H. Patten, Jr.

Job evaluation and job enrichment are two concepts in conflict and when juxtaposed today they collide. In this article I analyze the collision course and suggest the kinds of new thinking needed to harmonize the two JEs.

JOB STUDY AND WORK DESCRIPTION

For many years, the painstaking work of job analysis (leading to the writing of job descriptions and the meticulous evaluation of all the jobs so described) was advocated by industrial compensation specialists. It was needed during an industrial era when chaos prevailed in respect to defining work. Leaders in the rationalization of work, the pioneer industrial engineers such as Frederick W. Taylor, desired to impose order on this chaos. For them, getting the job facts was essential to controlling work assignments, supervising the behavior and performance of employees, and establishing criteria for the recruitment, selection, training, development, and pay of all employees.[1]

The result of decades of work in job description and job analysis was the creation of industrial and governmental jobs throughout the United States that were clear in their scope, particular as to the qualifications allegedly required of the employees who filled them, and limited as to their potential for sustaining the incentive to work and for providing job satisfaction. Apparently, employers and unions unwittingly wanted jobs defined in this way. The ideal was, in fact, for all work organizations lacking traditional job analysis and job evaluation programs to adopt these kinds of programs. During both World War II and the wage-price freeze periods since then, employers stood to benefit, from an internal administrative standpoint, by having formal plans of job evaluation and wage and salary

---

Modified with permission from Thomas H. Patten, Jr., "Job Evaluation and Job Enrichment: A Collision Course?" *Human Resource Management* 16, no. 4 (1977): 2–8.

administration. It is clear that the scientific management movement, industrial engineering, and job evaluation stem from efforts made historically to rationalize the work place for the ultimate purposes of economy and efficiency.

JOB ENRICHMENT

The mechanical nature and rigidity of job evaluation systems administered by the tenets of scientific management led to their partial downfall in the 1930s and 1940s. The rise of industrial unionism brought with it negotiation over rates of pay for evaluated jobs.

Perhaps inspired by Charlie Chaplin's film *Modern Times,* ultra-specialization of work, and the evolving situation, social scientists were beginning to wonder if the human factor was not being totally ignored by work designed through the prevailing methods of job study and job evaluation in vogue. More specifically, they wondered if jobs should not have greater psychological depth than they ordinarily displayed. Henri DeMan was one of the first observers to obtain recognition for his concerns over joy in work.[2]

During the late 1960s and early 1970s the concept of job enrichment became very prominent. Reports of the "blue-collar blues," executive "blahs," and alienation of many types of employees, but particularly factory hourly rated production employees, and the unique types of employee resentment expressed at the General Motors assembly plant at Lordstown, Ohio, gave rise several years ago to national concern about the human impact of work in America.[3] There was apparently an intellectual, if not a managerial, crisis in the design of work.

When job enrichment fails, according to Hackman and his colleagues, it often typically flops because of inadequate diagnosis of the target job and employees' reactions to it. For example, sometimes job enrichment is *assumed* by management to be a solution to "people problems" but the root cause is never properly diagnosed. Or a particular diagnosis is incomplete, superficial, and inadequate. Job enrichment in these instances is misapplied. *The real cause of the failure is often that job enrichment was superimposed on an existing system. Job enrichment calls for a new approach to work and management. It cannot be "added" to a different philosophy or approach.*

THE COLLISION AT CLOSE RANGE

Clearly, the conceptions of job design and enrichment fly in the face of rational job study and job evaluation. First, the conceptions call for broadening jobs and reassigning to lower-paid workers tasks that have hitherto been assigned higher-paid employees. The result would dilute the work of staff specialists and line supervisors so that they should, under the logic of job evaluation, be paid less for work now of lesser responsibility. Employees with enriched jobs should be paid more. Job enrichment would thus tend toward equalizing job responsibilities and should, if installed, cause widespread pay adjustments that are likely to be unsatisfactory to many employees. Yet we have no evidence of which I am aware that this has taken place. Walters denies that it is a problem at present but suggests it could become one.[4]

Second, job enrichment would reduce managerial control over the limitations currently imposed on jobs because job boundaries would be expanded, potentially expansible, and not always clear. This would generate costs in restudying and reevaluating jobs. Unions would generally abhor the idea. Where management would be required to negotiate new rates with unions, the task of reviewing large numbers of jobs would be considerable and conflicts with the union would be energy-sapping. Union and employee jurisdictional problems over broadened jobs that have fuzzy boundaries can be imagined.

Third, management has no assurance that enriched jobs will pay off in reduced labor costs, greater productivity, improved employee retention, and the like. However, employees may be satisfied and more highly motivated to perform; and these changes should benefit management.

Fourth, the union, for reasons mentioned previously and because a managerial proposal for job enrichment may be interpreted as a threat to the collective bargaining relationship, may reject job enrichment out of hand. Unions typically concern themselves with the immediate issues of wages, hours, and conditions of work, taking the view that job enrichment is more of a far-out dream of the intellectuals than a serious issue with the rank-and-file. In fact, in one of the few studies which exist in this area, it was reported that there was almost a total lack of attention being given as of 1973 to motivational programs (including job enrichment) in collective bargaining.[5] The job enrichment committees extant in the automobile industry appear dormant at present to say the least.

In summary, job enrichment is a challenge to traditional personnel work and to concepts of job description and job evaluation. For the sake of maintaining employee incentive to perform, we need to keep our attention on the connection between enrichment and evaluation because the merits of job enrichment justify its consideration. On the other hand, the job evaluation barnacles of the 1940s are very thick, and they must be scraped away if job enrichment is to be tried in a work organization. Is there any way to do this?

INDIVIDUAL ROLE AND GENERALIZED JOB

We have seen that there is a collision between job evaluation and job enrichment. Until recently in organizational theory, the model of bureaucracy was thought to fit, and be worthy of emulation by, many large-scale work organizations in America. Bureaucracy is today conceived of as having an excessively rigid organizational structure. Jobs in organizations cannot be assumed to be frozen and unsusceptible to change, particularly managerial, professional, and technical jobs. And some specialists are pushing this thought to the logical conclusion that bureaucratic traditional job descriptions are conceptually obsolete.[6]

Job descriptions in the traditional sense are regarded as meaningless to adherents of this school of thought. However, unions cling to job descriptions and job evaluations. In their negotiation posture, their grievance posture, and many of their job activities, unions are very supportive of job evaluation and job descriptions, even when they do not overtly endorse the conceptual underpinning.

Beginning with and accelerating since 1965, a substantial body of knowledge has been developed by behavioral scientists and organizational theorists that has applicability to the personnel management processes in such areas as employee selection, motivation, job satisfaction, development and communications. Its impact upon job evaluation, however, has been as yet negligible. If job evaluation is to have multiple uses as a tool for management, it must reflect the findings of the behavioral scientists and organizational theorists about how people and systems interact in a dynamic organizational environment.[7]

Behavioral science findings are highly relevant to the methods used to identify and assess those factors that influence the nature of jobs. For example, as Atwood has pointed out, the bureaucratic view that organizations can be conceptualized without considering people is paralleled by the view that a job or position should be considered as something distinct from the employee.[8] Or to take another example, bureaucratic theory holds that tasks are assigned to positions in the structure, and positions—not people—have the authority, responsibility, accountability, and the means for carrying out tasks. The counterpart in job evaluation ideology is that in classifying jobs, it is their respective duties and responsibilities as subdivisions of the function of the organization as a whole—not of persons—which are the controlling desiderata. Job evaluation needs to break out of this frame of reference.

Despite the fact that a great deal is known about how the employee relates to, and functions within, an organizational context, this knowledge generally has not been applied to the job evaluation process. There may be, however, elements of the individual-organizational relationship that could assist the personnel and compensation specialist in identifying and assessing certain job factors that are not being fully considered by traditional job evaluation systems. More specifically, job evaluation of the future should require an assessment of the behavioral elements inherent in the duties performed by the particular individual who occupies the position. It would seem unrealistic, therefore, to separate the duties of the position from the individual who functions in that particular capacity. Consequently, a new approach to job evaluation would be to assess how the

Part V: A Perfect Tool: Evaluation   151

position and its incumbent relate in a multidimensional organizational environment, i.e., the agreement between nomothetic and idiographic role expectations. As Atwood has suggested, this would totally conflict with job evaluation ideology of the past. Yet it may bring us closer to a humanized view of the job which is the sine qua non of job enrichment. Under this new view of job evaluation,[9] the job is conceived of as one subsystem in a series of subsystems that constitute the whole system (or work organization itself). The required pattern of relationships on the job would be viewed more in the light of the incumbent's skills, experiences, attitudes, and knowledge and what he or she brings to the job and displays in performing it than the generalized requirements laid on a job based upon what the ideal incumbent would be expected to demonstrate according to bureaucratic theory. Emphasis would be placed on identifying and defining the interaction of the individual with the organization as an integrated dyadic system.

Job evaluation would make much more use than hitherto of the concepts of role (based upon the job incumbent's perceptions of the objectives of the job) and status (based upon the expectancies of the formal and informal organizations). The overall thrust would be toward greater personalization and opening the door for enrichment as the latter is being currently conceived.

NOTES

1. Thomas H. Patten, Jr., *Pay: Employee Compensation and Incentive Plans* (New York: Free Press, 1977), pp. 214–216, 247–250 covers some of the points developed in considerably more detail in this article.
2. Henri DeMan, *Joy in Work* (New York: Holt, 1929), *passim*.
3. See *Work in America*, Report of a Special Task Force to the Secretary of Health, Education, and Welfare prepared under the auspices of the W.E. Upjohn Institute for Employment Research (Cambridge: MIT, 1973), pp. 17–42; and also David Jenkins, *Job Power* (Baltimore: Penguin, 1974), pp. ix–xv, 155–175, and 188–326.
4. Roy W. Walters, *Job Enrichment for Results: Strategies for Successful Implementation* (Reading: Addison-Wesley, 1975), pp. 186–187, 214–215.
5. Albert A. Blum *et al.*, "The Effect of Motivational Programs on Collective Bargaining," *Personnel Journal*, Vol. 52, No. 7, July 1973, pp. 633–641. Other glimmers into the subject (from Europe) are found in: Henry Douar and Jean-Daniel Reynaud, "Union-Management Conflicts over Quality Working Life Issues," pp. 393–404; Yves P. Delamotte, "Union Attitudes Toward Quality of Working Life," pp. 405–415 in Davis and Chernes, *op. cit.*, Vol. II.
6. Robert E. Sibson, "New Practices and Ideas in Compensation Administration," *Compensation Review*, Vol. 6, No. 3, Third Quarter 1974, pp. 42–44.
7. J.F. Atwood, "Position Synthesis: A Behavioral Approach to Position Classification," *Public Personnel Review*, Vol. 31, No. 2, April 1971, p. 77.
8. *Ibid.*, p. 78.
9. *Ibid*, p. 81.

* * * *

McGregor referred to Peter Drucker's concept of management by objectives (MBO) as an appropriate approach for personalized performance appraisal. Umstot, Mitchell, and Bell examine the compatibility of job enrichment and goal setting. They identify a congruency and mutual benefit toward productivity and job satisfaction, the double goal that the nursing administrator must strive to attain. As research on both concepts individually and together is limited, they propose a model for job design containing both components.

29.
Goal Setting and Job Enrichment: An Integrated Approach to Job Design

Denis D. Umstot, Terence R. Mitchell, and Cecil H. Bell, Jr.

Even though interest in the quality of working life and job satisfaction is increasing,[1-3] task performance and productivity continue to be the dominant concern of most managers.[4] Productivity on the one hand and job satisfaction on the other are the major two dependent variables in much organizational research literature. Often these two outcomes are pitted against each other—which *one* is to be enhanced: productivity *or* job satisfaction? This article proposes that the two outcomes are not necessarily mutually exclusive or inherently in conflict with one another; it is possible to design jobs that simultaneously enhance both productivity and satisfaction.

This article is about job design and the two job design strategies—goal setting and job enrichment. "Job design refers to the deliberate, purposeful planning of the job, including any or all of its structural or social aspects."[5,p. 379] Goal setting is the process of developing and formalizing targets or objectives that an employee is responsible for accomplishing. Although the goal-setting process is important, of primary concern here is the end result of goal setting: the presence or absence of specific task goals, targets, or objectives for individuals or small groups. The job enrichment approach seeks to make jobs inherently more interesting and satisfying through adding such job characteristics as skill variety, task identity, task significance, autonomy, and feedback.[6]

What is needed is an integration of goal-setting techniques and job enrichment techniques with goals facilitating higher productivity and job enrichment promoting job satisfaction and improving the quality of working life for employees. This article attempts such an integration and builds a model of job design. Some pertinent questions to be explored include: Are goal-setting and job enrichment

---

Modified with permission from Denis D. Umstot, Terence R. Mitchell, and Cecil H. Bell, Jr., "Goal Setting and Job Enrichment: An Integrated Approach to Job Design," *Academy of Management Review* 3, no. 4 (1978): 867–879.

strategies compatible methods for improving productivity and job satisfaction? Can they be combined? With what effects? What are the moderating characteristics of individuals or organizations that enhance or degrade a combined job design strategy?

(See Part III, Job Enrichment Defined, for a discussion of the foundations of job enrichment.)

GOAL SETTING FOUNDATIONS

On one hand, most people intuitively believe that goals are related to performance. Even the most casual observation reveals that people with vague or indefinite goals often seem to work slowly, perform poorly, lack interest, and accomplish little. On the other hand, people with clearly defined goals appear to be both more energetic and more productive; they "get things done" within a specified time period and move on to other activities (and goals). Goals may be implicit or explicit, vague or clearly defined, self-imposed or externally imposed; whatever their form, they serve to structure time and activities for people. Goal clarity and goal difficulty may vary widely among people, but goal setting seems to be a ubiquitous phenomenon.

Locke[7] developed a theory of work performance stating that clear and difficult goals, if accepted, will result in increased performance. The major theoretical assertions of Locke's approach are as follows. First, specific goals result in greater output than a general goal like "do your best." Second, a difficult goal results in greater output than an easy goal. And finally, goals serve to motivate performance only if they are accepted. The empirical results from the laboratory[7,8] and the field[9,10] seem to support Locke's motivational approach: specific difficult goals, if accepted, do result in high performance levels. Two recent studies imply that goal setting may also be effective for increasing work satisfaction.[5,11]

One practical application of goal setting is to use it within the framework of a management-by-objectives (MBO) program.[12,13] MBO combines goal-setting, control, and appraisal systems to improve organizational objectives associated with an individual or a small group. MBO programs are top-down programs that often focus primarily on managerial levels. There is a great deal of anecdotal evidence that MBO works; however, few rigorous evaluations have been reported (see Steers and Porter[10] for a review).

Job enrichment appears to be primarily and directly related to job satisfaction, and goal setting appears to be primarily and directly related to productivity. It seems reasonable to examine the possibilities for simultaneous application of these two techniques. Although few organizational practitioners have attempted to combine job enrichment and goal setting, one notable exception is the work of Myers,[14] who considers goals to be an integral part of the job enrichment process.

Unfortunately, little empirical evidence has been reported by Myers to show the effectiveness of the combination.

THE INTERACTION OF GOAL SETTING AND JOB ENRICHMENT

How Goals and Job Characteristics Affect Each Other

Few studies exist relating the presence or absence of task goals to specific job characteristics. The following sections review the existing literature and pose some tentative explanations to explain the interactions between task goals and job enrichment characteristics. These sections explore both how goals may affect job characteristics and, when appropriate, how job characteristics may affect goals.

Skill Variety

One would generally expect task goals to have very little impact on this dimension unless the job was very bleak indeed. In particularly boring and repetitive jobs, some amount of mental skill variety might be added if the individual or group engages in such processes as keeping a tally of work performed, calculating the chances of goal attainment, and anticipating the rewards that might be associated with goal accomplishment. Thus, goal setting might add skill variety to dull, repetitive jobs by providing additional sources of mental activation and stimulation.

Task Identity

Goal setting may involve integration of individual task goals with departmental or organizational goals, thus creating a sense of wholeness to the job that may have been previously lacking. *This integration of goals gives work meaningfulness—a requirement for job enrichment.* Also, by focusing on objectives and accomplishments rather than activities there may be more sense of closure on the task. Some empirical evidence exists to support the proposition that goals affect task identity. In an experiment to examine the effects of goal setting and job enrichment, Umstot, Bell, and Mitchell[5] found that when a job was initially designed to include goal setting, employees saw their jobs as having significantly greater task identity than did employees working without goals or job enrichment.

Task Significance

Goals may create a sense of meaningfulness by providing the employee with a perspective for where his or her contribution fits in terms of the organization's end product or service. By seeing the "big picture," employees may better understand the significance of their jobs and may thus have an enhanced sense of worthwhile contribution to the organization. If meaningfulness improves, job characteristics theory[6] predicts that increased work satisfaction and internal work motivation will result.

Autonomy

Goals have both a direct and indirect impact on autonomy. The direct impact stems from the knowledge of the control over work outcomes that goal-setting strategies usually provide. Employees are no longer fully dependent on the supervisor to structure their daily or even hourly activities but have the knowledge to take responsibility for work outcomes. If employees are allowed to determine their own means of goal accomplishment, there is a direct, positive effect on autonomy. The indirect impact of a goal-setting program on autonomy stems from possible changes in supervisory behavior. When no goal-setting program exists, supervisors tend to become involved in overcontrol and detailed supervision of their subordinate's task, an expected approach since responsibility is centered around the supervisor rather than the worker. However, when a goal-setting program is implemented, individual employees become responsible for their own work outcomes, and supervisors may feel more comfortable about allowing their subordinates greater freedom to determine the means for task accomplishment. *This thinking is congruent with Gouldner's concept of indirect supervision and its positive effect on job satisfaction (see Article 9, "The Problem of 'Close Supervision'").*

The Umstot et al. experiment[5] found that employees with assigned goals had significantly higher autonomy scores than did employees with neither goals nor enrichment, but this result was obtained only in newly designed jobs. When existing jobs were changed to add goals (without participation), there was no significant change in autonomy. In fact, the trends were in the opposite direction: goal setting seemed to result in a lower degree of autonomy. Thus, the experiment implied that a contingency approach may be necessary. When new jobs are designed, it appears that goals can be established unilaterally by management with good results, but if employees have been working without goals, they may feel that goals interfere with their autonomy. Perhaps a participative approach to goal setting would have yielded different results; *in participative management, goal setting is a joint endeavor.*

The results of the above experiments highlight the importance of the goal-setting process. On one hand, goals may be perceived as restraining autonomy if they are unilaterally imposed. On the other hand, goals may serve to facilitate autonomy if they are jointly set and if the employee is allowed to select the means to accomplish the goal. The concept of participation is central to the autonomy-goals relationship. If participation is used and the employees actually feel commitment to the goals, the sense of autonomy and responsibility might be much higher than in a job without goals where the employees had to grope and fumble to get the job done.

While there is evidence that participation enhances goal setting effects, Steers and Porter[10] point out that the opposite position can also be supported—the literature is contradictory. Steers[15] found that need for achievement may moderate effects of participation in the goal setting process. High-need achievers performed well with or without participation—apparently the goal itself was enough stimulus. The low-need achieving people, on the other hand, performed best only when participation was used. Thus, need for achievement or individual differences may moderate this relationship. A recent correlation study in a public utility by Schuler and Kim[16] found that, in general, employees were more satisfied with their work when participation *and* goal setting were present than when only participation or goal setting alone were present. They concluded that employee participation significantly influences higher performance and job satisfaction. If full participation is used, goal setting may increase the sense of autonomy. The opposite effect may occur if goals are unilaterally imposed.

Feedback from the Job

By providing standards of performance, goals almost automatically enhance performance feedback *if* the employee has information regarding goal progress. Another important benefit of goals in the feedback process is to help individuals separate performance-relevant feedback from other types of feedback. Goals can also serve as intrinsic performance reinforcers and can facilitate external reinforcement strategies. One indication of the influence of feedback on jobs is that both major approaches to job enrichment (Herzberg[17] and Hackman and Oldham[6]) consider feedback an integral part of the job enrichment process.

A review of the literature concerning knowledge of results or feedback shows that goal setting and feedback are perhaps inextricably woven together, so that it is very difficult to extract the effects of one from the other. Locke, Cartledge, and Koeppel argue that the effects of knowledge of results on performance are really a goal-setting phenomenon. They assert that knowledge of results will be motivating to the extent that "(a) specific goal setting is facilitated, and (b) the goals are hard or difficult goals."[18, p. 483] An additional conclusion is that "when the two effects are separated (goal setting and knowledge of results), there is no effect of (knowledge of results) over and above that which can be attributed to differential goal setting."[19(a), p. 482] After reviewing three studies on the effects of feedback on performance, Latham and Yukl[9] concluded that frequent relevant feedback is necessary for goal-setting success but that more research is needed, especially in terms of experiments where feedback and goals are manipulated in a controlled environment to isolate their effects. Kim and Hamner, in a field experiment that tested the effects of intrinsic and extrinsic feedback in a goal-setting environment, concluded that:

> The results show that it is possible for goal setting alone to enhance performance, without a formal feedback program, but when self-generated knowledge of results plus supervisory generated knowledge of results and praise was added to a formal goal setting program, performance was generally enhanced even more.[19(b), p. 56]

Erez[20] conducted a laboratory experiment to isolate the effects of feedback in the goal setting-performance relationship. When individuals were given feedback about their test scores, the correlation between self-set goals and performance was .60 ($p < .01$). The goals-performance correlation for individuals who did not have feedback about their scores was .01. The study concludes that feedback is a necessary condition for a goal or intention to affect task performance. Thus, feedback provides vital information to energize the goal-setting process. It also reinforces progress toward meeting the goal. Without the reinforcement of feedback, it seems unlikely that people would pursue goals as a desirable outcome.

Baird[21] conducted a laboratory experiment with 103 undergraduate volunteers using a stimulating task (in basket) and a nonstimulating task (math problems) in feedback and no feedback conditions. People assigned to groups with the stimulating task were significantly more satisfied than those with the nonstimulating task. However, there was no difference attributable to the feedback or no feedback conditions. Baird concluded that individuals working in stimulating jobs give themselves feedback and that "the advantage of goal setting (in the feedback process) is that the person's internal evaluation has a higher probability of being in line with the external feedback."[21, p. 73]

One barrier to unravelling the relationships between goals and feedback is a general lack of understanding of the feedback construct. Greller and Harold[22] have attempted to clarify the concept by identifying and studying several different sources of feedback: the supervisor, coworkers, the task itself, one's own feelings, the formal organization, and clients and customers. Goals may be formally or informally associated with any of these sources of feedback.

In summary, it appears that feedback (either self-administered or externally administered) is an essential element of the goal-setting process. Without feedback, there is no reinforcement to sustain efforts toward goal accomplishment. In addition, goal setting may serve to clarify and enhance feedback so that it is of a higher quality. Thus, goal setting and feedback seem to be naturally complementary. *Goal setting in performance appraisal adds the necessary component of feedback to make job enrichment possible.*

Other Ways that Goals Affect Jobs

Goals Enhance Role Clarity

Goals can serve to clarify the person's role in the organization and to enhance the person's understanding of the relationships between his or her role and roles of others. By understanding and clarifying the goals for a job, a significant source of role ambiguity is eliminated, and heightened clarity of expectations should be experienced.

Goals Provide Job Challenge

Challenge appears to be related to goal difficulty, in that the more difficult the goal, the more challenging the job. Locke[7] summarized a number of studies showing that hard goals result in higher performance. Oldham[23] found that challenge was related to quality of output but not quantity of output. *This finding is congruent with Herzberg's reference to the job satisfaction of doing a good job and the need to love the product.*

Hall and Lawler[24] found that job challenge, with quality pressure as an intervening variable, was related positively to both job involvement and organizational performance. Job challenge also seems to be related to attitudes toward the job. In a study of 6,950 U.S. Government Civil Service employees, 42.6 percent of the variance in job satisfaction was explained by job challenge.[25] Thus, setting hard goals may result in enhanced perceptions of job challenge and also in increased performance. Of course there are limits to the amount of challenge that will be accepted. If the goal becomes extremely difficult, it will most likely be rejected. There is considerable controversy in the literature concerning the nature of the relationship between goal difficulty, goal acceptance, and performance. (For a review of this issue, see Steers and Porter.[10])

Goal Setting Facilitates Individual-Organizational Goal Congruence

Argyris[26,27] has pointed out that when there is an incongruence between the needs of the individual and the requirements of the organization, the individual will experience frustration, psychological failure, a short-time perspective, and conflict. Goal setting, especially if it is conducted in a mature participatory manner, could serve to provide the individuals with a sense of self-control and longer time perspective. If individual and organizational goals are congruent, then goal setting might increase the number of mature healthy individuals in organizations. However, if the goals of the organization were incongruent with those of the individual, then goal setting might increase conflict and frustration.

The authors' meaning is not clear here. If goal setting of congruent goals between organization and individual is not possible in a participative management atmosphere, the institution is not a place for employment of humans.
Effects of goals on job characteristics are presented in Table 29-1.

Interactions with Organizational Characteristics

In addition to the specific effects of goal setting on individuals and jobs, it is important to know how the effects of goal setting on enrichment might differ in terms of some broader characteristics of the organization such as hierarchical level, structure, climate, and technology.

Organization Hierarchical Level

No studies were found that related goal setting to different organizational levels. Most MBO programs have been focused on the managerial level, while most field studies of goal setting alone (without the more elaborate MBO techniques) have been conducted at the blue-collar level. Therefore, it is hard to draw any conclusions with respect to this issue. Studies are needed that measure the effects of goal setting and MBO for different hierarchical levels. It seems probable that enrichment characteristics would change substantially from the lowest working level to top management and that the differences of existing job characteristics at various organizational levels would interact with the goal setting. The results of an unpublished study by Bell, Umstot, Whitney and Rosenzweig support the hypothesis that jobs become more enriched as the individual goes up the organizational ladder. *This finding is of special concern to the nursing administrator who is attempting to enrich the job of the professional nurse, since the professional nurse*

Table 29–1 The Interaction of Goal Setting with Job Characteristics

Job Characteristic	Predicted Effect of Task Goals on the Job Characteristic
Skill Variety	No Change
Task Identity	Enhance
Task Significance	Enhance
Autonomy	Enhance if Participation Used
	Degrade if Participation Not Used
Feedback from Job	Enhance
Role Clarity	Enhance
Challenge	Enhance
Individual-Organizational Goal Congruence	Enhance

functions at a low position on the hierarchy of a centralized organization—at the patient's bedside.

Since job characteristics vary widely across the hierarchical spectrum one should also expect differential effects of goal setting on job design. On one hand, goal setting at higher organizational levels, especially if participation was used, might make a good job even better without resorting to a combination goal-setting–enrichment program. On the other hand, jobs lower in the organization may be so unenriched that an enrichment strategy must be combined with goal setting to make any goal-setting program effective. At lower organizational levels, goal setting alone is predicted to be less effective than goal setting and job enrichment combined.

Organization Structure

Little evidence exists for this dimension even though it appears that structure would be an important element in goal setting. If the organization structure is decentralized with cost centers at the lowest levels of the organization, goal setting at the task level may be considerably facilitated. Conversely, centralized organizations may provide so little autonomy and such poor measures of performance at lower organizational levels that goal setting is impractical. Other structural variables such as size, span of control, and centralization of authority, are potential facilitators or inhibitors of goal-setting programs, but little is known about these relationships. *Further research on organizational structures is needed. Because the recent changes in organizational structure are relatively untested, nursing administrators who attempt to institute one or another of them need to do so with an appropriate research approach so that they can add to organizational data in these areas.*

Organization Climate

Hollmann[28] found that managers' perceptions of the supportiveness of the organization climate and perceived effectiveness of the MBO process were significantly correlated between climate and overall satisfaction with MBO as it related to their jobs. In a study of primary school children, Hall and Hall[24] also found that goal setting only worked in a supportive climate. In climates with low support, personal goals were not related to performance or success. A central theme of most change literature, including MBO, is the importance of top management support to create unfreezing or willingness of the organization to adopt a new program such as MBO or job enrichment. An open, supportive climate would seem to create the trust and collaboration necessary for effective goal accomplishment and implementation of enrichment programs. *The nursing administrator often has more control over organizational environment than organizational structure.*

Technology

The degree of interdependence between tasks is a key moderator in the goal-setting process. If tasks are highly independent and outputs are easily measurable, goal setting will be facilitated. If tasks are interdependent, such as in process organizations or on assembly lines, the goal-setting process will be inhibited because the output of individual employees is not measurable. *Since most nursing roles are interdependent, this measurement of individual output is of special concern to the nursing administrator.*

Table 29-2 summarizes some possible relationships between organizational characteristics, goal setting, and job enrichment.

The relationship between job characteristics (enrichment) and goal characteristics is generally favorable to combining the two approaches. Organizational moderators also seem to be congruent with an integrated approach, although there are many contingencies associated with the process that need to be more fully understood.

Table 29-2 The Moderating Effect of Organizational Characteristics on the Goal Setting/Job Enrichment Process

Organizational Characteristic		Predicted Effect on Goal Setting
Organizational Level	Higher	Goal setting alone most successful
	Lower	Goal setting *and* job enrichment most successful
Organizational Structure	Decentralized	Goal setting most successful
	Centralized	Goal setting least successful
Organizational Climate	Supportive	Goal setting most successful
	Non-Supportive	Goal setting least successful
Technology	Independent Tasks	Goal setting most successful
	Dependent Linked Tasks	Goal setting least successful

CONCLUSIONS AND IMPLICATIONS

A review of the literature has suggested that most of the interactive effects of goal setting and enrichment are positive. Thus, there seems to be no inherent reason why jobs should be designed for *either* job enrichment *or* goal setting. An integrative approach seems more appropriate. On one hand, job enrichment seems to have a major effect on work satisfaction but little effect on productivity. Goal setting, on the other hand, improves productivity and, in some instances, may improve work satisfaction.

Even though the evidence is quite convincing that task goals improve productivity, problems sometimes appear where task goals are incorporated into an elaborate MBO program.[10,29,30] One explanation for the lack of success of many goal-setting programs might be that goal-setting variables by themselves are an incomplete statement of task motivation. It seems quite plausible that most of the job enrichment variables (skill variety, task identity, task significance, autonomy, and feedback from the job) also seem to be essential for an effective motivational effort. For example, without feedback, goal attainment would not be reinforced, and motivation might decline. Without autonomy, the employee may feel that the means to reach the goal are incompatible; thus, he or she will not work toward goal attainment. Without task significance, the goal would have little meaning and would probably not be accepted. A somewhat weaker case might also be made for the interaction of skill variety and task identity with the goal-setting process. In short, it appears that goal setting and job enrichment, when combined, make a more complete model of work motivation than either does alone.

Figure 29-1 shows a general conceptual model of the variables that may be necessary for a more complete statement of job design. The model is only a partial description of the complexities of the job enrichment-goal setting process. The dotted arrow between the key job characteristics is a simplification of all the relationships summarized in Table 29-1.

Individual moderators are those given by Getzels and Guba in their model (see Article 1, "The Getzels-Guba Model"). Organizational moderators are outlined in Table 29-2. The open vertical channel between individual moderators and organizational moderators signifies that most of these moderators appear to affect both enrichment and task goals (exceptions include goal acceptance and goal commitment which seem more related to the goal-setting process). The size of the arrows in the model represents, albeit quite roughly, the relative power of the relationships. For example, the broad arrow between enrichment and satisfaction indicates a strong causal relationship while the narrow arrow from enrichment to productivity indicates a much weaker effect.

A major practical reason for building an integrated model for job design and work motivation is the outcome or result that might be expected from each technique. Goal setting has been consistently related to higher performance, while

Figure 29-1 An Integrated Model of Job Design

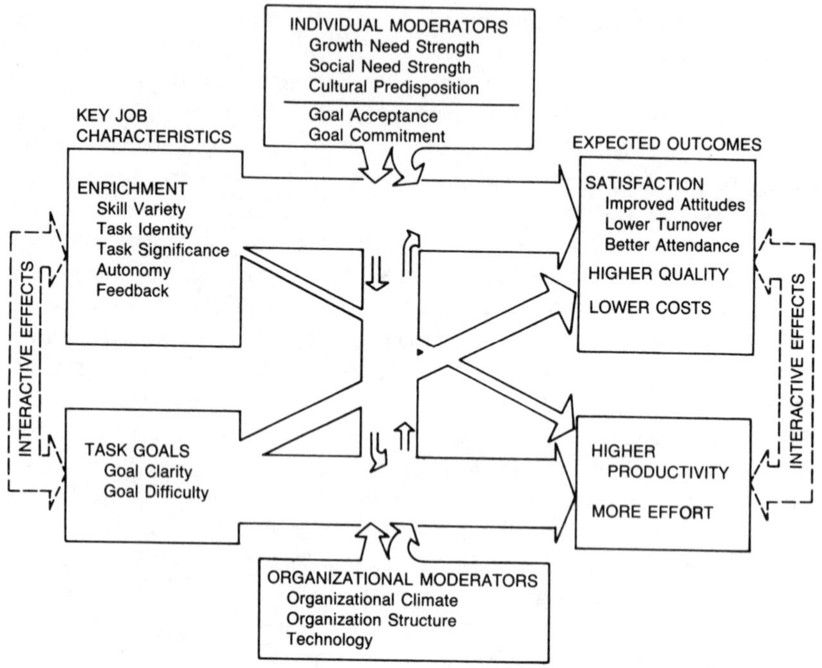

job enrichment has been more consistently related to work satisfaction than to performance. If the two are combined, simultaneous and sustained increases in both performance and satisfaction are the predicted result.

Although our understanding of the enrichment and goal-setting moderator variables is incomplete, it appears that both approaches are influenced by individual differences, especially growth need strength or need for achievement, and by certain organizational variables such as climate, structure, and technology. A convergent trend seems to be forming with both enrichment and goal setting being moderated by similar variables.

We have attempted to integrate goal setting and job enrichment into an overall model for job design. The research support for the model is limited in many areas, more persuasive in others. Thus, this article poses as many questions as it answers. Continued experimental research in both the field and the laboratory is needed to test the tentative relationships posed here. Although the integrated approach to job design introduces more complexity into designing work motivation systems, it also seems to offer the potential for improving both productivity and the quality of working life.

NOTES

1. Campbell, A., P.E. Converse, and W.L. Rodgers. *The Quality of American Life* (New York: Russell Sage Foundation, 1976).
2. Mills, T. "Human Resources—Why the New Concern?" *Harvard Business Review*, Vol. 53, No. 2 (1975), 120–134.
3. *Work in America*, Report of a special task force to the Secretary of Health, Education and Welfare (Cambridge, Mass.: MIT Press, 1973).
4. Scott, W.G. "Organization Theory: A Reassessment," *Academy of Management Journal*, Vol. 17 (1974), 242–254.
5. Umstot, D.D., C.H. Bell, Jr., and T.R. Mitchell. "Effects of Job Enrichment and Task Goals on Satisfaction and Productivity: Implications for Job Design," *Journal of Applied Psychology*, Vol. 61, No. 4 (1976), 379–394.
6. Hackman, J.R., and G.R. Oldham, "Motivation Through the Design of Work: Test of a Theory," *Organizational Behavior and Human Performance*, Vol. 16 (1976), 250–279.
7. Locke, E.A. "Toward a Theory of Task Motivation," *Organizational Behavior and Human Performance*, Vol. 3 (1968), 157–189.
8. Locke, E.A. "Personnel Attitudes and Motivation," in M.R. Rosenzweig, and L.W. Porter (Eds.), *Annual Review of Psychology* (Palo Alto, Calif.: Annual Reviews, Vol. 26, 1975).
9. Latham, G.P., and G.A. Yukl. "A Review of Research on the Application of Goal Setting in Organizations," *Academy of Management Journal*, Vol. 18 (1975), 824–845.
10. Steers, R.M., and L.W. Porter. "The Role of Task-Goal Attributes in Employee Performance," *Psychological Bulletin*, Vol. 81 (1974), 434–452.
11. Ivancevich, J.M. "Different Goal Setting Treatments and Their Effects on Performance and Satisfaction," *Academy of Management Journal*, Vol. 20 (1977), 406–419.
12. Drucker, P. *The Practice of Management* (New York: Harper, 1954).
13. McGregor, D. *The Human Side of Enterprise* (New York: McGraw-Hill, 1960).
14. Myers, M.S. *Every Employee and Manager* (New York: McGraw-Hill, 1970).
15. Steers, R.M. "Factors Affecting Job Attitudes in a Goal Setting Environment," *Academy of Management Journal*, Vol. 19, No. 1 (1976), 6–16.
16. Schuler, R.S., and J.S. Kim. "Interactive Effects of Participation in Decision Making, the Goal Setting Process and Feedback on Employee Satisfaction and Performance," *Academy of Management Proceedings* (1976), pp. 114–117.
17. Herzberg, F. "The Wise Old Turk," *Harvard Business Review*, Vol. 52, No. 1 (1974), 70–80.
18. Locke, E.A., N. Cartledge, and J. Koeppel, "Motivational Effects of Knowledge of Results: A Goal Setting Phenomena?" *Psychological Bulletin*, Vol. 70 (1968), 474–485.
19(a). Herzberg, F., B. Mausner, and B.B. Snyderman. *The Motivation to Work*, 2nd ed. (New York: John Wiley & Sons, 1959).
19(b). Kim, J.S., and W.C. Hamner. "Effect of Performance Feedback and Goal Setting on Productivity and Satisfaction in an Organizational Setting," *Journal of Applied Psychology*, Vol. 61 (1976), 48–57.
20. Erez, M. "Feedback: A Necessary Condition for the Goal Setting-Performance Relationship," *Journal of Applied Psychology*, Vol. 62, No. 5 (1977), 624–627.
21. Baird, L.S. "Feedback: A Determinant of the Relationship Between Performance and Satisfaction," *Academy of Management Proceedings*, 1976.

22. Greller, M.M., and D.M. Harold. "Sources of Feedback: A Preliminary Investigation," *Organizational Behavior and Human Performance*, Vol. 13 (1975), 244–256.

23. Oldham, G.R. "The Impact of Supervisory Characteristics on Goal Acceptance," *Academy of Management Journal*, Vol. 18, No. 3 (1975), 461–475.

24. Hall, D.T., and F.S. Hall. "The Relationship Between Good Performance, Success, Self-Image, and Involvement Under Different Organization Climates," *Journal of Vocational Behavior*, Vol. 9 (1976), 267–278.

25. Branson, P.A., and W.R. Peacock, Jr. *A Study of Job Satisfaction of Air Force Civilian Employees* (Masters thesis, Air Force Institute of Technology, Wright-Patterson AFB, OH, 1976).

26. Argyris, C. *Personality and Organization* (New York: Harper, 1957).

27. Argyris, C. "Personality and Organization Theory Revisited," *Administrative Science Quarterly*, Vol. 18, No. 2 (1973), 141–167.

28. Hollmann, R.W. "Supportive Organizational Climate and Managerial Assessment of MBO Effectiveness," *Academy of Management Journal*, Vol. 19 (1976), 560–576.

29. Owens, J. "The Values and Pitfalls of MBO," *Michigan Business Review*, July 1974, 11–14.

30. Raia, A.P. *Managing by Objectives* (Glenview, Ill.: Scott, Foresman, 1974).

* * * *

Administrators at the Bishop Clarkson Memorial Hospital began over a decade ago to study and revise the organizational and management approaches that affected employees. As part of their work, they incorporated goal setting into their evaluation process of professional and nonprofessional employees. Their materials, including special written instructions for management personnel and special forms, show how the performance evaluation process can be used for job enrichment and how administrative philosophy and management behavior determine the motivational components of the evaluation process.

30.
The Evaluation Process

Bishop Clarkson Memorial Hospital

We spend a great deal of time in people-management talking about the importance of looking at jobs, not only in terms of their activities, but in terms of the end results which they are designed to accomplish. We have seen the kinds of problems that can develop in an individual's performance when he does not fully understand what is expected of him. It is important to people, therefore, to have a clear understanding of what is expected of them, and, to a certain extent, this goes beyond simply knowing and understanding what the major end results are.

Individual needs for fulfillment, recognition or achievement within an organization typically require some kind of grading system to be established. In this way, we can recognize varying levels of performance and provide some type of reward for the individuals, based on their performance levels.

Additionally, and more importantly, the establishment of standards of performance allows us to continue to support the growth of subordinates by recognizing various performance levels and developing plans which will continually increase the individual's performance and, therefore, enhance his career development. There are essentially five reasons why people do not perform as desired. They are:

1. Not knowing what is expected of them.
2. Not knowing how to perform the tasks that are expected of them.
3. Not knowing why they are performing the task.
4. Not being physically able to perform the task.
5. Not wanting to perform the task.

Through the performance appraisal, we can tell an employee what is expected in terms of the end results to accomplish; the standards of performance related to those end results; and the allowable methods of operation. This will enable the

---

Modified with permission from Bishop Clarkson Memorial Hospital, "Appendix Number 552," *Performance Planning and Appraisal Process: Guidelines for the Appraiser* (Omaha).

employee to know where he is going and provide information to the manager and the employee which allows both to cover and/or reorganize and then take action regarding those areas where the subordinate is failing.

The administrative uses of performance appraisals all hinge on generally subjective ratings or rankings of performance and potential. These are management assessments and management decisions. But the other (even more critical) side to appraisals is the motivative side. How is this different from the process of rating performance for salary and promotion? The administrative side focuses on past performance while the motivative side focuses on future performance.

The motivative side involves determining where a person stands now, and (more importantly) determines the steps to take to meet current job requirements better . . . or prepare for future assignments. That is, the motivative performance appraisal session is a matter of working together on future performance, rather than on rating past performance. The motivative kind of appraisal aims for improved performance through planned actions. It includes communication to improve the person's understanding of the job and to give specific directions and time limits to the improvement process.

So, not only do we need to focus on the administrative function, we also need to focus on performance planning. To do this, we need the use of performance ratings in joint planning sessions to attain these results:

1. Find out how your employees view their own performance. How do they view what the job is and what it requires? Do they have a realistic view of where they stand? One of the prime reasons for performance being below par is that the person has the wrong understanding of what he should be achieving.
2. Next, we must help each employee to a better understanding of what is expected of him. Once he knows what is expected, he becomes his own best critic on a day-to-day continuing basis.
3. Together, you should come to an agreement on expected results and time limits for improved performance. It is essential that expected results be the employee's and not only yours . . . that they flow from an understanding of what is required and not just from the manager's demand.

The biggest factor in achieving these results is the approach that you take. Should you be a critic or a counselor? It is important that you place proper emphasis on developing and understanding performance standards for the coming year and not just on the absolute rating itself. You, as appraiser, should attempt to divorce yourself from the role of rater/critic and adopt the role of counselor, coach, and instructor.

As a counselor, you will want to keep in mind the following information regarding human reactions during sessions:

- criticism and defensiveness . . . Research has shown that criticism by the appraiser generally produces a defensive reaction by the subordinate. The result? A negative effect on future performance. So even though criticism may be necessary, overly done, it can set up blocks for getting at the real issues and motivating people toward improved performance. Frequent criticism constitutes so strong a threat to a person's ego and self-esteem that it disrupts rather than improves subsequent performance.
- participation . . . Employees with a high participation level in the planning sessions generally react more favorably than those with a low participating level, unless they are employees who have traditionally been accustomed to low participation in their daily relationships with their managers/supervisors.
- establishing expected results . . . How important is this part of the process? Far superior results are obtained when the appraiser and the employee together set specific results to be achieved, rather than merely discussing needed improvements. The process of getting a person to set his own targets, willingly and realistically, becomes a continuing part of the working relationship between the employee and the appraiser.
- coaching . . . Coaching should be day-to-day and not a once-a-year activity:
  a. People seem to accept suggestions for improved performance if they are given in a less concentrated form rather than from comprehensive sessions. Isolated criticisms and suggestions are a lot easier to take than the massive combination of months of shortcomings.
  b. Some appraisers have a tendency to save items and incidents where improvement is needed in order to have enough material to conduct a comprehensive discussion of performance at a review.
  c. Necessary criticism should be made as soon as the deficiency is noted and not at the time of a formal performance appraisal.

The purpose of this program, then, is to give you a planned approach to handling the "Performance Planning and Appraisal Session" so that you and your employees will gain the most from it and be able to take constructive steps toward improving performance.

ESTABLISHING STANDARDS

There are certain key points to keep in mind when developing measurements:

1. In developing measures, efforts should be made to identify tangible indicators so that the subjectivity is limited and attention is focused appropriately.
2. The more subjective the measures, the more multiple indicators of evaluations should be used.

170   SELF-ACTUALIZATION FOR NURSES

3. Measures should relate to specific accountabilities of a position and the emphasis (priority) dictated by the operating environment. The key to sound management is the question . . . "Will these measurements show the degree to which required end results have been produced?"
4. If an evaluation by another party is necessary to measure achievement, list in advance who will perform the evaluation and on what basis.
5. Standards should be set so that most of your employees would be expected to achieve the standard with a normal amount of effort. *This does not imply "averaging," but rather a realistic approach to goal setting. A standard must be achievable; success is an important component in self-esteem.*
6. Standards should cover specific accountabilities of the position as defined in the job description, *but the job description should be flexible enough to allow individualized goal setting as part of the evaluation.*
7. Management functions of planning, organizing, leading, and controlling (POLC), operational functions, like expense, revenue, and productivity, as well as technical functions inherent to the position, should be covered by standards.
8. Standards should be no more extensive nor detailed than necessary to satisfy the appraiser's need to evaluate and control and the subordinate's need for recognition.

Some examples of potential performance measurements are:

1. Filing, manual and administrative procedures of office activity are kept current so that there are no more than three variances a year to accepted procedure.
2. Daily mail is distributed within one hour of receipt.
3. Medications are given to the patient within one hour of the order 100% of the time.
4. Regulatory requirements (JCAH, OSHA, etc.) are adhered to 100% of the time.
5. Supply of office inventory items are maintained so that they do not fall below the minimum department standard more than three times per year.
6. Exceptions to hospital policy/departmental regulations occur no more than three times per year.

POSITION ANALYSIS

There is group involvement in the development of each position description. For example, the Nursing Management Conference prepared the following description of the RN team leader position.

Summary Statement

Responsible for providing and supervising total and comprehensive nursing care to an assigned group of patients on a nursing unit. This will be accomplished by: planning, organizing, leading, and controlling the work of the personnel assigned to her/his team, and by utilizing the nursing process to document an individualized plan of nursing care for each patient which is in correlation with the medical plan of care.

Typical Duties and Responsibilities

1. Administers safe, effective, timely, and accurate patient care in accordance with established policies and procedures.
2. Ensures that written records of all patients on her/his team accurately reflect each patient's condition, progress, education, and treatment in conjunction with the individualized patient care plan.
3. Assesses patients' needs through both direct and indirect interaction with the patient and/or family to formulate, implement, and document a plan of care.
4. Administers medications (including I.V. therapy) skillfully, safely, and timely in accordance with established policy and procedure.
5. Plans, prioritizes, supervises, and evaluates nursing care given by team members.
6. Teaches, guides, motivates, counsels, corrects, and commends team members. Formally evaluates and documents the performance of subordinates as assigned by the Head Nurse/Assistant Head Nurse.
7. Maintains close communication with the Head Nurse/Assistant Head Nurse and team members in all matters relating to patient care. Communicates with the medical staff and other departments, as necessary, in carrying out the plan of care.
8. Communicates, supports, and enforces hospital policies and division policies and procedures to team members and to patients and visitors as necessary.
9. Supports hospital Philosophy and Objectives; follows proper chain of command when problem-solving is necessary.
10. Provides patient teaching by assessing and evaluating patient needs and implementing a teaching plan.
11. Conducts patient-centered team conferences, provides for ongoing unit staff education, and assists new personnel, as delegated, in the orientation process.
12. Is readily available to patients, family, physicians, and team members for consultation and assistance.

13. Utilizes all available resources efficiently and supports supply system control.
14. Promotes good public and intrahospital relations.
15. Performs other functions as delegated by the Head Nurse/Assistant Head Nurse.
16. Maintains confidentiality of all matters pertaining to patient care.
17. Attends floor meetings when scheduled and keeps informed by reading postings on bulletin boards which are related to Hospital, Division, or Nursing Unit specialty policies, procedures, or other pertinent information.

Education, Training, and Experience

1. Minimum required for entry into the position:
   A. Formal education or equivalent: (Include any licensure or registration requirements)

   Graduate of an accredited school of professional nursing. Currently licensed as a Professional Registered Nurse in the State of Nebraska.

   B. Previous experience required: (Actual work experience in this or other organizations)

   Experience or education which has provided opportunities to refine competencies in clinical nursing practice.
   PROMOTES FROM: R.N. Entry Level
   PROMOTES TO: Head Nurse, Assistant Head Nurse/ Patient Care Coordinator

2. Position training: (Minimum training . . . type and length . . . for satisfactory performance after entry into position)

   A probationary period of 90 days is required during which time the employee will satisfactorily complete the formal orientation program. The R.N. Team Leader will complete the mandatory learning modules for the position within the first two weeks of employment. The R.N. Team Leader will receive further orientation by individual unit nursing staff regarding the performance of additional skills and nursing duties.

3. Assignment, review and approval of work: (Degree of supervision received)

   The duties of the R.N. Team Leader are assigned, reviewed, and approved through supervision by the Head Nurse/Assistant Head Nurse. The R.N. Team Leader supports the management of the nursing unit and reports exceptions to the Head Nurse.

4. Physical skills/equipment operation:

   The R.N. Team Leader displays and demonstrates the ability and knowledge of appropriate scientific principles utilized in performing those nursing skills associated with the operation of specific equipment needed to carry out nursing procedures efficiently, accurately, and safely.

5. Relations with others:
   A. Within the hospital staff: (Outside own department)

   An R.N. Team Leader will have contact with all of the diagnostic, therapeutic, and supportive services within the hospital to aid in the coordination of treatments or maintenance of planned care. The R.N. Team Leader maintains confidentiality in regard to the patient's medical record.

   B. Outside the hospital staff:

   Fosters positive interpersonal relations in dealing with the patient's family and/or friends.

   Membership and participation in professional organizations is encouraged.

6. Work direction of others:

   Registered Nurse
   Nursing Student
   Private Duty Nurses
   L.P.N.
   Nursing Assistant
   Unit Clerk

7. Performance measurement:

   Performance is measured based upon the R.N. Team Leader's ability to perform accurately and efficiently the required skills defined as listed in the position analysis and as well as according to previously determined performance standards.

8. Dimensions:
   A. Displays ability to make decisions based on the logical thinking process.
   B. Demonstrates leadership ability.
   C. Shares ideas and information by communicating effectively.
   D. Serves as a role model for the team members through her/his example of consistent professional behavior.
   E. Is consistent and fair with all members of her/his team.
   F. Creates and readily accepts new ideas which will improve patient care.
   G. Possesses a working knowledge of team nursing.
   H. Possesses knowledge and skill in human relations.
   I. Demonstrates the ability to teach others.
   J. Demonstrates ability to utilize computer system.
   K. Attends scheduled CPR classes.
   L. All R.N.'s are required to pass medications at B.C.M.H. and in order to qualify for medication administration, the R.N. must:
      1. Successfully pass the Pharmacology Pre-test offered at B.C.M.H. within two weeks of starting date.
      2. Receive formal orientation to Clarkson's medication policies and procedures.

9. Additional information:
   A. The R.N. Team Leader demonstrates self-control and emotional stability in a variety of demanding situations. She/he must be interested in helping people and have a sincere desire to constantly improve nursing knowledge and skills.
   B. Because of the variety of patient diagnoses the R.N. may come in contact with, she/he is potentially subject to injury or infection which could occur due to improper use of equipment, body mechanics, or improper application of infection control policies and procedures.
   C. Based on the Division Policy, may be assigned to another unit or shift and must be able to work every other weekend or the equivalent. May be called for duty in the event of an emergency or disaster.

Part V: A Perfect Tool: Evaluation   175

PERFORMANCE EVALUATION

Employees will receive a performance evaluation at the completion of six (6) months, and twelve (12) months thereafter, for each position that the employee has held. The standards are as follows:

1. The responsibilities and duties of each position are defined in a job description and communicated to the employee by the manager.
2. Standards of performance are established by the manager for each position and agreed upon by the employee.
3. The appraisal session is conducted by the manager with the incumbent to determine progress against standards and areas of improvement to be concentrated upon during the next period.
4. The results of the session, including deficiencies noted, improvement plans and new standards, are to be documented in writing and signed by the incumbent and the manager for inclusion in the employee's personnel file.
5. The manager or supervisor is accountable for conducting the interview and completing the performance appraisal form (Exhibit 30–1).

Exhibit 30–1 Nursing Service Division Employee Progress Review: R.N. Position

NURSING SERVICE DIVISION Non-Exempt Employee Progress Review
R.N. Position
Bishop Clarkson Memorial Hospital
Omaha, Nebraska

Employee's Name:	Date of Employment:	Date Issued:
Department Name:	Date Employed in Position:	Date Due:
Supervisor's Name:	Period Covered by Review: to	Date Returned:

OBJECTIVES:

TO HELP THE SUPERVISOR OBSERVE AND EVALUATE THE VARIOUS ASPECTS OF EMPLOYEE PERFORMANCE; AND,

Exhibit 30–1 continued

TO HELP THE SUPERVISOR AND EMPLOYEE FOCUS ON OBJECTIVES THAT WILL HELP TO INCREASE THE EMPLOYEE'S LEVEL OF PERFORMANCE.

Please refer to Personnel Policy #119, Personnel Procedure #304 and Appendices #530 and #552 for guidance in the review process.

RATING GUIDELINES:

BELOW STANDARD
The employee is not meeting standards of the position. This may constitute a performance problem or may be an employee who is new to the organization or position.

MEETS STANDARD
The employee is meeting the standards and duties of the position. The employee clearly performs all that is normally expected of the position.

EXCEEDS STANDARD
The employee is exceeding the agreed-upon standards of the position and is clearly achieving more than would normally be expected of the position.

SECTION B: Standards for this section are to be established for each individual position by the accountable manager. Additional pages may be added if necessary.

DIRECT PATIENT CARE

DOCUMENTED STANDARD:
Consistently administers safe, effective, timely and accurate patient care in accordance with established policies and procedures. Able to complete patient care activities as described in the job description.
☐ BELOW STANDARD
☐ MEETS STANDARD
☐ EXCEEDS STANDARD

COMMENTS

DOCUMENTATION

DOCUMENTED STANDARD:
Insures that written records on all assigned patients accurately reflect each patient's condition, progress, education, and treatment.
☐ BELOW STANDARD
☐ MEETS STANDARD
☐ EXCEEDS STANDARD

COMMENTS

NURSING CARE PLANNING

DOCUMENTED STANDARD:
Develops, maintains and documents individual nursing care plans on assigned patients. Care plans include nursing interview, assessments, approaches, long and short term goals and teaching plans in correlation with medical plan of care.
☐ BELOW STANDARD
☐ MEETS STANDARD
☐ EXCEEDS STANDARD

COMMENTS

Exhibit 30-1 continued

	DOCUMENTED STANDARD:	
MEDICATION ADMINISTRATION	Administers medications (including I.V. therapy) skillfully, safely, and timely in accordance with established policy and procedure.	☐ BELOW STANDARD ☐ MEETS STANDARD ☐ EXCEEDS STANDARD
	COMMENTS	

DOCUMENTED STANDARD:	
	☐ BELOW STANDARD ☐ MEETS STANDARD ☐ EXCEEDS STANDARD
COMMENTS	

DOCUMENTED STANDARD:	
	☐ BELOW STANDARD ☐ MEETS STANDARD ☐ EXCEEDS STANDARD
COMMENTS	

DOCUMENTED STANDARD:	
	☐ BELOW STANDARD ☐ MEETS STANDARD ☐ EXCEEDS STANDARD
COMMENTS	

DOCUMENTED STANDARD:	
	☐ BELOW STANDARD ☐ MEETS STANDARD ☐ EXCEEDS STANDARD
COMMENTS	

Exhibit 30–1 continued

SECTION C: PROGRESS NOTES

The performance standards have been agreed upon for the next review period.

Appraiser Signature:	Date:	Incumbent Signature:	Date:
Appraiser Signature:	Date:	Incumbent Signature:	Date:
Appraiser Signature:	Date:	Incumbent Signature:	Date:
Appraiser Signature:	Date:	Incumbent Signature:	Date:

*   *   *   *

The Bishop Clarkson Memorial Hospital performance evaluation program clearly demonstrates a participative management philosophy. It meets the vertical loading principles of sharing control of evaluation between supervisor and nurse, increasing accountability for meeting mutually set goals, and providing feedback on goal achievement. As is clear from these documents, this hospital has a team nursing approach to delivery of care. Such an approach is more difficult to incorporate into an adhocracy than the primary nursing approach. The forms, however, can easily be adapted for a nurse in a primary nurse role.

Peer evaluation adds another element of expertise to performance appraisal. The professional nurse's performance is evaluated by a co-worker who shares day-to-day activities, background, and expectations. Often the nurse's administrative supervisor and/or professional superior (for example, clinical specialist) are also on the peer evaluation team, giving the evaluee different perspectives of work. O'Loughlin and Kaulbach describe a peer review appraisal process used by an all-RN staff of primary nurses. There is a great need for trust among peers if peer evaluation is to be a success. This trust is usually built up only over a long period of working together. Peer review also requires extensive, clear criteria for evaluation.

31.
Peer Review: A Perspective for Performance Appraisal

Elayne Lowe O'Loughlin and Dolores Kaulbach

How do you measure professional accountability objectively, reliably, and accurately? We faced this problem when we implemented primary nursing on a new 19-bed neurosurgical unit with an all-professional nursing staff. It was important for us to evaluate each nurse's delivery of quality nursing care according to established criteria; thus, we had to develop a mechanism for weighing work performance.

The evaluation of work performance is traditionally the responsibility of nurse managers. However, inherent in most performance appraisals is the belief by those being evaluated that the appraisal process is subjective and not reflective of actual work performance. In an effort to reduce subjectivity in our appraisals, the nursing staff agreed to institute a system of peer review based on a mutually agreed-upon set of standards.

Peer review can be defined as a process by which practitioners of the same rank, profession, or setting critically appraise each other's work performance against established standards. Title XVIII, Public Law 92-603 states that health care professions must institute measures to ensure quality patient care.[1] This law mandates peer review for physicians. Peer review is new to the nursing profession and there is little information in the nursing literature on its use.

Passos looks on peer review as the hallmark of professionalism and the mechanism by which the nursing profession would be held accountable to society.[2] Ramphael suggests that it should be the method nurses use to regulate their practice if they hope to maintain its standards.[3] Although other professions have been using peer review for some time, the nursing profession is only now slowly moving to develop peer review standards and conduct reviews.

Modified with permission from Elayne Lowe O'Loughlin and Dolores Kaulbach, "Peer Review: A Perspective for Performance Appraisal," *Journal of Nursing Administration* 11, no. 9 (1981): 22–27.

Part V: A Perfect Tool: Evaluation   181

Primary nursing lends itself particularly well to peer review, since each primary nurse is held responsible and accountable for all of the care given to a specific number of assigned patients. Under a primary nursing care delivery system it becomes possible to evaluate the total range of the nurse's professional skills from the admission of patients to discharge teaching and follow-up. Primary nursing is listed as a structural prerequisite in the model for nursing professional review developed by Hegyvary and Haussmann.[4]

Thus, to provide for fair, reliable performance appraisal on our primary nursing unit, our objective was to institute a peer review process that would:

1. Provide a feedback mechanism for sharing ideas and giving constructive criticism on a peer level
2. Identify areas for growth and development
3. Provide increased job satisfaction through recognition by peers
4. Increase personal and professional growth
5. Identify behavior not in compliance with standards, and define expectations for correcting deficiencies.

DEVELOPING THE APPRAISAL TOOLS

In developing standards and expectations for the primary nurse, it is important that the appraisal tools provide information that will identify:

1. Technical competency
2. Whether the patient care outcomes reflect the nurse's technical competency
3. What the professional nurse does, as primary nurse, that is unique
4. Superior work worthy of recognition and commendation
5. Areas for growth and development.

Due to their lack of experience developing appraisal tools, the nursing staff agreed to try whatever tools we could find to implement the peer review process. However, finding existing appraisal tools that could help us assess these five areas was difficult. The first tools used by the staff, while effective in helping assess technical competency, were inadequate for assessing professional skills. The thrust of each tool revision was to shift the focus from technical to professional skills.

The nursing staff recognized a need for defined standards because interpretations of quality care differ. We decided to use the ANA standards for neurological and neurosurgical nursing practice[5] and to incorporate Dorothea Orem's framework for nursing practice,[6] in the development of a "Professional Skills Appraisal Tool" for measuring and recording data about performance. This approach enabled us to assess both the technical competency of the nurse and her ability to use the nursing model framework.

The Professional Skills Appraisal Tool (Exhibit 31–1) assesses various behaviors based on minimum standards. The measurement tool aids the peers in evaluating how each standard is met and the rationale for the nursing decisions made.

Profiles for assessment are:

1. Technical competence
2. Communication skills
3. Organizational skills
4. Originality
5. Judgment
6. Assertiveness/forcefulness
7. Achievement
8. Human relationship skills.

Guidelines (Exhibit 31–2) are provided to assist reviewers in ranking the nurse in each area.

To assist the reviewers in completing their assessments, we also developed a patient interview tool which focuses on the outcome of the use of the nursing process and not on the nurse herself. We were interested in the nurse's intervening and assisting actions to improve, maintain, and preserve the patient's health status and in her implementation of discharge plans.

The patient interview assesses the nurse's ability to identify the patient's support system, his emotional status, and his physical abilities. The interviewer questions the patient about specific problems and assesses how the patient and/or significant others deal with them.

In addition, we developed guidelines to assist the peers who review patient records, kardexes, and care plans. Both the patient interview tool and the guidelines aid the review panel in completing the Professional Skills Appraisal Tool.

CONDUCTING THE PEER REVIEW

The peer review process involves five stages:

1. Review of the charts, kardex, and care plans of patients cared for by the nurse being reviewed
2. Interview of these patients
3. Observation of the nurse
4. Summary of findings by the review group
5. Presentation of findings and recommendations to the peer.

Exhibit 31-1 Professional Skills Appraisal Tool

Items in heavy type represent profiles for assessment and minimum standards. Numbered items beneath each profile and minimum standard are the outcomes to be measured by observations and chart audit. The actual appraisal tool also includes space in which the reviewers rank the nurse in each area and provide a rationale for each ranking.

I. TECHNICAL COMPETENCE

a. Demonstrates the ability to utilize the nursing process to identify patient problems as she/he develops and directs the plan for nursing care to assigned patients/clients.

b. Demonstrates the ability to utilize a patient-centered approach in planning, implementing, and evaluating care given to assigned patients.

1. Audit of chart for documentation of:
   a. Data collection.
   b. Development of patient care plans.
   c. Implementation of care plans.
   d. Evaluation of care given.
   e. Inclusion of diagnostic procedures and tests, preparation for surgery, discharge preparation, rehabilitation, etc., in patient/family teaching plan.

2. Evidence that a continuous and therapeutic relationship is established with the patient/family and that the nurse is involved with them throughout the hospitalization.

3. Evidence that there is documentation of assessments of patient/family through admission interview, observations, and physical examination to determine agency, self-care deficits, and nursing assistance required in doing for, teaching, guiding, supporting, providing a developmental environment, and referral.

4. Evidence that the nurse gives care to the patient.

5. Evidence that the nurse performs procedures according to guidelines in the nursing procedure manual.

6. Evidence that positive patient care outcomes identified from audit criteria reflect nursing care actions.

7. Evidence that patient/family are assisted in developing long- and short-term goals, are involved in patient care conferences where appropriate, and are prepared for discharge.

8. Evidence that the nurse supports the patient's rights to make decisions affecting his/her care and assures that the patient/family understands health care options.

9. Evidence given that the patient/family is able to identify the nurse as primary care giver.

Exhibit 31-1 continued

c. **Demonstrates the ability to accept responsibility and be held accountable for the care given to assigned patients.**

Evidence is given that the nurse:

1. Plans safe, economical, and efficient nursing care that meets the standards of ANA and AANN.
2. Communicates significant changes in her patient to the N.C. and the physician.
3. Keeps nursing care plans current and plans for improvement in nursing care via conferences and inservice education.

II. **COMMUNICATION SKILLS**

a. **Demonstrates the ability to communicate and coordinate the nursing care plan.**

Evidence is given that:

1. Information is made available to other members of the nursing staff about assigned patients and their illnesses.
2. The nurse reports observations of physical and emotional reactions to treatments and medications and the implications of such reactions to the physician. The implications of her observations are documented in the care plan and in the patient's chart.

III. **ORGANIZATIONAL SKILLS**

a. **Demonstrates the ability to organize workload and to set priorities in patient-care-related activities.**

Evidence is given that the nurse:

1. Directs and coordinates activities for assigned patients in a logical and systematic way.
2. Sets priorities in planning and implementing patient care activities.

b. **Demonstrates the ability to use time effectively.**

Evidence is given that the nurse:

1. Completes assignments in an organized manner.
2. Communicates pertinent information regarding plans and progress of assigned patients to assure adequate follow-up.
3. Obtains all pertinent information before proceeding to solve patient-care-related problems.

IV. **ORIGINALITY**

a. **Demonstrates the ability to utilize creativity, imagination, and ingenuity in the role of primary nurse.**

Evidence is given that the nurse:

1. Is resourceful in developing care plans which utilize a better way of doing or accomplishing a task.

Part V: A Perfect Tool: Evaluation 185

3. Information on plans and goals for patient is on a level that all can understand and carry out in her absence.
4. The plan of care is communicated to the kardex and the implementation of the care plan is documented in the patient's chart.
5. The nurse can express herself clearly, listen effectively, and communicate appropriate information.
6. Appropriate referrals are made and follow-ups done.
7. Multidisciplinary conferences are held when appropriate.
8. The nurse establishes rapport with patient/family through verbal communication.

b. **Demonstrates ability to coordinate and collaborate with other members of the health team in patient care planning.**

Evidence is given that the nurse:

1. Attends physicians' and interdisciplinary rounds, communicates with her patient's physician, and, when possible, is present when the physician sees the patient.
2. Refers appropriate problems to the dietitian, social worker, O.T., R.T., P.T., etc.
3. Communicates and coordinates the patient's activities with other members of the health team, giving suggestions, sharing information, comparing observations, and correcting health care practices that interfere with goals for health care delivery.

2. During team conferences, presents practical programs that could be used to improve patient care.
3. Contributes original ideas that benefit the goals of the patient's hospitalization plan.
4. Develops ideas presented by others into a workable plan for patient care.
5. Suggests unit projects, e.g., research designed to identify ways to improve patient care or to save cost.
6. Has a wealth of knowledge that she readily shares with the group, either on patient care or unit activities.
7. Is constantly seeking new ideas on how to provide the best care to the patient, and uses ideas presented at workshops or in articles to design new care plans.

V. **JUDGMENT**

a. **Demonstrates the ability to analyze problems and make sound judgments based on logical thinking.**

Evidence is given that the nurse:

1. Interprets and adheres to lines of authority, and uses proper channels for communication.
2. Uses resources adequately and appropriately.
3. Coordinates with other nurses and the nursing coordinator to maintain coverage of patients during absences from unit.

Exhibit 31-1 continued

4. Is able to set priorities in planning patient care, and can distinguish between the significant and the insignificant, the important and the unimportant.

5. Can provide rationale for decisions in both written and verbal communications.

6. Is able to set limits, knows limitations, and knows own strengths and weaknesses.

7. Can see long-range implications and act on them to avoid problems; plans patient care accordingly; is able to plan for future needs of the patient.

8. In administration of medications and treatments, uses good judgment to alter them within the limits of sound professional judgments based on the patient's physical and emotional needs. Knows why medications or treatment are given, what they are to do, how long before results, what results will look like, and adverse effects, if any.

9. Does ongoing assessments and evaluations of nursing acts, and revises care plans accordingly to reflect changes.

10. Questions physicians when orders are unclear, refuses to carry out orders if they are against her judgment or standard of care.

11. Requests and accepts constructive criticism regarding nursing judgments from appropriate resources.

VII. ACHIEVEMENT

a. **Demonstrates the ability to complete projects assigned without being prompted to do so.**

Evidence is given that the nurse:

1. Is resourceful because she/he accepts challenging topics or projects to work on that benefit the unit or patient care.

2. Is thorough when completing assignments, assessments on patients, nursing care plans, discharge teaching, and follow-ups.

3. Is thorough when completing projects assigned to the best of her/his ability; feels pride in paying attention to detail.

4. Is committed to unit objectives and his/her part in assigned objective; has objective completed by stated deadline without prompting from others.

5. Is motivated for own professional growth.

6. Maintains sense of personal satisfaction by keeping skills current through continuing education.

7. Meets or exceeds written standards for patient care.

VIII. HUMAN RELATIONS

a. **Demonstrates the ability to work well with peers, other members of health team, the patient and his family.**

Part V: A Perfect Tool: Evaluation   187

12. Suggests constructive changes in the delivery of care evidenced by updated written care plans and consultation from appropriate sources.

VI. ASSERTIVENESS/FORCEFULNESS

a. **Ability to influence the decisions of others through own assertiveness.**

Evidence is provided that the nurse:

1. Is a self-motivated, self-confident, poised, mature, dynamic personality; likes what she is doing, does it enthusiastically; has infectious energy.
2. Sees something to do and does it without being told; does not have to be reminded to complete a task.
3. Is assertive, open, honest, and approachable.
4. Stands by a decision if challenged, when convinced it is a right one. However, is able to accept constructive criticism.
5. Participates actively in staff meetings, team conferences—is not afraid to voice opinions.
6. Asserts self when unacceptable practices affect patient care or professional standards, by reporting and recording in a constructive manner.
7. Is knowledgeable about patients assigned, and can speak authoritatively about plan of care for patients.
8. Provides opportunities for the patient/family to set goals; reinforces positive behavior.

Evidence is given that the nurse:

1. Is able to promote harmonious working relationships within the unit.
2. Is able to use proper channels for communication.
3. Deals with conflicts on a one-to-one basis.
4. Does not take personal problems to work and does not relay them so that they affect the work of others, the functioning of the unit, or patient care.
5. Knows how to channel anger appropriately.
6. Is able to take constructive criticism in good spirit; benefits from mistakes.
7. Has optimistic outlook on life; good team spirit.
8. Upholds policies of the institution.
9. Is not selfish with ideas—shares ideas with others.
10. Is fair in dealings with others.
11. Recognizes feelings of others, gives credit when due.
12. Respects others' opinions, judgments, or abilities.
13. Is readily accepted by peers, and works well with others.
14. Recognizes and shows concern for what is right in the solution of problems. Is loyal, with professional integrity.

Exhibit 31–2 Ranking Guidelines for Use with Professional Skills Appraisal Tool

---

Rank each nurse according to instructions listed below. Each profile should be assessed and compared with the expected standards for each to come up with a score. The score given should reflect the degree to which the nurse met the minimum standard for the profile under assessment. Make sure you give a rationale for rank, identifying areas for growth as well as areas in which peer excelled. Recommendations should be given in constructive manner.

RANK 1: Primary nurse does not have the ability or fails to meet *any* of the listed expectations required to meet the minimum standards for profile being assessed.

RANK 2: Primary nurse has some ability to function in the role of primary nurse, but fails to meet some of the listed expectations required to meet the minimum standards for profile being assessed.

RANK 3: Primary nurse has the ability to function as a primary nurse, meets the minimum standards by carrying out many of the expected behaviors of the profile being assessed, but does not consistently excel in meeting them.

RANK 4: Primary nurse shows ability to function as a primary nurse by *demonstrating on a consistent basis* that she/he can meet all minimum standards by carrying out the expected behaviors required to meet the minimum standard. This nurse also demonstrates abilities not possessed by nurse in Rank 3.

RANK 5: Primary nurse shows *outstanding* ability to function as a primary nurse by demonstrating consistently that she/he possesses abilities easily identified by peers as more superior than peers. This person meets *all* the minimum standards and demonstrates all the behaviors of the profile being assessed. This person is an expert clinician, articulate, assertive, innovative, meticulous, role model, whose judgment is unquestionable, is respected by her peers, the doctors and other members of the health team. The person fits the role of the professional nurse in all his/her endeavors.

The review team consists of three primary nurses, one from the district of the peer being reviewed, the other two from different districts. *On some nursing staffs, the three-person review team includes one person from a higher position, for example, a clinical specialist or management person.*

The staff consists of 18 registered nurses who all function as primary nurses. Two reviews are scheduled each month, with each nurse being reviewed at least once per year.

The nurse to be reviewed is told in advance the date of her review but she is not told who her appraisers will be. The appraisers are also chosen at the same time, allowing for observation of the nurse prior to the date of the review.

On the day of the review, two appraisers review the charts, kardex, and care plans, using the guidelines to assess whether they meet the minimum standards listed on the Professional Skills Appraisal Tool.

Part V: A Perfect Tool: Evaluation 189

A third appraiser interviews the patient and/or significant other using the patient interview tool. Over a period of time prior to the review date this person also serves as the observer, following the nurse around and assessing her performance. The reviewer is usually a peer from the same district, since she has a better opportunity of observing the nurse over time. She bases her observations and comments on the minimum standards listed on the Professional Skills Appraisal Tool, and records them on a separate form.

After all reviews are completed, the three reviewers meet to discuss their findings. They complete the Professional Skills Appraisal Tool based on all of the information they have gathered. The final score is based on the nurse's ability to meet the minimum standards described on the appraisal tool. The reviewers concur on the recommendations for their peer. They give the results to their peer within 24 hours, with one reviewer acting as spokesperson for the group. The nurse is given a copy of the completed skills appraisal tool. The nursing coordinator, the assistant nursing coordinator, or the staff development instructor may be invited to sit in on the summary conference as consultants to the peer group, but this is optional. The nurse also usually does a self-evaluation, using the Professional Skills Appraisal Tool, and this information is presented to the review group and discussed in the conference.

The results of the peer review are then given to the nursing coordinator who reviews them with the nurse. Together they develop a plan of action for correcting deficiencies and establish a deadline. The deadline is set according to the seriousness of the identified deficiencies. All information from the appraisal, including commendations given, is kept in the nurse's file and used for the annual evaluation that is required by the hospital personnel department. Any follow-up to ensure compliance with the minimum standards is the responsibility of the nursing coordinator. Nurses who consistently get poor peer appraisals and fail to meet minimum standards by the set deadline are relieved of the primary nurse role for six months. If their performance does not improve within these six months, they are asked to resign. *Clearly, the emphasis of this evaluation is strongly "corrective."*

OVERCOMING PROBLEMS

When the subject of instituting a peer review mechanism for performance appraisal came up, the staff's reaction varied from interest to indifference. Some considered it necessary, while others found it threatening. Once we developed the Professional Skills Appraisal Tool, we presented it to all staff for critique and only minor revisions were suggested. Any suggestions given were incorporated into the final tool. All staff accepted the final tool. We found that the staff members working on the unit the longest period of time were more eager and interested to try this form of evaluation than were the newer staff members.

Many obstacles arose during the early days of planning when numerous existing tools were tried and discarded by us. The nursing staff either had difficulty using the tools or the nursing coordinator was not getting the information she required as to the nurse's professional ability to provide quality care. The constant change in tools was difficult and confusing. However, a lot of the difficulty was eliminated after the standards were presented and the actual behaviors expected of each nurse were understood.

Initially, the nurses did not feel qualified to appraise each other and left appraisal to the nursing coordinator, who was at that time included on the review team. However, the patient interview part of the process became ineffective because many patients were hesitant to give the nursing coordinator feedback on their assigned primary nurse. It was difficult to determine whether the patient felt threatened for himself or the nurse. Also, it was apparent that patients rated the nurse according to their own ideas of what a nurse should be, rather than by the care they received. The review was therefore subjective in spite of our efforts, and open to many interpretations.

In an effort to get accurate information, we developed more specific patient interview questions to shift the focus to *actions* of the nurse, and not the nurse herself. Also, removing the nursing coordinator from the review team and having only staff nurses do the review made a big difference. The patients felt freer to talk about their care.

Initially, a requirement for serving as a peer reviewer was three months' experience working on the unit. However, we found that three months was insufficient time for the nurse to feel comfortable reviewing her peer's performance. The time requirement was extended to a year of experience working on the unit.

Peer review is still not fully accepted by all staff members. The initial novelty of doing something that no one else at the hospital is doing wears off, resulting in some ebbing of enthusiasm. Some feel that peer review is an added burden, a chore that is being inflicted on them, or something they are not paid to do. Although the process gives an objective appraisal of how their peers see them, they are still hesitant about accepting it as the wave of the future.

PROGRAM EVALUATION

The current Professional Skills Appraisal Tool has been in use for three years. All staff members who have been on the unit for at least a year have used the tool or had it used to evaluate them. The peer review system is outlined for each new recruit so there is no surprise when she comes to work in the unit. *The method of evaluation is peer review*. The one-year waiting period between employment on the unit and participation in peer review has lessened the resistance of new personnel who may feel threatened by the process.

Initially, the appraisal process took an eight-hour day to complete. However, with education and repeated use of the tool, the staff have narrowed the time it takes to complete the review to three hours, except, of course, for observation of the nurse, which occurs over time prior to the review date. We have found that, in situations where staffing is compromised, the nursing staff are very reluctant to allot the time to do peer review.

Patients have benefited from the peer review process. An analysis of discharge summaries gives an objective view of the patient's discharge status in relation to the desired patient care outcomes. To date, no patient has been readmitted with complications resulting from nursing-care-related deficiencies.

Among the staff nurses, a feeling of competitiveness has prompted behavioral changes that result from peer pressure to give the best care they can. Sensitivity to the patients has increased, making the nurses more acutely aware of patients' rights and feelings, the rationale for certain treatments, and the cost of these treatments to the patient.

Some of the reviewers noted that they sometimes rated the nurse higher than she deserves. We have observed this situation in some of the conferences we sat in on. To minimize the difficulty in obtaining honest appraisals, we recently introduced a change whereby the results are given to the nurse by the nursing coordinator rather than by her peers, and the reviewers remain anonymous to the nurse. This change is still too new to evaluate, *although it is known that an approach of anonymity has been found useful by other nursing staffs. Dickson wrote of the practice at the University of Minnesota Hospitals in Minneapolis that "nurses are often reluctant to offer face-to-face evaluations to each other. Anonymous peer evaluations are an avenue for directing critical and supportive comments to fellow workers."*[7]

As peer review becomes more widely used, nurses will realize that peer measurement of performance against realistic and attainable standards of nursing allows them to state unequivocally that they are being held accountable and responsible for their nursing performance.

NOTES

1. U.S. Public Law 92-603, 92nd Congress, 1972, pp. 101–117.
2. Passos, J.A. "Accountability: Myth or Mandate?" *J. Nurs. Admin.*, 3(3): 17–22, 1973.
3. Ramphael, M. "Peer Review," *Am. J. Nurs.*, 74(1): 63–67, 1974.
4. Hegyvary, S.T. and Haussmann, R.K.D. "Nursing Professional Review," *J. Nurs. Adm.*, 6(9): 12–16, 1976.
5. American Nurses Association, *Standards-Neurological Neurosurgical Nursing Practice*, Kansas City: ANA, 1977.

6. Orem, D. *Nursing Concepts of Practice,* New York: McGraw-Hill, 1971.
7. Dickson, B. "Maintaining Anonymity in Peer Evaluation," *Supervisor Nurse* 10, (5): 21–29, 1979.

* * * *

In the past, managers have used performance evaluation to decide on salary merit increases and on retention, promotion, or termination. Now they can use evaluation as a motivational tool. The approach should be based on participative management. This joint responsibility for evaluation is established by joint determination of performance criteria and job descriptions, and by joint goal setting.

Nurses function professionally by establishing the standards by which they will be judged. Individual nurses accept responsibility for their own growth by establishing their own goals and holding themselves accountable for achieving them. The professional group of nurses, finally, can accept responsibility for monitoring their own members through peer review.

The job enrichment principles of vertical job loading involved in performance appraisal are the lessening of administrative control, increased accountability of the nurse, and provision of feedback. Thus, through performance appraisal, job enrichment and professionalism can be united in the health care institution.

Part VI

The Manager as Climate Setter for Job Enrichment

In this book, Maslow's identified human needs of self-esteem and self-actualization have been associated with Herzberg's motivators of achievement, recognition, work itself, responsibility, advancement, and growth. The nurse manager is in a key position to permit or deny these motivators to the nursing staff.

Sherwin introduces this area in "Strategy for Winning Employee Commitment." He draws on the theories and writers discussed earlier, but he also looks at management as an ongoing process that requires hiring, firing, and disciplining, regardless of the philosophy of the manager. He views power as antithetical to a leadership style that inspires commitment and followership.

In "Is There Love in Your Leading?" Silber further develops the concept of love introduced by Herzberg. While Herzberg spoke of employees' love of work, Silber speaks of managers' love for their employees (their work). Both are approaches still uncommon in management literature. Silber develops followership through listening, needing, being aware of needs of others, avoidance of "lording," and instilling a sense of oneness with the employees.

Fuszard, in "Management Concepts That Work: Sponsorship," offers nurses an opportunity to put "love in their leading." A high octane of oneness with the staff will permit the nursing administrator to identify ways of helping them.

A leadership style which permits job enrichment is the 9,9 grid style developed by Mouton and Blake, and described here by Jongeward. Jongeward sees the 9,9 management style reflected in a total organizational support system through Likert's System 4.

Coaching and counseling is an appropriate skill of the 9,9 manager. Its step-by-step process developed by Buzzotta, Lefton, and Sherberg operationalizes the leadership style described by Sherwin as necessary to instill followership.

As told by Mahler, the story of Pygmalion and the power of high expectations is a final message to the manager on how to effectively work with employees, and the manager's success, according to Maslow, depends totally upon her own self-concept!

32.
Strategy for Winning Employee Commitment

Douglas S. Sherwin

Lack of commitment by employees is behind much of the behavior blamed for high costs and poor service. Students of the management art, therefore, have devoted themselves to understanding the causes of commitment and alienation among employees. Their insights have resulted in persuasive new approaches aimed at gaining commitment and changing behavior. Participative management, Theory Y styles of supervision, management by objectives, sensitivity training, job enrichment, leadership and human relations training are some of the products of this creative effort.

Business executives are anxious to see employee attitudes improved. Appreciating that the results they get come from existing behavior, and that better results require different behavior, they doggedly—though perhaps not always hopefully—try out new ideas for altering attitudes and behavior. But the results are often disappointing. When the training has been given and the employee returns to his job, managers usually find the employee backsliding to his old habits, attitudes, and behavior. They end up feeling disillusionment and lack of conviction toward training programs and other techniques designed to change personality, attitudes, or behavior.

What is the explanation? It lies, I believe, in the most basic assumptions of organization. Commitment, far from being something that has to be created in employees, is a natural, psychological need of every person. *This is the identification with work, work place, employer, and workgroup described by Herzberg and McGregor.* But we in management frustrate it at the source by assumptions and practices that we apply in the organizing process. Because these assumptions are intrinsic to organizing and are made prior to any functioning of the organization, their influence is always present and maintains a kind of irreducible level or core of

---

Modified with permission from Douglas S. Sherwin, "Strategy for Winning Employee Commitment," *Harvard Business Review* 50, no. 3 (1972): 37–47.

employee alienation. So when the employee returns to his job after training, he comes again under their influence and eventually resumes the behavior observed before the training.

According to contemporary thought, organization is a strategy for achieving goals.[1] Based on this criterion, our strategy has to be judged incomplete; the organization has not permitted its members to satisfy their psychological and social needs. *This is a raw description of the diverse goals of individual and organization identified by Getzels and Guba.*

POWER OR LEADERSHIP?

The organization hires, separates, changes duties, transfers, penalizes, promotes or does not promote, sets and resets pay, changes locations, and may even sell itself, or part of itself along with its employees, to some other organization. But it is less the actual exercise of power than the *concept* itself that discourages commitment. That concept can be stated simply. Power is an innate right of the organization. It is not only inherent but indispensable. For without it, how can the organization accomplish its mission?

This concept of power divides employees into two classes with apparently divergent interests. It places the organization unmistakably on the side of the owners' interests and *opposed to the employees' interests*. What else is power for if not to control employees? This orientation of the organization and its management employees to the owners' purpose separates the other employees from that purpose. Thus the organization in effect *renounces* any employee commitment to the organization.

Power, to the employee, is clearly the differentiating quality between the organization and himself. The organization has it; he does not. His reaction to this fact is ambivalent.

∇ On the one hand, he resents it; and when the organization is unresponsive, frustration and impotence can escalate his resentment to hostility. Resentful employees, consciously or unconsciously, may do the organization harm in large or small ways. They certainly do not identify with it.

Δ On the other hand, the employee never questions that power is inherently a right of the organization or doubts that it is indispensable to the organization's task. For, plainly, it must have power to deal with him. Otherwise, he reasons, lack of discipline, anarchy, chaos, unfairness, and failure would follow. These he does not want.

Thus the astonishing thing is that the employee totally accepts the organization's concept of power. Still, he senses unpleasant implications. If the organization needs power to deal with him in order to secure its purpose, then his interests must somehow be at odds with the organization's interests, and vice versa. The objectives of the organization must not be his. As he sees it, therefore, it is a case of "them and us"—or even "them and me": two classes. Rejected by the organization, the employee rejects it. He "decommits." He perceives himself as excluded and subordinate—an object.

But he accepts this condition as a price he has to pay to earn his bread. Thus, work becomes a means to an end instead of a worthy end in itself, and he makes no commitment to it or to his organization. For when people commit themselves, in my observation, it is to ends, not means. Without a commitment to the organization, the job and its wages are simply a commodity to the employee—undifferentiated from another job. One employment opportunity resembles another. Loyalty has no basis.

Impending Bankruptcy

Having exercised power for so long, we managers seldom wonder at its origin. We merely take it for granted as the natural state of things. Still, thinking about its origin can be revealing.

Perhaps unconsciously we suppose power is bestowed on the organization by the owners. Yet that assumption does not stand up when we reflect on it. Owners have an objective: to receive income and profit from risking the diminution or even entire loss of their ownership. When they select a board of directors, they delegate to it the authority to decide and act for them on certain matters. The directors delegate further to the officers. Through this process, the management becomes the owners' agent.

But that is the be-all and end-all of authority. While managers receive authority from owners to act for them, nothing in this itself invests them with authority over employees. The owners' purpose is not to organize people; not to hire, pay, or fire people; not to punish or reward; not to use power over anyone. These are *means* selected by the owners' agents, the management, to achieve the owners' purpose. Power is not really a necessary attribute of management; it is a recourse that management chooses.

If the organization does not derive power from ownership, then from where is it derived? Without running abstract discussions of terms into the ground, I think it helps to make one distinction between authority and power—terms which share many meanings:

▽ I see *authority* as something passed on to others in the interest of efficiency. It is passed on freely, as a pragmatic thing, to get things done. It can be delegated down, as in the process just described, or up, as in the

case of citizens' delegating authority to representatives to make the laws.
Δ On the other hand, *power* connotes something arrogated to oneself. It is taken, rather than given. It is primarily for the benefit of those who possess it rather than those from whom it has been taken.

Power seems always to be associated with the ability to make someone choose between alternatives—one of which is to be avoided. Do what the organization asks, or face an undesirable economic alternative; choose between doing the job satisfactorily or separation, between obeying the rules or receiving penalties, between average performance at average pay or superior performance with increased pay and perquisites.

A second source, surprisingly, has nothing to do with the organization. It comes directly from what we might call the work ethic. It is the particular system of values held by our *employees* that says having a job is good, that hard work is good, cooperating and doing your part are good, loyalty is good, obeying the rules is good, and so on. In other words, employees do what the organization asks, not solely because of the difficult economic alternatives, but because to do otherwise is to make themselves outlaws of their own value system. Thus, they themselves have been a source of the organization's power.

Now, what is happening to the two sources of organizational power? We already see the near-bankruptcy of economic power. For one thing, the organization's ability to make the employee face alternatives has been narrowly circumscribed. Government has limited the organization's actions by legislation, regulation, and court judgment. Organized labor presents countervailing power. Penalties and separations are subject to grievance procedures or strikes. Promotions are subject to seniority.

Wages are set for the contract period, making rewards for superior performance unavailable as means of influencing performance. Where there is no contract, management's actions are still influenced by the union, waiting in the wings to promote itself from a real or imagined abuse of power.

What is more, the economic alternatives have become less severe. The government's commitment to a full employment policy has lessened the impact of separation, so that loss of a job no longer signifies extended unemployment. Pay is also comparable for similar work in a given area; benefits vest earlier; unemployment benefits are substantial. Finally, the employee's own view of work as a commodity is a factor: if he regards one employment like another, he is not going to be so much influenced by penalties or the threat of being fired.

Actually, there is reason to suspect that corporate economic power has not been very effective for some time. We have really been operating on employee's acceptance of the work ethic—and therefore on their sufferance. But a changing ethic now threatens this source too. Despite radicals at the fringe of society, the great majority of people do not deny the work ethic. But they are questioning and *qualifying* it. Having a job is good, but not any job; hard work is good, but not necessarily of itself; making money is good, but how it is made is important; sacrifice for family is good, but doing your thing is important too; loyalty is good, if to a worthy cause; doing your best is good, but does the end justify it? More than ever before, work is going to be on the employee's terms.

How far will values change? Businesses have so far been spared revolts against power such as witnessed in church and university. But conditions in the business situation make it vulnerable to a changing ethic. Employee dissatisfaction with management exists in almost every business—dissatisfaction with the investment results of pension plans, with incentive plans whose value is affected by management's performance, with the business philosophy of management, and with loss of employment when management fails to do its job well enough. Such dissatisfaction can crystallize, given the right spark of activism from employees seeking involvement or recourse, and result in opposition to, and eventual neutralization of, the organization's power.[2]

Power thus seems more in tune with the way things have been than with the way they are going to be. With only a little bit of it in our future, how are we going to get our job done?

PROMISING ALTERNATIVE

We have a choice: we can defend every inch of the way to conserve what economic power remains—in the end losing it anyway to angry and indignant employees. We can be keepers of the gate, so to speak, enjoying while they last the prerogatives fortuitously accorded us by the work ethic. Or we can accept the decline of organization power and start developing a concept that lets us accomplish things without the threat of arrogated power. I advocate the latter. The alternative I propose is a new concept of leadership.

Leadership means enlisting all members of the organization in the purpose of the organization. Therefore it is inextricably bound with purpose. Leadership without purpose has no meaning; purpose exists only because a leadership formulated it. Like the mountain and valley of the philosophers' ancient puzzle, one concept cannot exist without the other. Leadership is prior to purpose and purpose is prior to managing—both chronologically and logically. It is just this priority that gives leadership primacy over managing.

Leadership is also a relationship between leader and follower. It cannot exist by itself; it exists only *if* followership is produced. Doubtless there are special qualities of leadership. But looking beyond this, it is plainly something that elicits a positive response from those led. Followership then becomes not a happy accident of certain qualities of the manager but the essential meaning of leadership itself. Leadership really begins, therefore, not with the leader, but with the follower.

What creates in a follower a desire to follow a leader? The key to followership is that every individual is always striving to meet his own psychological needs. What leadership does is enable the individual to satisfy his psychological needs by his own actions, which are the very actions sought by the leader to achieve the purpose of the organization.

Leadership not only replaces power; it is made *possible* by disregarding power. For power is anathema to leadership. Power does not produce followership; it antagonizes it. Power is the root of the managing group's attitude as enforcer, driver, superior, privileged, and causative. But attitudes beget attitudes, and this one creates a negative response from employees.

The Managerial Job

We can give managing new meaning and importance by conceiving of it as the tool of leadership to achieve the organization's purpose. Managing, in this view, becomes art, technique, systematization, method, and economics. And where leadership is emotions, feelings, spirit, and purpose, managing is cool, impersonal, objective, and imaginative; it connotes professional *action* for getting results—including followership. If we embrace this view, we would think of ourselves at every level of management first and primarily as leaders—and then as practitioners of the art and science of managing.

Thus, it becomes every manager's responsibility to enlist the people in the organization's cause and to provide the requirements of followership. We do not know what all these requirements are. We have to assume that work can satisfy many of them if, by creative managing, we introduce psychological satisfiers (*motivators*) into the work situation and eliminate, neutralize, or compensate for nonsatisfiers (*hygiene factors*) already present. We want followership not to depend on accidental or even instinctive qualities in a manager. We want it produced by rational, conscious, purposive managing that *understands* the requirements of followership as it understands the requirements of *patient care in the hospital setting*; and that creates conditions for followership as it creates conditions for success in these other areas.

Every major project requires certain inputs to achieve its objectives. Management is *one* of the necessary inputs. It may be a scarcer and more expensive resource than others, but it is not sufficient; it is not above the other inputs, nor is it better than they. In the concept proposed here, it is simply equal to the other necessary inputs.

Supplying the management input now becomes simply the duty of the appointed manager. It is not a nobler duty; it is but one function cooperating with other functions to achieve the purpose of the enterprise.

What is described is a humble concept of managing. But no inference should be made that management operates with a low profile, that it is a mere facilitator, or that its decisions can be determined by vote, consensus, or democratic process. It must be tough. It must do its duty, contribute its input without vacillation, apology, or guilt, and *in spite of* sympathy and empathy for individuals adversely affected, although managers most certainly will have such feelings. Otherwise the management input is antileadership, failing everyone.

How Much Difference?

Pragmatist philosopher William James once observed, "A difference that *makes* no difference *is* no difference." So what is the difference if after all the manager continues—as he must—to hire, fire, transfer, promote, penalize, and direct much as he did before, using power?

The difference is in the way that employees interpret management actions. As things stand, employees tend to view managers' actions as self-serving and for the benefit of the owners—only incidentally and indirectly in the interests of the employees. They see the purpose of the organization as the owners' purpose and achieving it as management's objective.

The subordination of power, on the other hand, makes it possible for nonmanagement employees to share in the purpose and objectives of the organization. For without power, managers must *enlist*, rather than force, the contribution of employees. Enlisting their contribution (which is of course only another way of saying "securing their followership") implies that a process must take place. In that process information and judgments are exchanged and an understanding of conditions is built. Out of the process come objectives and means—different, perhaps, and hopefully better than they otherwise would be, but in any case deserving of support by employees because the employees shared in making them. The employee becomes more involved in the social system of the company and thereby satisfies certain of his psychological needs. And as a result of the process, managers' actions can be *accepted* by employees as the necessary input that managers make as their obligation.

If management does its job, enlisting the commitment of all employees to the shared objectives, there is less need for discipline. Where that need nevertheless arises, the employee's peers can be expected to support disciplinary action, and the employee himself is more disposed to accept it.

CONCLUSION

What will happen if we do not find a way to let our employees meet their psychological needs on the job? How long will we be permitted to keep the present industrial system if we do not? These are frightening questions. Let us dream a little and imagine what matters might be like if we do meet the need.

A committed man is a Theory Y man. It will be remembered that Douglas McGregor used the now familiar categories of Theory X and Theory Y to refer to assumptions about people which he thought underlay contrasting styles of managing. Theory Y people have integrity, work hard toward objectives, assume responsibility, desire to achieve, want their organization to succeed, and will make decisions; on the other hand, Theory X people are not very interested in the organization, its performance, on-the-job achievement, assumption of responsibility, or hard work. What manager would not be excited to think what he could accomplish if his department were filled with Theory Y people!

Unfortunately, Theory Y remains but a potential. I remember once counseling one of our general managers, who was then having a lot of people problems, not to regard his hourly employees as Theory X. "But Doug," he said, "they *are* Theory X." And he was right!

Theory X behavior is what we observe all around. This may be due in part to employees' earlier environments in the home and school. But the working environment, I believe, makes a final contribution. Can we really expect much from a Theory Y style of managing if it is simply overlaid onto assumptions of organizing that prevent the employee from meeting his psychological needs? Environment *selects* behavior, and the business organization selects Theory X behavior. Until the basic assumptions of organizing are adapted to the Theory Y hypothesis of man's nature, Theory Y behavior is likely to remain only a matter of faith.

Suppose we could wave a wand and instantly introduce the changes proposed in this article. Would we get greatly increased commitment from our employees? Perhaps not immediately. Followership (like leadership) is weak. The cause is lack of exercise. Our employees have been conditioned by experience to suppress their feelings and withhold commitment. To change that behavior, management will need to provide employees with a very different body of experience on the job. Adapting our organizing concepts to human needs is certainly the first imperative. In addition, employees must be allowed to experience the attraction and excitement of pursuing a shared mission. Finally—and this is crucial—every instance and demonstration of employee commitment, even when critical of management, has to produce an affirmative and supportive reaction from managers. When this happens, we will know we are making progress.

NOTES

1. See, for example, Alfred D. Chandler, Jr., *Strategy and Structure* (Cambridge, MIT Press, 1962); and Wilbur M. McFeely, "Organization as a System of Response," *The Conference Board Record,* April 1970, p. 41.

2. For a revealing survey of businessmen's views on employee participation and activism, see David W. Ewing, "Who Wants Corporate Democracy?" HBR September-October 1971, p. 12; and "Who Wants Employee Rights?" HBR November-December 1971, p. 22.

* * * *

What can the nurse manager do to create this Theory Y environment that Sherwin says is so necessary for followership? Silber feels that managers must introduce love into their leading through listening, asking, needing, and permitting themselves to be needed. A final approach he suggests is enthusiasm, which he refers to as the high octane of oneness, of spirit.

33.
Is There Love in Your Leading?

Mark Silber

LOVE is a four letter word. But seldom is this four letter word found in public places on plaster. Songs are written, songs and sonnets are sung, plays project this theme and persons pursue this goal in life. Ministers, rabbis, and priests preach love, many people long and lust after love, some deny love to self, of self, and to others. But little on love is written on leadership . . . can a leader be lovable, is there love in leadership, is there love *in your leading*?

Three weeks ago I was invited to conduct a two-day executive retreat for senior officers and administrators in a plush executive conference center. The objective of the intense two-day session was the processing of organization and management values-styles, helping this major company address their futurism and how they would choose to live with each other. During this Organization Development process the Vice President of Manufacturing asked me, "Dr. Silber, do managers have to love each other? Give us some of your thoughts on love in managing." As I am a corporate psychologist, not a poet or minister, I engaged them in the process of exploring mature manager love . . . the mutual search for their definition of what love *meant to them* as executives living together.

Here were twenty-six experienced heavy industry executives fully involved in a heated dialogue on love in leadership! A silly, sissy search? Not at all! A waste of time . . . not at all. The outputs of this one section of my manager development conference with them were a K.R.A. (Key Result Area).

This K.R.A. possibly paid for the whole growth process . . . people producing a mutually defined system of values as they now and will live together in obtaining company results. Twenty-six experienced executives exercising their minds and viscera toward a common objective . . . putting love into their managing! *This process of identifying common values is the same as that followed by a group of*

Modified with permission from Mark Silber, "Is There Love in Your Leading?" Unpublished paper, 16776 Bernardo Center Drive, Suite 110B, San Diego, California 92128.

nurses identifying the philosophy of nursing of a new unit, such as intensive care or rehabilitation.
Love sustains and builds self-esteem and self-worth in the individual employee. It also reflects role identity, wherein we identify ourselves in relation to another.
<u>Love</u> is four letters.

L

Leader love is not lazy listening. I am asked to speak on human relations with supervisors and mid-managers and during these seminars lazy listening is often a focal point. If we, as leaders, are going to put relations into human interaction, then care and concern is critical. Do you really care about the other person? If you really do, you will listen actively. If you are really concerned about another person, then your listening will be active and undivided. Uninterrupted listening really communicates to other people that *they* are important. Who is important in your conversations? Loquaciousness is not love . . . loquaciousness is not listening.

Leader love locates the needs of others. We have heard it said, "I feel good when I am with you." What we understand this to mean is that you locate and listen to and for my needs. We all have a need to be noticed, needed and nurtured! Leader love translates into real behavior between people which encourages the *other* person to be noticed. When you, as a leader, are with others do they have to notice you? One of the most primitive needs of humans is the need-to-be-needed; as a leader who loves, do you get the verbal and non-verbal signals across to others that you need them? Do you nurture the other person in your peer relations, do you nurture your staff people in that relationship, are you mature to nurture your boss? I recently saw a sign on the desk of one of my client executives . . . "Even bosses need love too."

Leader love lets go of the luxury of lording. Leaders look up to people, not down at them! Which direction, in your attitudes and behaviors, comes across to others when you interact with them . . . "He looks down at me when we talk," or "I feel adequate and a *somebody* when we talk together about an opportunity or problem." Dr. Mort Feinberg, a distinguished psychologist internationally, in a recent conversation shared the importance of being a boss without bossing, a competent in corporate life without being caustic or cutting; he observed that mature managers work *with* people rather than do things *to* people. The luxury of lording has little place in effective leadership . . . maybe it is time we lose our own egos, lengthen our listening to others, laugh at ourselves, thereby losing our lordship.

O

Leader love contains the octane of oneness. Outputs which make a *real* difference, rather than activity and attendance, are the objectives of leading. As I have observed effective leaders in their facilitation of others obtaining outputs, a recurring ingredient is contained in their influencing these results, that is, an infectious octane of spirit. There is indeed a zest in leading, an enthusiasm of commitment. That empathy is the common bond of oneness . . . we, together, can make it happen . . . we, together, will make it happen . . . we, together, are one through which we both need each other.

Omitting omniscience, the belief in one's universal knowledge, is leader love. Immature, insecure managers feel that they were not appointed into management, they were annointed! When a person operates with omniscience, that person's behaviors reflect "oughts" . . . you ought to do it my way, you ought to do, you ought to do, you ought to do. You ought because I know the only way, the correct way, the politic way, the only way to do things right. Leader love, by contrast, takes the position that the other person is knowledgeable; the other person is a freethinking adult, the other person wants to outreach. Letting the other person outreach is letting the other person grow, develop, stretch, and take risk. If leaders can omit the dominance of their egos, omit their superimposing their "oughts" on others, and omit their need to dominate at others' expense, then leaders will become lovable and grow in their own effectiveness of being an adult and manager of adults! Omniscience is the enemy of the effective person . . . as person and as leader. To focus on obtaining outreach is a key to the art of leading . . . outreach of thinking and performance from others. *A study of values identifies whether one is a Theory X or a Theory Y manager. The Theory Y leader will be able and proud to bond himself with his employees for synergistic results.*

V

The way we manage is based on our values. How we place value on relations with humans, how and where we prioritize our values in the search for managerial power, love, and achievement, how our values are aligned determine how we behave. Where we place value . . . that's where we behave and allocate our time. Find out how a manager uses and allocates time, and you will discover his values! Love is allocating time to our values, which are the basis for our decision making; we make decisions based on what and who is of value to us. If you want to discover what holds meaning for a manager, observe his behavior and investment of time. Do you really place value on human beings, or are they merely means to your ends? Do you really value your persons who report to you; if so, are you spending enough time with them, listening to them, being open with them? Leader love does not mean "talking about your human values," but putting your time in the same place as your espoused values. Is your manager behavior in agreement and alignment with your mouthed values? Values are the sources for decisions, what is and what is not of importance. Where are your priorities, and what holds meaning for you as a leader? Possibly this would be a great time for you to rethink what are your leader values, what are your assumptions or values about others, how you give definition to others in your relationships on and off the job. Simply, is there love in your values?

The Latin word is *valere* or *valens*. In management education we call it *valence*. Leader valence is the degree of binding power in a relationship, the degree of power which exists between persons (or substances), causing them to unite to produce a specific effect upon each other. When leaders compete against their employees to prove to them that they are better or brighter, valence is lost and the other person feels like a victim. Might I ask you in the privacy of your own honesty, when you deal with others do you play the role of victor and they become a victim? Victory results from valence between and with others . . . the winning of relations and the obtaining of objectives are the outcomes based on the degree of valence between the leader and the led. Valence is the cement that binds manager to manager, manager to employee, producing a *mutual* power to produce. Through valence the employee permits a specific impact to occur from the manager and the manager permits and is accepting of employee impact on him. Leader valence means mutual power and potency for productivity, in which and through which both are victors!

E

E stands for effectiveness, as well as efficiency. The difference between the two is that of quality versus quantity. Both are needed. Peter Drucker, in his classic management textbook, *The Effective Executive,* makes the excellent point, "There is nothing so meaningless as to do something with great efficiency which should not have been done at all." A secret in living, a key to managing effectiveness, is to focus on not only doing things *right,* but doing the *right things.* Effectiveness in your child rearing, effectiveness in your marriage, leadership effectiveness based on the identification of the right things . . . the things which make a real difference. Leaders need to invest the time in identifying those target areas of performance which make a difference, not focusing on maintaining what they inherited, the status quo, the tradition, or "sacred cows." As time and circumstances change, so must our thinking about effective outcomes. Success comes to those individuals who invest the time to think . . . to think about what differentiates what is important *now* from what once was important. Effectiveness is the process of defining what is success now, the effectiveness of outcomes and outputs which truly make a difference now. The *E* in leader love stands for the effectiveness in your planning, play, and relations. Are you emphasizing effectiveness or just living and leading efficiently?

E also stands for effluence, the outpouring of transactional strokes on others. An eminent clinical psychologist in Chicago, Dr. Arnold Carson, has spent years in therapeutic aspects of marriage enrichment and growth with couples in their mutual defining of love. Dr. Carson relates love to acceptance of the other person's esteem. When people enjoy each other, there is exhilaration and an effluence. Effluence is the flowing out of endearment, attention, and the positive "emotional strokes" of affection from one person to another. Do you take the time to really listen to the other person? As a leader, do you invest enough time with your staff personnel to really listen to the other person? As a leader, do you invest enough time with your staff personnel to really know them as individuals? Can you and do you show the earnest exhilaration of responding to their creativity, ideas for improvement, the excitement of their success as they experience victories and wins in their lives? Esteem is reinforced and validated when employees experience this exhilaration shown by leaders to their wins, gains, and growth. Whose esteem is important when you are with others . . . the other person's or yours? Esteem is how we as individuals see ourselves and how others reinforce that image of who we are as persons. Our personhood is our self-esteem. Do you accept the other person as he is, or are you in the business of re-engineering and remolding other people to fit your needs? Enjoying and enriching the esteem of the other person is one of the secrets of leading, influencing, and a happy marriage.

E, *finally, is elan, the glorious pursuit of excellence. The Theory Y leader, the bonded leader, the excited, striving leader will carry employees to the excellence of performance that permits self-fulfillment in a total job well done.*

Drucker calls it . . . Executive Effectiveness. Batten calls it . . . Tough-Mindedness. Silber calls it . . . Elan. Elan is the pursuit of excellence, the spirit of achievement, the zest for accomplishment in a climate for results. One of the prime contributions of leadership is casting a giant shadow of elan, a leader atmosphere which encourages excellence in a work group. Is your leader shadow which falls over your group's morale one in which individuals feel your sense of urgency, your need for achievement, your spirit and sense of the necessity of their jobs? Employees feel necessary when their leaders feel the jobs in which they are incumbents are necessary. Our jobs are us! If our tasks and assignments are necessary in the eyes of our leader, then we are necessary and important as individuals. Elan is a shadow or climate, a climate which is contagious for excellence, a contagious climate containing the expectations of leadership which stimulate, sustain and support performance of excellence, not mediocrity or just a "standard day." Could it just be that corporations and leaders only get a "standard day" from employees because that is all they expect? Expect excellence, encourage excellence, and you may well obtain excellence! Accept mediocrity, reward mediocrity, and you will witness a work group functioning at a mediocre level. The factor which can make the difference between excellence and mediocrity is leadership elan.

Love is a four letter word. Is there love in your leading? Is there love in your relations with others? You see, to be lovable means to be worthy of love. If leaders are to be lovable . . . worthy of love . . . then their behaviors, as described in the preceding paragraphs, must be living testimony of the *L*s, the *O*s, the *V*s, and the *E*s.

* * * *

One way we can demonstrate love in our leading is through the concept of sponsorship. This concept, so familiar to other professions, is new to nursing. For too long this powerful tool has been available to us, yet gone unused.

34.
Management Concepts That Work: Sponsorship

Barbara Fuszard

Nursing literature has been focusing on the reality shock of the new nurse's first encounter with the nursing work world. Other professions, such as medicine and dentistry, have also been concerned with the evolution of the professional in their own disciplines. One of the helps toward that professionalization which is in use in other professions, but which has not appeared in nursing literature, is *sponsorship*.

Sponsorship has been defined as "the process of exerting continuing influence on the career of the newly certified professional."[1] It begins with the nursing faculty of the new professional's school of nursing and is completed in the institution where she accepts her first position. Of special interest to the nursing administrator is the role of institutional personnel. As nursing has not used this technique for socialization of the new registered professional nurse, we need to look to the other professions for examples of sponsorship.

Physicians, dentists, engineers, etc. sponsor neophytes in two ways: in launching their professional careers and in fitting them into social circles. To launch their careers the professionals suggest areas of office space or take them in as partners. They introduce them to other professionals who can refer clients; share their own methods of accounting; offer to train their new office personnel in their own offices. A familiar sight in a hospital is an attending physician with his arm around the shoulders of a new colleague, walking down the hall. He introduces him to administrators, shows him the layout of the institution, and lets everyone see that he is backing, is the friend of, this new physician.

The other professionals also sponsor the novice professional socially. The neophyte is introduced to persons and groups with whom he will want to associate. The seasoned professional helps him get membership in a favored club. Wives share information about baby sitters, cleaning ladies and hairdressers. The new

---

Modified with permission from Barbara Fuszard, "Management Concepts That Work: Sponsorship," *Facilitator* 6, no. 1 (1980): 2.

professional and his family are quickly assimilated into the professional community, and he is launched easily onto his new career.

How often we decry the lack of cohesiveness among nurses. Have we failed to lay the groundwork for such bonding by not utilizing sponsorship? Do we rather see nurses withholding information, little tricks of the trade, from one another? "I had to learn the hard way, and by . . . she can too." Or the competition of nurses of different educational preparation: "Let's see how much Miss Baccalaureate Degree knows."

A recent article in *The Facilitator* by Vicki Elfrink Doty discussed an orientation program for new graduates which permits both the staff development and the unit personnel to act as sponsors of the new graduate.[2] Or perhaps we could use the one-to-one approach physicians use. Some hospitals reimburse their employees who recruit a new nurse—a definite step of bonding which implies it's "O.K." to have friends and support them at work.

Is it not time for nursing to ensure its preparation of professionals by using some of the proven tools of other disciplines? Sponsorship seems to be getting results in other professional groups that we want in ours.

How can we more fully utilize this concept in nursing? Can we help the new nurse with her personal life? Just like the new physician, she needs to know about schools for her children. She needs to know about baby sitting, discount stores, uniform shops that give discounts, and recreation and entertainment available in the area. More than the physician, she needs to know her way around the institution, especially the mores and red tape. She needs to know the informal as well as the formal structure, and role expectations of the various power persons and groups.

As the "new recruit" moves to "old hand" in the institution, she will need to know about promotions or new roles becoming available, and how to prepare for them. She will need to know about educational opportunities, professional advancement in nursing organizations, opportunities for research and publications. What a joy for a nursing administrator if she could even sponsor one of her nursing staff into the prestigious American Academy of Nursing! Sponsorship is important for the new nurse, the new employee. How much more important, and rewarding for the sponsor, however, when the relationship continues through the growth of the nurse in her professional life.

NOTES

1. Basil J. Sherlock and Richard T. Morris, "The Evolution of the Professional: A Paradigm," *Sociological Inquiry*, 37:1 :27–46 (Winter, 1967).
2. Vicki Elfrink Doty, "Orientation as Socialization," *The Facilitator* 5:2 (March-April 1979), pp. 7–8.

Part VI: The Manager as Climate Setter

* * * *

Jongeward now looks at two contemporary management theories and their impact on job enrichment. Blake and Mouton's grid approach looks at the supervisor's behavior, whereas Likert's System 4 and System 4T speak to a whole-systems approach.

35.
The Effect of Management Style on Job Enrichment

Dorothy Jongeward

Several years ago Drs. Robert Blake and Jane Mouton integrated a large amount of leadership research that had been previously conducted by other investigators. They called their new conceptual framework "The Managerial Grid." This name was derived from the following two-axis diagram which they created to identify differing managerial leadership styles.

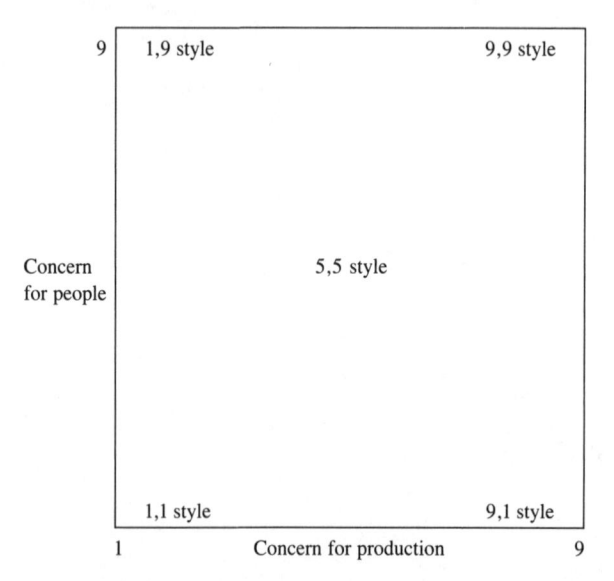

```
         9 | 1,9 style                    9,9 style
           |
           |
           |
Concern    |            5,5 style
for people |
           |
           |
           |
           | 1,1 style                    9,1 style
           |_____
           1         Concern for production      9
```

Modified with permission from Dorothy Jongeward, *Everybody Wins! TA Applied to Organizations* (Reading, Mass.: Addison-Wesley, 1976) pp. 276–277 and 283–290, 298–300, 302. Copyright © by Dorothy Jongeward, Dorothy Jongeward Associates, Inc. 724 Ironbark Court, Orinda, CA 94563.

212

In their conceptualization, the vertical axis represents a manager's concern for people (or how much attention and energy he spends on individuals as they work). The horizontal axis represents a manager's concern for production (or how much attention and energy he gives to getting work tasks accomplished). Each axis is divided into nine units with 1 representing the lowest degree and 9 standing for the highest degree of concern on each scale.

Although it is theoretically possible to plot 81 points on such a 9 by 9 grid, Blake and Mouton identified five points on it as symbolizing different basic managerial styles. A 9,1 leadership style is typical of a manager who has an extremely high concern for accomplishing production tasks but a very low concern for his people who must achieve them. A manager using this style explicitly or implicitly assumes that efficiency in work results from arranging the procedures and conditions of work in such a way that human elements can interfere, at most, to a minimum degree. Conflicts between work requirements and people's needs are nearly always resolved in favor of work, with no effort to integrate the desires of individuals.

A 1,9 leadership style is typical of a manager who has an extremely high concern for the people he works with but a low concern for the productive work which they achieve. An individual who manages with this style assumes that thoughtful attention to the needs that people have for satisfying relationships will lead to a comfortable and friendly organizational climate. This style is perhaps identical to the old "human relations" school of thought, i.e., "If you're kind to people, they will be happy and have high morale. This, in turn, will cause them to produce more." Interpersonal conflict is seen as negative and harmful to relationships, so it is ignored if at all possible.

The 1,1 leadership style is typical of a manager who has a low concern for both people and production. An individual who manages with this style assumes that the exertion of minimum effort to get required work done is appropriate for sustaining organizational leadership. He may philosophize, "People work best when you leave them alone!" Conflict is largely ignored.

The 9,9 leadership style is typical of a manager who has a high concern for both his people and the work they do. An individual managing with this style assumes that giving high priority to solving both people problems and work or task problems results in committed and trusting workers and also high productivity results.

The 5,5 leadership style is typical of a manager who attempts to compromise his moderate concern for his people with his equally moderate concern for production results. An individual who manages with this style assumes that adequate organizational performance is possible only through trading-off the need to get work out with the need to maintain satisfactory morale. His behavior often fluctuates between "being tough on people to increase productivity" and "being nice to people to increase their sagging morale." Conflicts are usually negotiated, with compromises being sought to resolve most situations.

A leader does not provide job enrichment for his employees. But appropriate leader behavior can permit job enrichment to happen. The 9,9 leadership style is most congruent with job enrichment because of the 9,9 leader's support of employees and his high expectations. Likert puts the 9,9 leadership style into a comprehensive organizational climate for job enrichment.

WHAT MAKES LIKERT'S SYSTEM IV WORK?

As a young man Rensis Likert worked as a laborer for the Southern Pacific Railroad. From this early work experience he observed that the manner in which the employees were supervised often seemed to influence work outcomes more than quality standards or statements issued by those with formal authority. Dr. Likert has spent much of his professional life conducting research on this early personal observation.

This research has included studies of numerous organizations with various locations, sizes, purposes, and degrees of effectiveness. Until his retirement in 1970, Dr. Likert was the Director of the Institute for Social Research (ISR) at the University of Michigan, a position which he held from 1946. With Likert's leadership, ISR invested 25 years in investigating why some organizations are able to accomplish the end results which they set out to achieve, whereas others fail to do so. Using a multiple choice survey technique in which Likert had played a prominent role in developing in the early 1930's, ISR staff members continuously refined their investigations and conclusions. The following concepts are among the current results of this research.

Causal, Intervening, and End-Result Variables

Through their studies, Likert and his colleagues tried to find cause and effect relationships between their measurements of management actions and the end results achieved by management. From their efforts they concluded that all organizations are significantly influenced by three different kinds of variables. These are causal variables, intervening variables, and end-result variables.

Causal Variables

These are described as the most important ones, since they begin a series of actions which greatly influence later events. Likert confines his definition of causal variables to those things which management can *directly* influence and change. He excludes influences such as national economy and government regulation which management cannot directly modify.

Likert's causal variables include the following:

1. Available technology and competence of individuals in this technology
2. Facilities
3. Organizational policies
4. Organizational structure
5. Organizational climate that is established by the actions of top management in the following areas:
   a) Management's willingness to be influenced by the ideas and perceptions of individuals at lower levels in the organization
   b) The process management uses in making decisions
   c) Its assumptions and actions regarding lateral coordination and collaboration with peers in other functions

   The variable of organizational climate greatly influences two other equally important causal variables:
6. Supervisory leadership
7. Peer leadership

Likert describes effective supervisory leadership as being comprised of four factors:

a) *Supportive leadership style.* To use Likert's words ". . . The relationship between the superior and subordinate is crucial. This relationship . . . should be one which is supportive and ego building. The more often the superior's behavior is ego-building rather than ego-deflating, the better will be the effect of his behavior on organizational performance. It is essential to keep in mind that the interactions between the leader and the subordinate must be viewed in the light of the subordinate's background, values, and expectations. The subordinate's perception of the situation, rather than the supervisor's, determines whether or not the experience is supportive."[1]
b) *Emphasis on high performance aspiration and goals.* Likert describes this factor in the following way: "A firm must succeed and grow to provide its employees with what they want from a job: pride in the job and company, job security, adequate pay, and opportunities for promotion. Economic success is a situational requirement which can be met only if the organization, its departments and its members have high performance goals. Superiors consequently should have high performance aspirations, but this is not enough. Every member should have high performance aspirations as well. Since these high performance goals should not be imposed on employees, there must be a mechanism through which employees can help set the high-level goals which the satisfaction of their own needs requires."[2]

c) *Time and effort spent on team building.* Team building concentrates on behaviors between work group members which will first create and then maintain healthy and productive interpersonal relationships.
d) *Work facilitation.* Accomplishing work through the efforts of group members is, of course, a primary function of supervisory leadership. Supervisory behaviors which serve to develop or provide effective work methods, facilities, equipment, and know-how for accomplishing the group's work goals are described as work facilitation. The amount of work facilitation which a supervisor does is perhaps also an indication of how much commitment he has to the work team, its goals, and his supportive feelings toward its members.

Peer leadership, or leadership executed by work group members of the same level on each other, is made up of the same four factors which comprise supervisory leadership: (a) supportiveness, (b) high-performance aspirations and goals, (c) team building, and (d) work facilitation. Research evidence seems to indicate the following conclusions about peer leadership.

a) In work groups the total amount of peer leadership is at least as great as the total amount of supervisory leadership.
b) Peer leadership is at least as important as supervisory leadership, and possibly more so, in accomplishing work group goals.
c) Supervisory leadership will often influence the amount of peer leadership found within a work group.

Of the seven causal variables described, Likert and his associates have developed survey tools for measuring only the last three: organizational climate, supervisory leadership, and peer leadership. (*These are included in the Likerts' book "New Ways of Managing Conflict."**)

Intervening Variables

Likert describes intervening variables as those factors which reflect the internal state and health of the organization. They are directly influenced by the causal variables described earlier and have a major impact on end-result variables. They include the following collective aspects of a group's working processes:

1. Motivation of individuals
2. Individual and group problem solving

---

*Rensis and Jane Gibson Likert. *New Ways of Managing Conflict* (New York: McGraw-Hill, 1976).

3. Decision making
4. Coordination
5. Communication

End-Result Variables

In Likert's theoretical framework, end-result variables are always dependent on both the causal and intervening variables and reflect the observable achievements of the organization. They include such organizational outcomes as productivity, costs, earnings, scrap loss, and quality performance.

Several other "costs of doing business" are also end-result variables and reflect in somewhat different terms the effectiveness and efficiency of the total management system. These include employee turnover, grievances, employee attendance, and employee satisfactions.

In addition to the three causal factors mentioned earlier, Likert and his associates have also developed survey tools to measure the intervening variables and the end-result employee satisfactions.

How A Management System Works

Each of the variables described above influences at least one or more of the other variables. Collectively they tend to operate somewhat like a closed-loop system as diagrammed in Figure 35–1.

The causal variables of organizational policies, structure, and climate (I-C, I-D, and I-E) are determined by the behavior of a few key individuals in top management. As shown in the diagram, these causal variables, in turn, greatly influence supervisory leadership behaviors (I-F). And supervisory leadership behaviors are critical in determining peer leadership behaviors (I-G). Collectively these variables largely determine the kind of behaviors occurring within the work group in relation to the intervening variables of motivation, problem solving, decision making, coordination, and communication (II-A, II-B, II-C, II-D, and II-E). This entire sequence of behaviors determines the kind of end results that the organization is able to achieve (III-A through III-G).

Since top management executives usually monitor the end-result variables very closely, they tend to take action whenever the end results fall short of their expectations. This action is normally in the form of executive behavior which either modifies or reinforces the causal variables of organizational policies, structure, and climate (I-C, I-D, and I-E). These variables, in turn, influence supervisory leadership behaviors (I-F), etc. Thus, the chain of management behaviors become cyclical.

Figure 35-1 Likert's Management System Conceptual Sequence

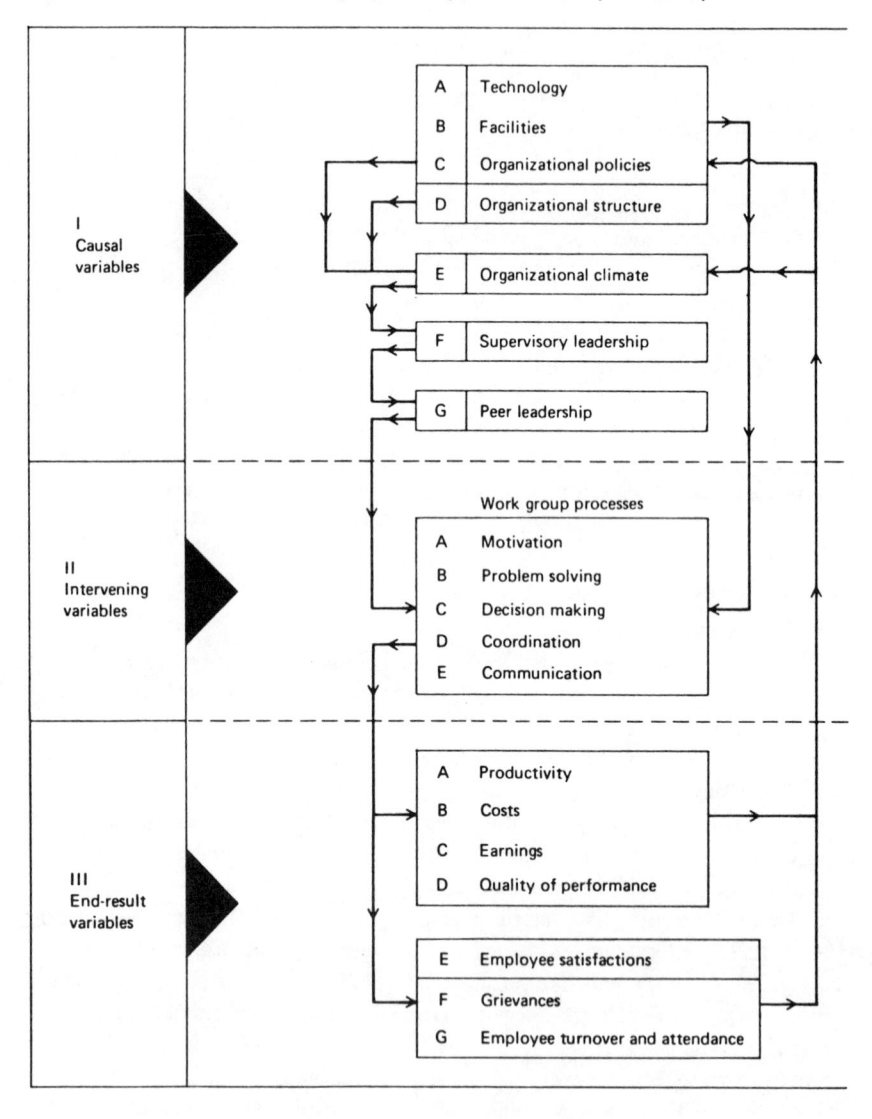

I Causal variables

A	Technology
B	Facilities
C	Organizational policies
D	Organizational structure
E	Organizational climate
F	Supervisory leadership
G	Peer leadership

II Intervening variables

Work group processes

A	Motivation
B	Problem solving
C	Decision making
D	Coordination
E	Communication

III End-result variables

A	Productivity
B	Costs
C	Earnings
D	Quality of performance
E	Employee satisfactions
F	Grievances
G	Employee turnover and attendance

Systems I to IV

Likert and his associates have constructed questionnaires to obtain employee perceptions of causal and intervening variables of the management system in which they work. Each item on the questionnaire is constructed as a continuum. At one end of the continuum, the described behavior is of an exploitative authoritarian nature. A management system which is characterized by a series of behaviors at this end of the measurement continuum is labeled System I by Likert.

At the opposite end of the continuum on each questionnaire item, the described behavior is characterized by a high degree of individual participation. A management system which is characterized by a series of behaviors at this end of the measurement continuum is called System IV. Likert has also identified two intermediate kinds of management behaviors which fall between the two extremes of exploitative authoritarian management and highly participative management. He calls these System II (benevolent authoritarianism) and System III (consultative). In summary, each item on a Likert questionnaire is constructed as a continuum which measures four types of management behavior.

System I	System II	System III	System IV
Exploitative authoritarian	Benevolent authoritarian	Consultative	Participative

Differences between the Systems are demonstrated in Table 35–1. Only System I and System IV examples are given, since they are the extremes of the continuum.

System 4T is a term introduced by the Likerts in "New Ways of Managing Conflict." It is considered the ideal system for job enrichment, encompassing all the variables of human aspects of an organization. A System 4 Total (System 4T) Model Organization is one in which the organization rates high on all the variables discussed here.[3]

Table 35–1 Comparing Likert System I and System IV Management Characteristics

Management Characteristics	Likert System I Characteristics (Exploitative Authoritarian)	Likert System IV Characteristics (Participative)
	ORGANIZATIONAL CLIMATE CAUSAL VARIABLES	
Attitudes toward other members of the organization	Subservient attitudes toward superiors, coupled with hostility; hostility toward peers and contempt for subordinates; widespread distrust.	Favorable, cooperative attitudes throughout the organization, with mutual trust and confidence.
Adequacy of upward communication via line organization	Very little.	A great deal.
At what levels of the organization are decisions formally made?	Bulk of decisions at top of organization.	Decision making widely done throughout the organization, although well integrated through linking process provided by overlapping groups.
How adequate and accurate is the information available for decision making at the place where the decisions are made?	Partial and often inaccurate information only is available.	Relatively complete and accurate information available based on measurements and efficient flow of information in organization.
Extent to which technical and professional knowledge is used in decision making	Used only if possessed at higher levels.	Most of what is available anywhere within the organization is used.
	SUPERVISORY LEADERSHIP CAUSAL VARIABLES	
Accuracy of perceptions by superiors and subordinates	Often in error.	Usually quite accurate.
Manner in which goal setting or ordering is usually done.	Orders issued from the top.	Except in emergencies, goals are usually established by means of group participation.

NOTES

1. Rensis Likert, *The Human Organization: Its Management and Value* (New York: McGraw-Hill, 1967), p. 51.
2. *Ibid*, p. 51.
3. Rensis and Jane Gibson Likert. *New Ways of Managing Conflict* (New York: McGraw-Hill, 1976), p. 49.

* * * *

Coaching is an example of the functioning of a 9,9 manager in the process of encouraging employees to develop to their highest potential. Buzzotta, Lefton, and Sherberg give step-by-step guidelines on manager behavior in coaching and counseling, using performance evaluation as an example.

36.
Coaching and Counseling

V.R. Buzzotta, R.E. Lefton, and Mannie Sherberg

Coaching and counseling is probably the most common form of training in organizational use today. Formal training programs, seminars, courses of one kind or another are all done intermittently—from time to time—in most organizations. But coaching and counseling is done every day, probably even several times each day. And it's done not only by professional trainers, but by managers, supervisors, and executives of every kind and at every level. Because most organizations spend large amounts of time and money on coaching and counseling, it's important that it be done *right*.

But that's not the problem. In many cases, it *isn't* done right. In fact, a lot of people who coach and counsel aren't even aware of the fact that there's a right way (and a number of wrong ways) to do it. They just do "what comes naturally." As a result, they—as well as their subordinates and their organizations—suffer some pretty serious consequences.

WHAT IS IT?

Coaching and counseling is (1) the use of managerial power (2) to elicit self-analysis by the subordinate which (3) combines with the manager's own insights and knowledge (4) to produce self-understanding on the part of the subordinate, commitment to mutually accepted goals, and a plan of action for achieving them.

(Strictly speaking, coaching is distinguished from counseling in that coaching focuses on improving job skills and job knowledge, whereas counseling focuses on problems of attitude and motivation or on interpersonal hangups. If a salesperson, say, doesn't know the correct way to demonstrate the benefits of a product,

---

Modified with permission from V.R. Buzzotta, R.E. Lefton, and Mannie Sherberg, "Coaching and Counseling: How You Can Improve the Way It's Done," *Training and Development Journal* 31, no. 11 (American Society for Training and Development, 1977): 50-60.

coaching is needed; if the person refuses to mail call reports to the district manager because she thinks "the call report system is a lot of baloney," counseling is needed. In common usage, however, the two words are combined into a single phrase.)

As this four-part definition makes plain, coaching and counseling should lead to (1) optimal results for the organization and (2) optimal development for the subordinate, *as described in the Getzels-Guba model*. It should produce some kind of improvement in the subordinate's performance or attitudes—and the improved performance or improved attitudes should in turn produce improved results.

In the broadest sense, any contact between a manager and a subordinate for purposes of developing the subordinate can be called coaching and counseling. But, as a rule, the term is used in a somewhat narrower sense, to refer to a specific kind of development. Table 36–1 shows how coaching and counseling (center column) is usually distinguished from the less formal daily contacts between boss and subordinate and the more formal annual performance appraisal. We will concentrate on the middle column.

All of this sounds fairly simple. But it isn't. Coaching and counseling is a deceptive . . . almost treacherous . . . phrase—as many a manager has learned sorrowfully. The words themselves are as clear as the windshield on a brand-new car: to coach is to train, and to counsel is to advise. But that's exactly what many managers fail to do. To see why, let's look at a Dimensional Model of Coaching and Counseling; as we do, we'll see the difference between what coaching and counseling should be . . . and what it frequently is.[1]

Table 36–1 Three Subordinate Development Methods

Type	Daily or periodic contact	Coaching and counseling	Annual performance appraisal
Nature	Informal	Semiformal	Formal
Subjects	Immediate problems and decisions and objectives	Skills and progress toward master plans	Master plans and objectives
Time Orientation	Solve now	Measure immediate past performance. Improve immediate future performance.	Measure past year's performance against objectives. Set next year's objectives.
Time to Conduct	3–10 minutes	15–60 minutes	2–6 hours

FOUR BASIC WAYS

Based upon two fundamental measures, or dimensions, of interaction—dominance-submission and hostility-warmth—the model distinguishes four basic ways of coaching and counseling, or what's called coaching and counseling. (See Exhibit 36–1.) If these four kinds of coaching and counseling are compared with our definition, it becomes plain that the first three (Q1, Q2, and Q3) aren't really coaching and counseling at all.

Carping and censuring is a better name for so-called Q1 coaching and counseling. Or crabbing and condemning. Or complaining and criticizing. Whatever it's called, it aims to produce fear and apprehension, not planned, intelligent change. Cooling-it and copping out is what Q2 coaching and counseling really is. The manager's goal is to keep people in line and maintain the status quo; she has little

---

Exhibit 36–1 Dimensional Model of Coaching and Counseling

DOMINANCE

Quadrant 1 (Q1)	*Quadrant 4 (Q4)*
Tries to produce change through coercion or threat. Assumes most people are lazy and unwilling, and that they won't make an effort to improve unless they're pressured or forced. The basic message is: Do what I say . . . or else. Believes that intimidation can work wonders with most people.	Believes people will make an effort to improve when they understand what they'll get out of it, and when they've had a chance to participate in analyzing their performance or attitudes and in working out ways to do better in the future. Believes that productive change occurs only when people see the connection between their own needs and those of the organization.

HOSTILITY ──────────────────── WARMTH

Quadrant 2 (Q2)	*Quadrant 3 (Q3)*
Doesn't really try to produce change at all. Assumes that people will change if and when they're ready to do so, and that nothing the manager does can influence them; in effect, the manager is at the mercy of his/her people, since they decide when they're going to improve. Sees coaching and counseling as useful for keeping people in line, but not much else.	Tries to produce change by accentuating the positive and eliminating the negative. Assumes most people will make an effort to improve if they get enough encouragement and support. Sees self as a cheerleader, whose job it is to keep subordinates from becoming discouraged or demoralized.

SUBMISSION

use for change and curbs and cautions, cramps and confines, in an effort to avert catastrophe and calamity.

Compassion and companionship are what Q3 coaching and counseling provide ; change is stifled in the process. As the manager compliments and compromises, congratulates and comforts, she either chokes off or frustrates productive change. Only Q4 coaching and counseling fits our definition. In Q4 coaching and counseling, real communication occurs between manager and subordinate. The coaching session is characterized by give and take, discussion, candor, a genuine two-way exchange—all characteristic of communication as opposed to browbeating (Q1), cautioning (Q2), or undeserved praising (Q3).

In Q4 coaching and counseling, the assumption is that optimal results for the organization and optimal development for the subordinate go hand in hand. The word optimal is worth noting; it means, of course, the best obtainable—and that's what Q4 coaching aims at: the best results obtainable under the circumstances. In other words, it doesn't shoot for pie-in-the-sky results; it shoots for realistic results—the highest results achievable under existing conditions.

Contrast this sensible, hard-headed approach with what happens in so-called Q1, Q2, and Q3 coaching and counseling. The Q1 approach isn't really concerned about optimizing results for the subordinate; it focuses on optimizing results for the organization, and sees the subordinate mainly as an instrument for doing this. The Q2 approach isn't interested in optimizing results, period; it's concerned with preserving existing results—with keeping things on an even keel, not with improving them. The Q3 approach zeros in on happy results, not optimal ones; it has nothing against optimal results but, if such results necessitate pushing or exerting or challenging the subordinate, the Q3 approach prefers to settle for less-than-optimal (and therefore more comfortable) results. Only the Q4 approach tries to produce optimal results for *both* organization and subordinate.

Finally, as our definition requires, Q4 coaching and counseling trains and advises. It's the only approach in which real teaching and real learning occur, where advice is based on genuine understanding and commitment. In Q4 coaching and counseling, change is real because it's internalized by the subordinate; it happens because of conviction, not concern.

HOW IT'S DONE

The significant question is not "Does Q4 coaching and counseling work?" (it does), but "How does a manager *do* it?" After all, it's a fairly simple matter to chew out and bully a subordinate (Q1), or to hem and haw and refuse to come to grips with issues (Q2), or to sweet talk a subordinate and pretend there are only silver clouds, no linings (Q3). But how does a manager go about communicating with a subordinate so as to produce optimal improvement in the subordinate's performance or attitude and, thereby, optimal improvement in results?

To answer that, it should be emphasized that Q4 coaching and counseling is a four-phase process that follows a very deliberate and systematic format. The phases are:

1. Precoaching
2a. Coaching: Identifying improvement areas
2b. Coaching: Action-planning
3. Review

In what follows, our examples will refer to coaching (as opposed to counseling), but it should be kept in mind that the format is the same for both.

Phase 1: Pre-Coaching

Q4 coaching stays in close touch with the real world. The manager doesn't waste time talking to subordinates about their performance as she guesses it to be; they are counseled about their performance as she observes it. The manager goes into a coaching session armed with facts, data, records, evidence, and gets this evidence by doing intensive precoaching work.

Take, as an example, *a nurse manager who uses the Q4 approach and has been asked to assist a staff nurse prepare for charge nurse responsibilities*.

Prior to a coaching session (perhaps several times) *she works with the staff nurse on her unit,* watching, listening, silently evaluating. This fieldwork, which is indispensable if she is to know what's being talked about in the coaching session, follows a four-step format:

a. Before *even going onto the unit,* the manager explains the reason for the visit. And she levels. *If the nurse manager is going to make general observations, she will say so. If she has another purpose, such as investigating a complaint that has been lodged against the staff nurse, she will say so.* After all, *the staff nurse can't improve if treated like a kid who can't take the truth.*

b. Next, the two agree on ground rules for the day (How will the manager's presence be explained to *patients, physicians, other nurses?* Will she intervene under any circumstances? And so on). Everything possible is done . . . before starting out . . . to eliminate surprises.

c. During the day, the manager pays close attention to everything *the staff nurse* does, focusing on both content (what's said and done) and process (How it's said or done). She is alert to all that's going on—to content and process and the interaction between the two, alert to what's plainly discernible, and alert to "hidden" or "obscure" data—subtleties that disclose much about the *staff nurse's* strengths and weaknesses. This is hard, fatiguing work . . . but it must be done if sensible coaching is going to result. *During the day, and after certain events, the nurse manager and the staff nurse may compare notes, and the staff nurse may be given ideas on how to handle common situations.* (These "curbstone conferences" are no substitute, however, for the full-blown coaching session, which comes later.)

d. Finally, and privately, at the end of the day the manager evaluates what she has seen and heard—puts it into perspective. She separates the *nurse's* strengths and weaknesses, decides where improvement is needed, and determines the topics to stress in the coaching session, organizes her thinking and tries to form a picture of the *staff nurse* that's based not on imagination, bias, or hunch, but on observed evidence. The *nurse* is asked to prepare, too, outlining those areas in which she should privately and systematically be evaluated. This way, they'll both be ready for the coaching session. (The session may come at the end of the day, or on a later day.)

In brief, to do Q4 coaching the manager must "tell it like it is." But she can't until first learning it like it is. That's what precoaching is all about. (Learning it like it is does not, of course, always require observation in the field.) The crucial point is that all coaching and counseling . . . by all types of managers . . . depends upon careful, thorough gathering of evidence prior to the coaching session—and analysis of that evidence by both manager and subordinate. To repeat: telling it like it is demands learning it like it is.

Phase 2a: Coaching: Identifying Improvement Areas

The next phase is the actual coaching session—the face-to-face meeting in which manager and subordinate grapple with this question: How is the subordinate doing, and how can she do even better? The coaching session is a two-stage session because it tries to answer a two-part question. The first part (how is the subordinate doing?) underlies the first stage of the coaching session (identifying improvement areas); the second part (how can the person do even better?) underlies the second stage (action-planning). *As the purpose of this coaching and counseling is to have a better employee, the whole tone of this four-step approach must be exchange of information rather than punishment.*

In a way, coaching is mapping; it gives the subordinate a "map" showing where to go next, and how to get there. But a map is useless unless you know where you're at now. So the manager devotes the first stage of the coaching session to laying out the coordinates showing subordinates where they're at—how they're doing, what their strengths and weaknesses are, where they most need to improve. She does this in six steps:

a. The manager first explains the purpose of the session in terms that mean something to the subordinate. It is made plain that this is not a trial, not an ordeal, not punishment, but a chance to grow in ways that pay off. Or, if the idea of growth frightens the subordinate, the manager talks about coaching as a way to build stability on the job. Whatever the approach (and that depends upon what motivates the subordinate) the manager makes sure the subordinate understands "what's in it for me." *The employee must be sure that the changes suggested are for her benefit, not the benefit of management.* Then the ground-rules are set out, emphasizing that the subordinate can say what she wants at any time. Candor and openness by both of them are to characterize the session.

    b. Now the manager finds out how the subordinate thinks she is doing—by asking. This is crucial. If the manager forces her views on the subordinate and plays "Big Mommy," one of two things may happen: the subordinate may resent the conclusions (and may rebel) or may never learn how to evaluate her own performance (and thus become overly dependent on the manager). But the purpose of coaching is not to generate rebellion or dependency—it's to generate autonomy. This means the subordinate must be encouraged to do her own thinking—and to voice it. So the manager probes to find out what the subordinate thinks about her own performance . . . plus and minus . . . and why. The manager digs for evidence and wants to know why the subordinate sees herself in a certain way. The manager is not interested in mere impressions, but in their justification. (Of course, even the most skillful probing may not produce much data if the subordinate hasn't "done the homework"—her share of precoaching preparation. Once again, precoaching is vital.)

    The manager does more than merely probe, however; she listens attentively (*a quality of loving*), comparing ideas, listening interpretively and asking: "What's my subordinate really saying? Are there other meanings hidden or submerged beneath the words?" If there seem to be, the manager probes still further to find out what they are.

    At no point does she argue, interrupt, or blame, but probes, and listens at a thinking level—analytically. If the subordinate seems too generous to herself, if she paints too rosy a picture, or is downright wrong, the manager probes these areas with special care and may even interpose facts to set the record straight. But—primarily—she probes, trying hard to get the subordinate to present a balanced, factual account of what's going on, and then asks the subordinate to summarize her evaluation.

    c. Once the subordinate has described the job performance as she sees it, the manager offers her own views, setting forth pluses and minuses, explaining how the pluses can be maintained or strengthened, and assigning priorities to the minuses, with those most urgently needing improvement at the top of the list. Throughout, reasons are given, based upon observation and data, for her view. No punches are pulled. The manager is candid, thorough, and to the point.

    d. Now the two are ready to compare views. The manager asks the subordinate to stack her own impressions against the manager's, and to draw whatever conclusions seem justified. Once again, she probes to get to the facts. If the subordinate claims the manager's analysis is unfair, the manager asks why. If the subordinate seems too quick to agree with the manager, the manager probes to find out if the agreement is genuine.

All the while, something else is done: the manager compares her own views with the subordinate's, asking if her own ideas should be revised (or even rejected) in the light of what has been heard. If the manager decides that her original thinking is weak or wrong, she admits it. The whole idea is to get at the truth about the subordinate's performance. That requires openness to new evidence and willingness to discard shaky assumptions. *This candid search for objective truth gives the employee security in her self-esteem, since her own self-esteem is based on the combination of how she sees herself and how the nurse manager sees her.*

e. After the two agree on the subordinate's strengths and weaknesses, they work together to (1) clearly identify the strengths and ways to reinforce them (this is important; many subordinates are unaware of, or underestimate, their strengths), and (2) set priorities for those weaknesses that most require attention. The idea is to identify the most serious shortcomings, those most damaging to results, those that must be eliminated (or diminished) first. It's unrealistic to expect anyone to change many aspects of behavior at one time; it's more realistic to concentrate on a few changes, zeroing in on those that really count. (At no time does the manager develop a "laundry list" of weaknesses—a long, item-by-item catalog of faults. This would discourage change by making the effort seem futile. The manager concentrates on a limited number of significant liabilities.)

f. Finally, the subordinate is asked to state the understanding of her strengths and the improvement priorities—and to write it down. This has nothing to do with distrust. The clearest agreement may get hazy as time passes; the commitment to paper lends permanence to it. More than that, it lends significance as well. Spoken words evaporate; written words seem more tangible, more solid. They're harder to shrug off or ignore; long after they're put on paper, they're still there, stubbornly refusing to go away.

At this point, which is only the mid-point of the session, the manager and the subordinate agree on what needs to be done, but haven't discussed how to do it. The subordinate has, so to speak, a map showing where she is and where she ought to be headed—but is not yet clear on how to get there from here. That's the goal of the second stage.

Phase 2b: Coaching: Action-Planning

At this point, the subordinate is like a traveler with a map showing her present position and the place she wants to go to, but nothing in between—no road, footpaths, routes of any kind. The problem is to find the fastest, easiest, most efficient way to travel the distance between the two points—without getting lost or detoured. Discovering that passage . . . the most direct path to the job-improvement goal . . . is what the second part of the Q4 coaching session is all about. The format of this second stage is much like the first:

  a. The manager asks the subordinate for specific ideas on how to effect the improvements they've agreed on. She wants the subordinate's detailed thinking—step by step—about what should be done to diminish . . . or get rid of . . . the liabilities they've identified. Generalities, good intentions, vague pledges—none of these will do. The manager wants particulars.

  b. Next, the manager presents her own ideas about what needs to be done, being as specific as the subordinate is expected to be. For example, *a nurse manager* who thinks the *staff nurse* needs to manage time better doesn't just say so and let it go at that; she gets down to cases, spelling out ideas about *organization of her work, the opportunities for delegation, and so forth*. When possible, the manager quantifies . . . getting down to numbers, hours, minutes. This is not nit-picking. It's the only way that a generalization like "you've got to do a better job of managing your time" can be brought to life and made workable.

  It comes down to this: there's a big difference between preaching and action-planning. Preaching relies upon vague injunctions to "do better." But these don't help the subordinate who knows she needs to do better. The question is how. Only detailed action-planning can answer it.

  c. At this point, two action-plans have been proposed: the subordinate's and the manager's. Now the manager asks the subordinate to compare them, to describe which will be the more workable, the more productive. (The subordinate may select parts of both plans; it's not necessary to assume that the two plans will be irreconcilable.)

  d. Out of this comparison and discussion comes a specific action plan—a list of things to do and when to do them—for improving in the priority areas. All pertinent details (when, who, how, etc.) are included. The "map" is now virtually complete, the manager and the subordinate agree on how to get from here to there, from where the subordinate presently is to where she should be. (If implacable differences do arise, the manager's judgment ultimately prevails. She strives . . . hard . . . for genuinely mutual agreement, but never capitulates or caves in and remains, throughout, the boss.)

  e. Now that the "route" has been settled, the subordinate writes it down step by step. This eliminates any chance of later wondering: "Was I supposed to travel by bus along Highway A . . . or by car along Highway B?" As far as the manager is concerned, no action plan is complete until it's in writing—and the subordinate does the writing.

  f. Finally, the two agree on a review procedure and set a date for the review. This is vital, for two reasons: the review gives the manager a chance to help the subordinate if the latter has trouble carrying out the action plan, and it gives both people a chance to change or modify the plan if circumstances require it. Unfortunately, the best laid plans of mice and managers sometimes go astray.

Phase 4: Review

a. Before the session, the manager collects data about how the subordinate is doing. Again, she will get in as much direct observation as possible and review whatever performance records are available. Once again, the manager wants evidence about the subordinate's progress.

b. The review session itself begins with the manager explaining its twofold purpose: (1) to find out what problems the subordinate may be having in implementing the plan of action, and to develop strategies for overcoming them, and (2) to find out if the plan is proving workable, and to change or revise it if necessary. In other words, the review focuses on both the subordinate and the plan of action. If the plan isn't working, the fault may lie with the subordinate (who isn't carrying it out effectively) or with the plan (which isn't sound) or with both. As always, the manager stresses the benefit of the review to the subordinate—and makes it plain that openness and candor are desired.

c. The subordinate is then asked to summarize the priorities and the action plan established in the previous coaching session. The point is to make sure that both people still agree on what the priorities are . . . and on what should have been done to achieve them. If there's any disagreement or misunderstanding, now's the time to clear it up by referring to the written record of the last session.

d. Next, the manager asks the subordinate's opinion of how she is doing, probing specifics. This is not a third-degree. The idea is to explore—not to entrap. That cannot be done if the manager assumes that whatever is wrong is the fault of the subordinate.

e. Having heard the subordinate's thinking about her progress, the manager offers her thinking, backing it up with examples. A complete picture is presented: where praise is merited, the manager praises; where weaknesses are apparent, she is candid; where the manager is responsible for failure of the action plan, she admits it. *As can be seen, the nurse manager and staff nurse are very much functioning here as colleagues, learning together and offering peer review.*

f. Now the manager asks the subordinate to compare the two analyses, probing to make sure the comparison is candid. Then, the two try to agree on what (if anything) needs to be done differently. They may hammer out changes in the action plan, they may change or modify goals, they may realign priorities. Their purpose is to emerge from the review with an updated action plan that fits today's realities . . . and tomorrow's anticipated realities.

g. Finally, the two agree on a new review date. Like its predecessor, today's action plan is not considered a document for the ages. It's a working tool, nothing more—and if it doesn't work as well as it should, then it, too, will be revised.

We've said that Q4 coaching and counseling produces optimal results for everyone concerned: the subordinate, the organization, and the boss. But, the closer we look at what's meant by optimal results, the more troublesome the word becomes.

Optimal results, as we've said, are the best results obtainable under the circumstances. They're rarely what you'd consider ideal results. They're almost never what you'd call "perfect." They're simply the best results the manager can hope to get from this subordinate at this time in this situation. When a manager thinks about optimal results, she doesn't ask: "What's the best outcome I can conceive of?" but asks: "What's the most I can get under these conditions?" Put another way, when striving for optimal results, she is not necessarily dealing with things as she would like them to be, but is dealing with things as they really are—with hard, sometimes unruly, realities. The manager, in effect, acknowledges working with people, not puppets.

To illustrate, let's ask this question: Ideally, what kind of results would a manager like to get out of every coaching and counseling session?

Obviously, we can't answer that question in specific terms, because the specifics vary from organization to organization. But we can answer it in general terms. Almost surely, here are two of the things a manager would *like* to get out of every coaching and counseling session.

1. Self-discovery. The manager would like the subordinate to discover . . . for herself . . . how she is really doing on the job and how it can be done better. The manager would like to produce an "Aha" effect ("Aha! Now I get it!"). Instead of hitting the subordinate over the head ("Now listen to me while I tell you what the score is"), the manager would like to make the light go on in her head.
2. Growth. The manager would like the subordinate to show evidence that she is capable of further development on the job and that, as a result of the coaching and counseling session, the subordinate is able to improve, to do better. *Theory Y requires managers to look upon employees in this way, and their belief in their own skill and the process of coaching and counseling requires that they anticipate results.*

These are two of the things the manager would like to see happen. They're ideal results. But . . . at this point . . . a whole series of "what-ifs" have to be asked:

- What if the subordinate can't or won't discover the truth for herself? What if the "Aha" never happens? What if the bulb never goes on?
- What if the subordinate doesn't want to grow but prefers to stay in her present niche? What if she is afraid to grow and prefers to shelter under the boss's wing? What if she can't grow and has all she can do just to stay at the present level of performance?

In other words, what if the results the manager would like to get and the results possible are two different things? What if ideal and optimal never meet?

In this example, in which the nurse manager is trying to prepare the staff nurse for a charge nurse position, her failure to change will result in her being denied the more responsible position. If change is necessary for the employee to keep her position, however, the situation is different. This leads to what we call the coaching and counseling dilemma. The problem leading to the dilemma is this:

1. Even though ideal and optimal may never meet, the manager doesn't want to forget about the ideal. Far from it. In fact, she wants to come as close to achieving it as possible, producing optimal results that approach the ideal.
2. But . . . as we've just seen . . . in some cases, there's going to be a wide gap between ideal and optimal—in spite of the manager's best efforts. Some subordinates simply aren't going to achieve much (if anything) in the way of either self-discovery or growth.

So much for the problem. Now let's look at the dilemma. Strictly speaking, a dilemma is a situation in which someone is forced to choose between unsatisfactory alternatives. A dilemma is a bind. When a manager is coaching a subordinate who either can't or won't achieve self-discovery and growth, the manager is in a classic bind, faced with two alternatives—both unsatisfactory.

1. She can acquiesce in the situation, simply shrugging it off and telling herself that nothing can be done to get better results from the subordinate.
2. The manager can impose her own ideas, goals, and plans; saying, in effect: "If you're not able or willing to think for yourself, you'll have to accept my thinking—you'll have to do things my way."

Either way, the choice is nothing to cheer about. But the manager has to choose, one way or the other. Which horn of the dilemma, then, should be grabbed?

The answer is: the *second* alternative. If the manager can't generate self-discovery and growth, she should impose her own decisions. This isn't an ideal answer, not by a long shot. But it is the optimal answer, the answer best calculated to produce some improvement in performance. The alternative is to settle for things as they are.

The solution to the dilemma can be depicted graphically as in Figure 36–1.

The diagonal line shows that where the subordinate demonstrates high capacity for self-discovery and growth, the need for the manager to exert tight control and impose ideas is quite low, approaching (although rarely reaching) the vanishing point. But, where the subordinate shows little or no capacity for self-discovery and growth, the boss must exert considerable control and structure during the appraisal, and must impose many of her own ideas. Any other course of action would be an abdication of responsibility. *In our concern for helping the employee fulfill her own needs, the manager still must ensure that the needs of the organization are met.*

Figure 36–1 Subordinate's Capacity for Self-Discovery and Growth

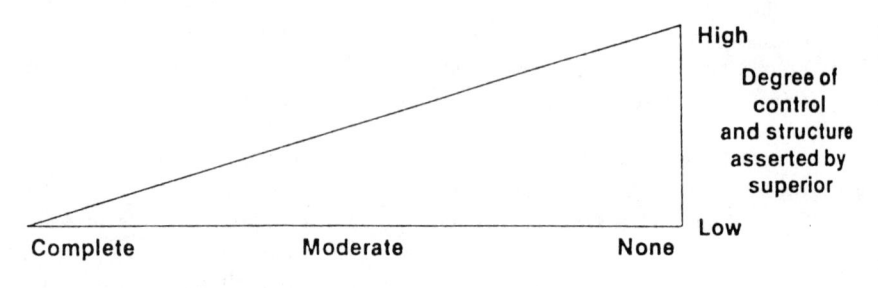

```
                                              High
                                              Degree of
                                              control
                                              and structure
                                              asserted by
                                              superior
                                              Low
Complete         Moderate            None
```

CONCLUSION

As we said at the outset, coaching and counseling . . . or training and advising . . . only *sounds* easy. It's not. It is, in fact, one of the toughest jobs confronting any manager. But it's a job that must be done and done well if optimal benefits are going to accrue to the organization and its people.

NOTE

1. The model is the basis on which coaching and counseling skills are taught in Dimensional Management Training and Dimensional Sales Management Training.

* * * *

As Buzzotta and his associates show, helping employees to reach their full potential can be a difficult and time-consuming endeavor. Pygmalion was the mythical Greek god who so believed in his love and his own power that he caused a statue to come to life; perhaps transforming a human being is no less wonderful than bringing a statue to life. Mahler discusses Eliza Doolittle's transformation into a "fair lady" in order to demonstrate a remarkably simple way of developing an employee. It is simply by believing in the employee. Although the process is complex and not totally understood, excellent results have been effected by managers who have high expectations for their employees. These results have been documented in employee productivity, quality of performance, and career progress. The manager successful with this approach is the Theory Y manager described by McGregor. Most important is the manager's own self-concept.

37.
The Pygmalion Effect

Walter R. Mahler

Sterling Livingston, a professor of business administration at Harvard Business School, found interesting parallelisms between George Bernard Shaw's *Pygmalion* and the impact of executives on their subordinates. Livingston argues that:

> Some managers always treat their subordinates in a way that leads to superior performance. But most managers, like Professor Higgins, unintentionally treat their subordinates in a way that leads to lower performance than they are capable of achieving. The way managers treat their subordinates is subtly influenced by what they expect of them. If a manager's expectations are high, productivity is likely to be excellent. If his expectations are low, productivity is likely to be poor. It is as though there were a law that caused a subordinate's performance to rise or fall to meet his manager's expectations.
>
> The powerful influence of one person's expectations on another's behavior has long been recognized by physicians and behavioral scientists and, more recently, by teachers. But heretofore the importance of managerial expectations for individual and group performance has not been widely understood.[1]

Livingston contends that the evidence supports four rather provocative statements:

1. What a manager expects of his subordinates and the way he treats them largely determine their performance and career progress.
2. A unique characteristic of superior management is their ability to create high performance expectations that subordinates fulfill.

Modified with permission from Walter R. Mahler, *How Effective Executives Interview* (Homewood, Ill.: Dow Jones-Irwin, 1976), pp. 59–62 and Sterling Livingston, "Pygmalion in Management," *Harvard Business Review* 47, no. 48 (1969): 81–88.

3. Less effective managers fail to develop similar expectations and, as a consequence, the productivity of their subordinates suffers.
4. Subordinates, more often than not, appear to do what they believe they are expected to do.

The importance of one's self-concept was well illustrated by one case study reported upon by Livingston. In an insurance organization one group, based upon past records, was identified as an "average" group. However, the manager of this group refused to believe that he was less capable than the manager of the so-called "super staff," or that his agents were less capable than the agents in the top group. Acting upon his own assumptions, he led his group to make a greater proportionate increase in productivity than the top group.

Livingston reports that:

> It is of special interest that the self-image of the manager of the "average" unit did not permit him to accept others' treatment of him as an "average" manager, just as Eliza Doolittle's image of herself as a lady did not permit her to accept others' treatment of her as a flower girl. The assistant manager transmitted his own strong feelings of efficacy to his agents, created mutual expectancy of high performance, and greatly stimulated productivity.

He goes on to explain that:

> Unsuccessful salesmen have great difficulty maintaining their self-image and self-esteem. In response to low managerial expectations, they typically attempt to prevent additional damage to their egos by avoiding situations that might lead to greater failure. They either reduce the number of sales calls they make or avoid trying to "close" sales when that might result in further painful rejection, or both. Low expectations and damaged egos lead them to behave in a manner that increases the probability of failure, thereby fulfilling their managers' expectations.

McGregor's thesis was that an atmosphere of approval was vital to an effective superior/subordinate relationship. Livingston lends support to McGregor with the following observation:

> Managers cannot avoid the depressing cycle of events that flow from low expectations merely by hiding their feelings from subordinates. If a manager believes a subordinate will perform poorly, it is virtually im-

possible for him to mask his expectations, because the message usually is communicated unintentionally, without conscious action on his part.

Indeed, a manager often communicates most when he believes he is communicating least. For instance, when he says nothing, when he becomes "cold" and "uncommunicative," it usually is a sign that he is displeased by a subordinate or believes he is "hopeless." The silent treatment communicates negative feelings even more effectively, at times, than a tongue-lashing does. What seems to be critical in the communication of expectations is not what the boss says, so much as the way *he behaves*. Indifferent and noncommittal treatment, more often than not, is the kind of treatment that communicates low expectations and leads to poor performance.

In the following formula, ability includes knowledge, skill, and experience. Willingness refers to an attitude toward work, the aspect that the employer can strongly influence.

$$\text{Ability} \times \text{Willingness} = \text{Performance}$$

It is interesting to consider that the superior's expectation may have a powerful impact on the formula, particularly on the willingness factor.

It appears that managers are more effective in communicating low expectations to their subordinates than in communicating high expectations. It is astonishingly difficult, according to Livingston, for managers to recognize the clarity with which they transmit negative feelings to subordinates.

Livingston observes that something takes place in the minds of superior managers that does not occur in the minds of those who are less effective. The answer, it appears, seems to be the superior's own self-concept. His or her own record of success gives the superior confidence in his or her own ability to select, train, and motivate subordinates.

Livingston concludes his provocative article with the following statement:

> Industry has not developed effective first-line managers fast enough to meet its needs. As a consequence, many companies are underdeveloping their most valuable resource—talented young men and women. They are incurring heavy attrition costs and contributing to the negative attitudes young people often have about careers in business.
>
> For top executives in industry who are concerned with the productivity of their organizations and the careers of young employees, the challenge is clear: it is to speed the development of managers who will treat their subordinates in ways that lead to high performance and career satis-

faction. The manager not only shapes the expectations and productivity of his subordinates, but also influences their attitudes toward their jobs and themselves. If he is unskilled, he leaves scars on the careers of the young men, cuts deeply into their self-esteem, and distorts their image of themselves as human beings. But if he is skillful and has high expectations of his subordinates, their self-confidence will grow, their capabilities will develop, and their productivity will be high. More often than he realizes, *the manager is Pygmalion.*

NOTE

1. Sterling Livingston, "Pygmalion in Management," *Harvard Business Review*, 47, no. 48 (1969): 81–88.

Index

A

Ability, 237
Abrahamson, Mark, 2, 28
Absenteeism, 104, 106-107, 116
Accountability, 111, 150
   professional, 180
Accreditation process, 18
Achievement, 91
   appraisal of, 186
   goal, 179
   need for, 167
   recognition for, 64
Action-planning, 229-230
Acute phase of co-care, 132-133
Adhocracy, 87, 90-99
   defined, 92
   value of, 98-99
Adjusted individual, 8
Adler, Alfred, 35
Administration
   behavior of, 11
   failure of, 9
   nursing, 114
   organizational chart for, 96, 97
   process of, 3

rational-bureaucratic behavior of, 11
   traditional behavior of, 11
Administrative director, 93
Advancement, 64, 118, 141
Advertising, 17, 22
Agricultural revolution, 121
Alfano, Genrose, 95
American Academy of Nursing, 210
American business philosophy, 82
American Nurses Association (ANA), 20
   Proposal for 1985, 15
American way, 83
ANA. *See* American Nurses Association
Analysis
   See also Appraisal; Evaluation; Review
   vs. appraisal, 142
   position, 170-174
Andrews, I. Robert, 102
Animal nature, 63
Appraisal
   See also Analysis; Evaluation; Review
   vs. analysis, 142
   development of tools for, 181-182

motivative kind of, 168
performance. *See* Performance appraisal
of professional skills, 188
self-, 142
Apprenticeship training, 15
Argyris, C., 159
Art, 51
Ascendance, 6
Assertiveness, 187
Association of Research Nurses and Dietitians, 128
Associations, 18, 21, 23, 123
See also specific associations
Attitudes, 144
data on, 103
employee, 194
job, 65
Attributes of professions, 13
Atwood, J.F., 150, 151
Australian Commonwealths Scientific and Industrial Research Organizations, 125
Authority, 150, 196
collegial, 31
defined, 196
hierarchy of, 29
horizontal, 31
hospital, 2
justification of, 28
physician, 2, 27
vs. power, 196
professional. *See* Professional authority
unilateral, 31
vertical, 31
Autonomy, 2, 153, 156-157
and goals, 156
of professions, 27
of units, 92
Avoidance-dissatisfaction, 64

B

Bagadia, Kishan Shyamlal, 51, 52, 74, 75

Baird, L.S., 158
Bakr, M.M., 51, 52, 74, 75
Batten, 207
Behavior
motives for, 6
prohibited, 5
required, 5
social. *See* Social behavior
Behavioral science, 65-66, 150
Bell, Cecil H. Jr., 138, 152, 153, 155, 160
Benefits, 55
Biological needs, 64
Bishop Clarkson Memorial Hospital, Omaha, Nebraska, 138, 166, 179
Bishop, Janet K., 87, 90
Blake, Robert, 193, 211, 212, 213
Blount, Mary, 113
Boredom, 47, 48
Bragg, J.E., 102
Brooten, Dorothy A., 21
Bucklow, M., 102
Bureaucracy, 2, 28, 31, 41, 90-91, 149-150
characteristics of, 28, 30
decisions in, 29
"indispensability" of, 29
and specialization, 30
and technology, 29
Burge, Suzanne, 113
Burnout, 47
Business philosophy, 82
Buzzotta, V.R., 137, 193, 221, 222, 234

C

Calling, 24
Campbell, J.P., 102
Care
continuity of, 131
coordinated. *See* Coordinated care
planning of, 111, 112
Career concept, 12, 24
Carping and censuring, 224
Carson, Arnold, 206, 207

Cartledge, N., 157
Causal variables, 214-216, 217
Censuring, 224
Census Bureau, 13
Challenge, 67
 and goals, 159
 intellectual, 48
Chaplin, Charlie, 148
Christman, Luther, 17
Chrysler, 84
Clarity of roles, 159
Client-professional relations, 20-21
Climate of organization, 161
Clinical director, 93
Clinical expertise, 117
Clinical ladders, 116-119
Clinical nurse specialist (CNS), 88
 influence of, 113-115
Closed-systems thinking, 93, 95
CNS. *See* Clinical nurse specialist
Coaching, 169, 193, 221, 222-234
 in job enrichment, 78
Co-care. *See* Coordinated care
Codes of ethics, 14, 20
Cohesiveness among nurses, 210
Collaboration, 123
Colleagueship, 21, 112
Collective bargaining, 149
Collegial authority, 31
Collegial model, 91, 93
Commitment of employees, 194-201
Communication, 56, 96, 114, 225
 gaps in, 131
 skills in, 184
 two-way, 57
 written, 30
Community sanction, 18
 and professions, 14
Companionship, 225
Company A., 84
Company Z, 84
Compassion and companionship, 225
Competence, 183-184
Competition, 21, 22
 vs. cooperation, 124
Compromise, 213

Confidence, 137
Confidentiality, 19, 127
Conflict
 individual, 8
 institutional, 8
 personality, 8, 9
 role, 8, 9
Consultation, 22
Control, 21
Control groups, 104
Conventional performance appraisal, 140, 141
Cooling-it and copping out, 224
Cooperation vs. competition, 124
Coordinated care (co-care), 129-135
 conferences on, 133
 phases of, 132-134
 teams in, 134
Coordination, 96
Copping out, 224
Corn Products Co., Latin America, 124
Counseling, 168, 193, 222-234
Courses in management, 117
Crigler, Lee, 113
Criticism, 169
Culture
 nonprofessional, 23
 professional, 14, 22-25
Cybercultural revolution, 121

D

Decentralization, 97-98
Decision making, 2, 127
Decision making
 in bureaucracy, 29
 group, 93-95
 participative. *See* Participative decision making
 responsibilities in, 75
Defensiveness, 169
DeMan, Henri, 148
De-mystification, 28
Department heads, 96
Dependency, 123

Desire to serve, 1
Development
  of appraisal tools, 181-182
  professional, 114-115
  subordinate, 223
Dickson, B., 191
Dilemma, 233
Direct action managers, 54
Discharge planning, 132
Discipline, 200
  formal, 22
  informal, 22
Dishoprick, Dean, 91
Disinterestedness, 21
Dissatisfaction-avoidance, 64
Division of labor, 29
Division managers, 96
Donnelly Mirrors Co., 100
Doty, Vick Elfrink, 210
Drucker, Peter, 152, 206, 207
Duties, 171-172

E

East-West Center, Honolulu, Hawaii, 124, 125
Economic power, 197, 198
Education
  See also Training
  centers for, 22
  formalized, 15
  nursing, 15
  patient and family, 132, 133
  requirements for, 172-174
Effective Executive, The, 206
Effective Motivation through Performance Appraisal, 137
Effectiveness, 206, 207
Efficiency, 47, 148, 206
Effluence, 206
Elan, 207
Eli Lilly, 84
Employees
  See also Personnel; Subordinates
  attitudes of, 194
  commitment of, 194-201
  counseling of, 57
  role expectations of, 109
  trust and confidence in, 137
Equality, 43
Erez, M., 158
Error prevention, 44
Establishment of standards, 169-170
Esteem. *See* Self-esteem
Ethics, 127
  codes of, 14, 20
  professional, 14, 22
Etiquette, 22
Evaluation, 167-178
  See also Analysis; Appraisal; Review
  as job enrichment tool, 137-138
  peer. *See* Peer review
  performance. *See* Performance appraisal
  program, 190-191
Evans, Christopher, 120
Excellence, 207
Executive module, 96
Expectations, 3, 8
  institutional, 8
  perception of, 9
  role. *See* Role expectations
Experience, 237
  requirements for, 172-174
Expertise, 117
Experts, 95
Extraprofessional intercourse, 18
Extrinsic vs. intrinsic rewards, 51

F

Facilitation of work, 216
Facilitator, The, 210
Family education, 132, 133
Faulconer, Diane Ramy, 116
Feedback, 79, 138, 153
  and goals, 158, 179
  from job, 157-158
  performance, 157
Feinberg, Mort, 204
Finkelmeier, Betty A., 113
First Global Conference on the Future, 121
First wave, 121
Flexner, Abraham, 2

Float pools, 47
Followership, 198, 199, 202
Followup, 79
Forcefulness, 187
Ford, 84
Foreman, 105-106
Formal discipline, 22
Formalized education, 15
Formal organizations, 28
Formal performance appraisal, 139
Fractionating human lives, 60
Free professions, 30-31
Freidman, Eliot, 2, 27
Freud, Sigmund, 35
Fringe benefits, 55
Fulfillment, 167
Full employment, 197
Functional manager, 98
Functional nursing, 47
Functional organizational chart, 97
Functional specificity, 18, 127
Fuszard, Barbara, 34, 52, 82, 87, 90, 193, 209

G

Galsworthy, John, 61
General Electric, 84
General Motors, 75, 84, 148
Getzels-Guba model, 1, 30, 109, 163, 223
Getzels, Jacob W., 1, 3, 195
Global village, 121
Goals, 159-160, 215
   achievement of, 179
   and autonomy, 156
   clarity of, 154
   and feedback, 158
   idiographic, 1, 143
   individual-organizational congruence of, 159-160
   and job challenge, 159
   nomothetic, 1, 143
   and performance, 154
   and role clarity, 159
Goal setting
   defined, 153

   foundations of, 154-155
   and individual-organizational goal congruence, 159-160
   and job characteristics, 160
   and job enrichment, 153-164
Goble, Frank, 33, 35, 37
Godfrey, Marjorie A., 48, 49
Gouldner, Alvin, 33, 41, 42-43, 44, 45, 46, 156
Greenwood, Ernest, 2, 13, 127
Greller, M.M., 158
"Grotesque" unity, 60
Groups
   See also Teams
   decision making in, 93, 95
   interests and aims of, 23
   professional, 127
   self-criticism in, 16
   specialty, 123
   subcultures of, 127
Growth, 64, 91, 232
   psychological, 59
Guba, Egon G., 1, 3, 30, 109, 163, 195, 223

H

Hackman, J.R., 148, 157
Hall, D.T., 159
Hammer, W.C., 158
Harold, D.M., 158
Harper Dictionary of Modern Thought, The, 121
Harris, P.R., 88, 120, 127
Harvard Business School, 235
Haussmann, R.K.D., 181
Hawthorne effect, 68, 104, 108
Hayman, Laura Lucia, 21
Health care team and CNSs, 113
Hegyvary, S.T., 181
Herzberg, Frederick, 1, 33, 38, 51, 52, 53, 63, 74, 78, 85, 88, 100, 102, 105, 110, 129, 138, 157, 193, 194
Hewlett-Packard, 84
Hierarchy, 2, 3, 5
   of authority, 29
   of needs, 33

organizational, 160-161
  of relationships, 3
"Higher" needs, 40
High performance aspiration, 215
Hippocratic Oath, 20
Hollman, R.W., 161
Holy Cross Hospital, Salt Lake City, Utah, 110
Honeywell, 84
Horizontal authority, 31
Horizontal job loading, 48, 68, 72
Horowitz, J.J., 134
Hospital authority, 2
Hospital evaluation team, 96
Hughes, Everett C., 31
Human relations, 186-187
  training in, 56, 194
Human relations school of thought, 213
Humble concept of management, 199
Hygiene factors (nonsatisfiers), 62, 63-72, 199

I

IBM, 84
ICRD. See International Cooperative Research and Development Projects
Idaho State Hospital South, 93, 94, 96, 97
"Ideal types"
  See also specific models
Identification
  of improvement areas, 227-229
  of tasks, 153, 155
Idiographic (individualizing or personal) aspects of social behavior, 3, 6, 7, 30
  and goals, 1, 143
  and role expectations, 151
Imposition, 123
Improvement-area identification, 227-229
Indispensability of bureaucracy, 29
Individual, 3
  adjusted, 8
  conflict in, 8
  goal congruence of with organization, 159-160
  integrated, 8
Industrial engineering, 65-66, 147
Industrial revolution, 121
Industrial unionism, 148
Informal discipline, 22
Informal organization, 106
Institute for Social Research (ISR), University of Michigan, 214
Institutions, 3
  characteristics of, 3
  conflict in, 8
  expectations of, 8
  nature of, 4
  needs of, 1
Integrated individual, 8
Intellectual challenge, 48
Interdependence, 22, 123
  of physicians, 22
  between tasks, 162
International Cooperative Research and Development Projects (ICRD), 124
International Council on Industrial Editors, 56
Interpersonal relations, 123
Interprofessional recognition, 116
Intervening variables, 216-217
Intraprofessional relationships, 16
Intrinsic vs. extrinsic rewards, 51
Investigation, 16
ISR. See Institute for Social Research

J

James, William, 200
Job
  See also Position; Tasks; Work
  analysis of, 147
  attitudes about, 65
  challenge in, 159
  classification of, 150
  content of, 64
  development of, 51, 68
  diagnosis of, 77-78

Index 245

feedback from, 157-158
horizontal loading of, 48
participation in, 57
restructuring of, 76
study of, 147
Job characteristics, 155
  and goal setting, 160
Job descriptions, 51, 117, 147
  traditional, 150
Job design, 51
  defined, 153
  integrated approach to, 153-164
Job enlargement, 47, 51, 67, 71
Job enrichment, 66, 68, 71, 75-80, 148, 194
  coaching in, 78
  defined, 51
  and goal setting, 153-164
  implementation of, 78-79
  vs. job evaluation, 147
  vs. leadership behaviors, 108
  limitations of, 75-77
  and management style, 212-220
  managers as climate setters for, 193
  misconceptions about, 75-77
  orthodox, 52
  proper application of, 77
  restructuring work for, 87-89
  steps to, 72-73
Job evaluation vs. job enrichment, 147
Job loading, 67
  horizontal, 68, 72
  vertical, 68, 88, 115, 125, 129, 138
Job purification, 47, 51, 67
Job redesign, 51, 52, 68, 81, 85
Job rotation, 47, 51, 67
Job satisfaction, 1, 153, 154
Jongeward, Dorothy, 211, 212
Judgment, 185-186
  problems of, 144
Justification of authority, 28

K

Karraker, Dean L., 137
Kaulbach, Dolores, 138, 179, 180

Key Result Area (KRA), 203
Kim, J.S., 157, 158
KITA, 64
  motivating with, 53-58
  negative physical, 54
  negative psychological, 54
  positive, 54
Knowledge, 237
  base of, 115, 127
Koeppel, J., 157
KRA. *See* Key Result Area

L

Labor division, 29
Latham, G.P., 157
Lawler, F.S., 159
Leadership, 198
  vs. job enrichment, 108
  and love, 203-208
  peer, 216
  vs. power, 195-198
  project, 94, 96, 98
  union, 103, 108
Leadership styles, 43, 212
  supportive, 215
Lefton, Robert E., 137, 193, 221, 222
Liaison, 96, 98
Licensing, 19, 127
Likert, Rensis, 96, 193, 214, 215, 216, 217, 218
Likert's Systems, 193, 211, 214-220
"Linking pin" concept, 96
Listening, 204
Livingston, Sterling, 235, 236, 237
Locke, E.A., 154, 157, 159
Lockheed, 84
Long-term research, 104
Love, 51
  and leadership, 203-208
"Love Story," 60-61
Lowin, A., 102, 105, 108

M

Mahler, Walter R., 193, 234, 235
Management, 199-200
  appraisal skills of, 144
  as climate setters for job enrichment, 193
  courses in, 117
  division, 96
  expertise in, 117
  functional, 98
  functions of, 170
  humble concept of, 199
  liaison, 98
  participative. *See* Participative decision making
  people concerns of, 213
  personnel, 65, 67
  production concerns of, 213
  project, 94, 96, 98
  resistance of to performance appraisal, 140
  scientific, 148
  systems of, 217, 218
  theory X. *See* Theory X
  theory Y. *See* Theory Y
  trust and confidence in employees from, 137
Management-by-objectives (MBO), 118, 152, 154, 160, 161, 163, 194
Management styles, 51, 84
  See also specific styles
  and job enrichment, 212-220
Managerial grid, 212
Mapping, 227
Maslow, Abraham, 33, 35, 37, 38, 40, 41, 48, 51, 55, 58, 64, 126, 193
Material goods, 137
Matrix organizations, 93, 94
MBO. *See* Management-by-objectives
McGregor, Douglas, 33, 38, 39, 41, 51, 137, 138, 152, 194, 201, 234, 236
Measurement of performance, 170, 174
Megatrends, 121

Middle-class work values, 108
Mills, Donald L., 2, 11
Mintzberg, Henry, 92
Mitchell, Terence R., 138, 152, 153, 155
Modern Times, 148
Monopoly, 19, 20, 27
  in functioning, 127
  and professional authority, 23
Morale, 57, 118
Moses, James A. Jr., 89, 129
Motivation, 53-58, 63-74
  with KITA, 53-58
  myths about, 55-57
  natural, 51
  principles of, 62
  professional, 33
  psychology of, 53
  theories of, 33, 37
Motivation-hygiene theory, 62, 63-72
Motivative kind of appraisal, 168
Motivators, 199
  vs. hygiene, 63-72
Motives
  for behavior, 6
  self-seeking, 24
Mount Sinai Medical Center of Greater Miami, Miami Beach, Florida, 116
Mouton, Jane, 193, 211, 212, 213
Multidisciplinary teams, 92, 96, 123
Myers, M.S., 154
Myths about motivation, 55-57

N

Naisbitt, John, 121
Natural motivation, 51
Nature
  animal, 63
  of institutions, 4
  of roles, 4
Naylor, Mary Duffin, 21
Need-dispositions, 3, 6
Needs
  See also specific needs

achievement, 167
biological, 64
conflicts between work requirements and, 213
fulfillment, 167
growth, 64
hierarchy of, 33
"higher," 40
institutional, 1
personnel, 1
physiological, 39
psychological, 37
recognition, 167
self-actualization. *See* Self-actualization
self-esteem. *See* Self-esteem
sexual, 18
to be needed, 2
for work, 38, 59
Negative physical KITA, 54
Negative psychological KITA, 54
Networks, 123
professional, 22
New Ways of Managing Conflict, 216
Nomothetic dimensions of social behavior, 3, 6, 7, 30
and goals, 1, 143
and role expectations, 151
Nonprofessional culture, 23
work as, 51, 85
Nonsatisfiers. *See* Hygiene
Normative nature of institutions, 4
Norms, 23
Nurse coordinator, 130-132
Nurse practitioners, 19
Nursing administration and CNSs, 114
Nursing education, 15
Nursing theory, 17

O

Objectivity, 23
Oldham, G.R., 157, 159
O'Loughlin, Elayne Lowe, 138, 179, 180
Oneness, 204
Open-systems model, 91-92, 93, 94
Operating room department, 116
Operational functions, 170
Orem, Dorothea, 181
Organizational charts, 4, 96, 97
Organizational skills, 184
Organizations
See also Institutions
bureaucratic. *See* Bureaucracy
changes in behavior of, 104
climate of, 161
fluidity of structure of, 96-97
formal, 28
hierarchical level of, 160-161
individual goal congruence with, 159-160
informal, 106
matrix, 93, 94
power of, 197, 198
role specialization in, 28
stability of, 30, 91
structure of, 96-97, 161
theories of, 65, 66, 149
Orientation conferences, 132
Originality, 184-185
Orthodox job enrichment, 51, 52

P

Parsons, Talcott, 6, 18, 20, 21
Participation, 169
job, 57
Participative decision making (PDM), 87, 100-101, 102-110, 156, 194
attitudes toward, 106
Passos, J.A., 180
Patient and family teaching, 132, 133
Patient's advocate, 131
Patten, Thomas H. Jr., 137, 138, 146, 147
Patterns of work, 11
PDM. *See* Participative decision making

Peer-established standards, 127
Peer leadership, 216
Peer review, 138, 179
　defined, 180
　and performance appraisal, 180-191
　for physicians, 180
　and primary nursing, 181
　process of, 182-189
People concerns of management, 213
Perception
　of career, 12, 24
　of expectations, 9
Performance, 237
　evaluation of. *See* Performance appraisal
　feedback on, 157
　and goals, 154
　high, 215
　measurement of, 170, 174
　vs. personality, 144
　planning of, 168
　professional, 19
　standards of, 167
Performance appraisal, 138, 139-146, 167, 169
　conventional, 140
　management resistance to, 140
　and peer review, 180-191
Performance Planning and Appraisal Session, 169
Personality, 3, 6, 7
　conflicts in, 8, 9
　defined, 6
　vs. performance, 144
Personal needs, 8
Personal propensities, 6
Personnel management, 65
　triangle of philosophies of, 67
Personnel needs, 1
Physicians
　authority of, 2, 27
　interdependence of, 22
　matrix model of, 94, 130
　peer review for, 180
　responsibility of, 27
　rights of, 27

Physiological needs, 39
Pillsbury, 84
Planning
　action, 229-230
　care, 111, 112
　discharge, 132
　performance, 168
Planning, organizing, leading, and controlling (POLC), 170
Police power, 18, 19
Porter, L.W., 154, 157
Position analysis, 170-174
Positive KITA, 54
Post-acute phase of co-care, 133
Power, 21
　vs. authority, 196
　defined, 197
　economic, 197, 198
　vs. leadership, 195-198
　organization, 198
　organizational, 197
　police, 18, 19
　subordination of, 200
Pre-coaching, 226-227
Pre-discharge phase of co-care, 133
Primary nursing, 179
　defined, 110
　and peer review, 181
　and professional development, 111-112
Production
　as concern of management, 213
　team, 81-82
Productivity, 107-108, 153
　data on, 105
　rate of, 104
Professional associations, 18, 21, 22, 23, 123
　See also specific associations
Professional authority, 13, 16, 127
　and monopoly, 23
Professional culture, 22-25
Professional development, 114-115
　and primary nursing, 111-112

Professionalization, 1, 2, 11, 12, 27, 209
  concept of, 11
  scale of, 14
Professional performance standards, 19
Professional skills appraisal, 188
Professional synergy, 120-128
Professions, 13-25, 27
  abuses in, 20
  and accountability, 180
  attributes of, 13
  autonomy of, 27
  and client relations, 20-21
  ethics in, 22
  etiquette in, 22
  free, 30-31
  literature of, 114-115
  and motivation, 33
  networks in, 22
  norms of, 23
  relationships within, 119
  roles in, 31
  subcultures in, 127
  symbols of, 24
  and systematic theory, 13-16
  training for, 31
Program evaluation, 190-191
Progress in technology, 60
Project managers, 94, 96, 98
Project teams, 92, 98
Promotions, 64, 118, 141
Psychological growth, 59
Psychological needs, 37
Psychological satisfiers. *See* Motivators
Psychology of motivation, 53
Public Law 92-603, 18
Purposive nature of institutions, 4
Pursuit of excellence, 207
Pygmalion, 235
Pygmalion effect, 193, 234, 235-238

Q

Quality, 206
"Quality," 61
Quality circles, 84, 119

Quantity, 206

R

Rational-bureaucratic administrative behavior, 11
Rationality, 15, 23
Rationalization, 29
Reality shock, 209
Reciprocity, 22, 123
Recognition, 91
  for achievement, 64
  interprofessional, 116
  need for, 167
Records, 105
Reeves, Diane M., 116
Referral, 22
Regional Medical Programs (RMP) legislation, 129
Relationships
  colleague, 21, 112
  hierarchy of, 3
  interpersonal, 123
  intraprofessional, 16
  professional, 119
Research
  centers for, 22
  long-term, 104
  systematic, 15
Respect, 35, 40
Responsibility, 64, 72, 91, 150, 171-172
  decision-making, 75
  increased, 77
  physician, 27
  statement of, 142
  subordinate, 141
Restructuring of work for job enrichment, 87-89
Results, 169
Review
  See also Analysis; Appraisal; Evaluation
  in coaching, 231-233
  peer. *See* Peer review
Rewards, 51

Rice, George, 91
Rights of physicians, 27
Riley, Margaret, 89, 129
RMP. *See* Regional Medical Programs
Robbins, Stephen, 91, 92
Role expectations, 4, 6, 7, 8
  for employees, 109
  idiographic, 151
  nomothetic, 151
Roles, 3, 4, 7
  See also specific roles
  clarity of, 159
  complementary, 5
  concepts of, 151
  conflicts in, 9
  definitions of, 23
  personality conflicts with, 8
  professional, 31
Role specialization
  in bureaucracy, 30
  in formal organizations, 28
Rosenzweig, 160
Rules, 29
  screening functions of, 45-46

S

Saint-Simon, 28
Salary and promotion policies, 141
Sanborn, Cindi, 113
Sanction-bearing nature of
  institutions, 4
Sanction of society, 127
Scanlon Plan, 100
Schuler, R.S., 157
Scientific investigation, 16
Scientific management, 148
Second wave, 121
Self-actualization, 37, 40, 48, 58, 193
Self-appraisal, 142
Self-concept, 31
Self-criticism in groups, 16
Self-discipline, 22
Self-discovery, 232
Self-esteem, 35, 40, 48, 58, 140, 193, 207, 236

Self-fulfillment, 59
Self-image, 236
Self-regulative codes, 20
Self-respect, 35, 40
Self-seeking motives, 24
Semi-attached units, 92
Semi-autonomous work groups, 81-82
Sensitivity training, 56, 194
  workshops on, 103
Setting of goals. *See* Goal setting
Sexual needs, 18
Shareholder service index, 69
Shaw, George Bernard, 235
Sherberg, Manuel, 137, 193, 221, 222
Sherwin, Douglas S., 193, 194, 202
Shils, Edward A., 6
Significance of tasks, 153, 155-156
Silber, Mark, 193, 202, 203, 207
Skills, 14, 237
  See also specific skills
  communication, 184
  organizations, 184
  professional, 188
  variety of, 153
  variety in, 155
Social behavior, 3
  idiographic. *See* Idiographic social behavior
  nomothetic. *See* Nomothetic social behavior
Social role interactions, 23
Southern Pacific Railroad, 214
Specialization, 29, 84
  in bureaucracy, 30
  in formal organizations, 28
  ultra-, 148
Specialty groups, 123
Specialty teams, 116-119
Sponsorship, 208, 209-210
  defined, 209
Stability of organizations, 30
"Standard day," 207
Standards
  establishment of, 127, 169-170
  peer establishment, 127
  performance, 19, 167

for professional performance, 19
State boards for nursing, 19
Steers, R.M., 154, 157
Strengths and weaknesses of subordinates, 227, 229
Structure
 hierarchical. *See* Hierarchy
 institutional, 4
 organizational, 161
Submission, 6
Subordinates
 See also Employees; Personnel
 development of, 223
 responsibility on, 141-142
 strengths and weaknesses of, 227, 229
Subordination of power, 200
Supervision, 45
 close, 42-44
Supervisory coaching in job enrichment, 78
Supportive leadership style, 215
Symbols, 23, 24
Synergy
 and collaboration, 123
 defined, 121
 professional, 120-128
Systematic research, 15
Systematic theory, 13-16
Systematization, 16
Systems approach, 211

T

Task forces, 92
Tasks
 See also Job: Position; Work
 identity of, 153, 155
 interdependence between, 162
 significance of, 153, 155-156
Tavistock Institute of Human Relations in London, The, 123
Taylor, Frederick W., 47, 147
Taylorism, 84
Team Practice and the Specialist, 134

Teams
 building of, 216
 coordinated care, 134
 multidisciplinary, 92, 123
 production in, 81-82
 project, 92, 98
Technical competence, 183-184
Technology, 78, 162
 and bureaucracy, 29
 progress in, 60
Theoretical controversy, 16
Theoretical systematization, 16
Theories. *See* specific theories
Theory X, 33, 38, 39-41, 137, 201, 205
Theory Y, 33, 38, 39-41, 52, 82, 84, 137, 144, 194, 201, 202, 205, 207, 234
Theory Z, 52, 82, 83-85
Third wave, 121
Tobin, Marie, 87, 110, 111
Toffler, Alvin, 90, 92, 121
Tough-mindedness, 207
Traditionalism, 11, 15
Training
 See also Education
 apprenticeship, 15
 human relations, 56
 professional, 31
 requirements for, 172-174
 sensitivity, 56
Transfer, 118
Trust, 137
Turnover, 84, 108-109, 118
Two-way communication, 57

U

Ultra-specialization, 148
Umstot, Denis D., 138, 152, 153, 155, 156, 160
Unfreezing of system, 103, 108
Unilateral authority, 31
Unions, 105, 149
 grievances of, 109
 industrial, 148

leadership in, 103, 108
United States Census Bureau, 13
Unity, 60
Universalism, 20
University of Michigan, 214
University of Minnesota Hospitals, Minneapolis, 191

V

Vacancies, 116
Valence, 206
Validity of records, 105
Values, 1, 23, 197, 198, 205
　See also specific values
　middle-class, 108
Van Dam, Andre, 124
Variables
　causal, 214-216, 217
　intervening, 216-217
Variety of skills, 153, 155
Vertical authority, 31
Vertical job loading, 68, 88, 115, 125, 129, 138
Vested interests, 20
Vollmer, Howard M., 2, 11

W

Wages, 58, 197

Walters, Roy, 33, 44, 149
Weber, Max, 2, 11, 28, 29
Westinghouse, 84
Whitney, 160
Whole-systems approach, 211
Willingness, 237
Wilson, Kathleen K., 124
Work
　See also Job; Position; Tasks
　conflict between needs and, 213
　description of, 147
　facilitation of, 216
　flow of, 81
　fractionalization of, 47
　and middle-class values, 108
　as motivator, 51, 85
　need for, 38, 59
　patterns in, 11
　semi-autonomous groups for, 81-82
　simplification of, 47
　specialization of, 47
　standards for, 100
Work ethic, 197, 198

Y

York, Lyle, 52, 81
Yukl, G.A., 157